Some Segments of a River

On Poetry,
Mysticism,
And the
Imagination

George Franklin

©2019 George Franklin
All Rights Reserved

All rights reserved. No part of this publication may be reproduced, stored in a retrieval system or transmitted in any form, or by any means (electronic, mechanical, photocopying, recording or otherwise) without the prior written permission of the author and the publisher.

Published by: Nicasio Press,
                Sebastopol, California
                www.nicasiopress.com
Cover Design: Constance King Design

ISBN: 978-0-9818636-9-6

For Jonathan Shimkin

Table of Contents

A Few Words in Lieu of an Introduction	1
I. Stevens /Abhinavagupta	7
1. Abhinavagupta: A Metaphysical Cameo	9
2. Stevens/Abhinavagupta	21
3. The Sayable and the Unsayable in Mysticism and in Poetry	77
II. An Ecstasy of Associations	89
1. Detours and Divagations	91
2. New Thresholds, New Affinities	117
3. Abhinavagupta and the Four Levels of Speech	135
4. Concluding Unscientific Postscripts	159
III. Inescapable Romance	181
1. Keats' Middle Way and the Intelligence of the Heart	183
2. Blake's "London": On Inspiration and the Poetic Genius	211
3. Shelley: Beyond Idealism and the Daemonic Sublime	229
Envoi: Afterword as Prelude	251
Selected Bibliography	255
About the Author	257

A Few Words in Lieu of an Introduction

I wish to emphatically state at the outset what will become all too clear. Although the first section in this volume is concerned with a great medieval Indian saint, philosopher, and aesthetic theorist, Abhinavagupta, and a great American Modernist poet, Wallace Stevens, and though I go on to consider, whether in passing or at length, philosophers and poets both Eastern and Western, I am not a scholar. I am (or have been) something entirely more unofficial, a poet. I have, as well, been something still more unacademic, a would-be spiritual adept.

After having been introduced to the aforementioned Abhinavagupta by my spiritual preceptor or Guru, in whose ashrams I spent well over a decade, I began to read everything I could related to the nondual Shaivism of Kashmir, the scriptural tradition of which Abhinavagupta was the greatest exponent. I was continually struck by what seemed to me to be surprising analogies between the metaphysics and aesthetics of Kashmir Shaivism and the metaphysics implicit, and sometimes explicit, in the poetry and prose of several of the great English Romantic poets whom I had long read and revered. At the same time, along a kind of parallel track, I was struck by analogies between Kashmiri Shaivite metaphysics and aesthetics and the work of Walt Whitman and of the great Neo-romantic American poets, of whom Stevens is, of course, one.

Scholars of East Asian religious studies—some Western, most Indian—have over the last century done an enormous amount of work in unearthing, explicating, and finally translating into English the primary texts, and commentaries on these texts, of Kashmir Shaivism, a great spiritual tradition that was on the verge of slipping into near-total oblivion. To all such scholars I feel an immense debt of gratitude.

As for academic high priests of what used to be called the literary arts, I will simply aver that such scholars—with, it is important to recognize, a number of notable exceptions—have engendered, over the last several decades, a plague of what is quite simply execrably bad and inept writing, writing that seems to consider an incoherent obscurantism the guarantor of authenticity, and whose authors too often tout obligatory methodologies that are a confused patchwork of gleanings from the equally arcane writings of their confreres. I confess that I profess no such methodology.

The first part of this book, "Stevens/Abhinavagupta"—after a brief cameo that deals with, respectively, Abhinavagupta's metaphysics, then with his aesthetics—is an attempt at reading Stevens and Abhinavagupta in each other's light, or side by side, not wishing to assimilate one to another, but to trace the arc of whatever energies might flow between them. Here, at the outset, I must offer an apology to the reader, for whom being introduced, in the book's first chapter, to a dense precis of an alien metaphysics, and then to the work of a notoriously difficult poet, may well prove less than enticing.

The essay on Stevens, a famously difficult poet, is the longest in the book, and the most demanding of the reader, whom I would urge to consider this first section, and particularly my opening discussion of Abhinavagupta, as a kind of bridge that crosses a moat that leads to a refurbished, accommodating mansion of many rooms. There is no need to tarry on the bridge. Feel free to pass over it blithely, as lightly and trippingly as you please. Be assured that whatever is discussed in the first chapter will later be reiterated in a less forbidding, more relaxed key. Once inside the castle, I assure you, there will be no exam to be passed. Your host would never be so discourteous.

The second part of this book, "An Ecstasy of Associations," is more speculative in nature. Its first chapter, "Detours and Divagations," is a wide-ranging discussion of different kinds of mysticism, mostly Eastern, and of their relevance to a discussion of poetry in general and to the imagination in particular. It also examines the complementary relationship between contemplative and ecstatic forms of mysticism and of poetry. Its second chapter augments my discussion of Abhinavagupta's aesthetics with a discussion of his theory of language, and begins to explore a kind of middle way between subjective idealism on the one hand and either reductive forms of objective realism or logical positivism on the other. Its concluding series of Postscripts continues this exploration with my own tentative speculations on the relationship between the imagination and Consciousness.

The third and final part of the book is a discussion of several English Romantic poets in the light of what I see as their tentative explorations of the aforementioned middle way. It seems to me that it is somehow apt that this book, which begins with a quite granular discussion of Stevens, should end with a discussion that includes Keats and Shelley, who were the most significant of Stevens' Romantic forebears.

With respect, specifically, to the term imagination, I feel what Marianne Moore professed to feel about poetry: I, too, dislike it. It reflects, as a noun, the mind's, and particularly the Western mind's tendency to hypostasize or reify not only the abstract but also the dynamic into reassuringly stable, seemingly substantial categorical niches. The imagination is thus reduced, along with reason, to a supposed mental faculty. That which is hypostasized—as, for example, Freud's id, ego, and superego—accrues to itself something of the allure and prestige of a reassuringly stable reality that we associate with nouns that denote objects in the so-called real world. Whereas, in contradistinction, I would suggest that the imagination is un-categorical. It is not a faculty, but a force. Not a noun, but a verb. Not a fixable notion, but an energy, not knowable in itself but glimpsed in its fugitive instances. Who knows, it may even be dependent upon an energy that is in some way independent of the human mind, a force field upon which the mind draws, experiencing a subsidiary stirring, a resonance, generated by some greater vibration that pulsates indifferently through all thoughts and all things.

The memory represents to us, always unfaithfully, that which we have been. The imagination, drawing upon a vast reservoir of potential energy, represents that which we are and might become. Many of the essays that comprise this book are concerned with delineating a variety of different but related takes on the imagination, some drawn from Eastern sources, which will doubtless be unfamiliar to many.

One of the preoccupations of this book is the notion that imagination is vitally connected to some form of creative intuition, of what used to be called inspiration. I explore the terminology, and the particular nuances, of various mystical traditions, and of various poets, as they broach this topic. To state my position in necessarily simple terms, great works of art are often preceded by a kind of powerful, preconscious, synoptic intuition, an immediate foreseeing and apprehension of both what is to be unfolded as an articulate whole and some of its specific lineaments. The task of the poet is to translate these intuitions into fully articulated works of art. Similarly, many spiritual experiences involve the sudden irruptions of heretofore unrealized insights into the nature of reality, insights which are themselves also translated into action, into a changed comportment in relation to a world that seems transformed.

I wish here to acknowledge a sin of omission on my part. I restrict myself in this book primarily to poets and saints. I do not much discuss the workings of this creative, synoptic intuition, or indeed of the imagination, with respect to the adepts of a variety of other fields, an omission which is particularly regrettable with respect to the sciences. If one reads the biographies of great scientists, particularly those of the twentieth century, it is startling how often their key insights, too, are experienced as the sudden, intuitive irruption of previously unimagined solutions to difficult problems. I do fortunately mention that all of us have moments of this kind of insight, and that by attending to them our experience of the world can be revitalized and transformed.

There is another key aspect of the imagination that I have discussed insufficiently in this book. I am referring to the imagination's tendency to draw together, to connect, by means of a kind of analogy or metaphor writ large, domains of experience or knowledge that are usually thought of, if not as entirely unrelated to each other, then as only tenuously and distantly related. Such juxtapositions and analogies are often generative of startling and productive insights. I hope that my not sufficiently addressing this issue is mitigated by the fact this book is in large part an attempt to juxtapose, to draw analogies between just such disparate realms of experience

If not for my fear of seeming presumptuous, and for considerations of rhythm, the subtitle of this book would have read: *On Poetry, Mysticism, the Imagination, and Consciousness.* Any extended inquiry into the nature of the imagination naturally leads to speculations about the nature of Consciousness. And indeed such speculations are broached in this text, not only in my account of the centrality of Consciousness in Kashmir Shaivism in the book's first section, but in my own provisional attempts to address this daunting subject in its latter two sections. I am not, however, altogether naive. I am aware that questions regarding the nature of Consciousness are now a hot and generatively troublesome topic in several academic disciplines. I have kept adequately abreast of none of them. Or rather I have read just enough to know that the elusive nature of consciousness, and specifically of how we experience the subjective quality of things as we do, remains for the aforementioned disciplines—scientific, philosophical, psychological, and to a lesser degree literary—an unavoidable, conspicuously unsolved, hard problem. Indeed, among those vitally concerned with this subject, many suggest that by its very nature it will remain unsolvable.

It might seem the height of ignorance, folly, and presumption to have suggested a merely personal, and what to some might seem an uninformed, perspective on this topic here. I hope, however, that *seems* is the operative word. Because questions regarding the nature of consciousness, far from being a merely personal issue for me, are characteristic of the texts that I examine and explore. For virtually all of the mystical traditions and their exponents to which I refer in this text, and for many of the poets, the nature of Consciousness, or of some transcendent reality, whether conceived of theistically as God or non-theistically as some ultimate principle or power, or as some radically indeterminate state that challenges the status of what we think of as reality itself, is also a paramount concern, perhaps *the* paramount concern. For these traditions and their greatest exemplars that which is of paramount concern is not only an epistemological but also an existential/ontological issue. The only way to know Consciousness is to become, to realize, or to be that Consciousness, or God, or Ultimate Reality, or that which undermines all notions of reality and selfhood whatsoever.

In this book I have attempted to give at least a cursory glance at the quite different ways, suggested above, that the mystics of various traditions apprehend and express the nature of mystical experience. Most of the poets I discuss in this volume, though having affinities with mysticism and mystical experiences, are not themselves mystics. Though typically more flawed and fragile vessels than their more purely mystical peers, they are nonetheless charged with the task of translating what would otherwise remain inchoate intuitions into articulate forms, thereby rendering them accessible to others.

A friend of mine from my years in the ashram recently wrote to me of the emptiness, tediousness, and tendentiousness of the rhetoric of spiritual ultimacy. Though doubtless guilty to some degree of trafficking in such rhetoric, I hope for the most part to have avoided it by virtue of faithfully adhering, in this text, to considering the nuances of individual poets and their poetry. Ultimately, or primarily, this is a book about how poets in particular have felt, intuitively, the stirrings of Consciousness and the imagination, and about how they have translated these intuitions into surpassingly beautiful texts.

My primary focus throughout the book is on poets and poetry, the first term in its title. It begins, as mentioned, with a long, quite granular discussion of Wallace Stevens, and remains in close contact with poets and with what is uniquely characteristic of their work throughout. It ends with a less speculative and more pragmatic account of several of Stevens' Romantic forebears.

The preoccupation with the individual, the exceptional, the original, is itself, broadly speaking, more characteristic of Western than of Eastern thought. And so this book is also in some sense a fraught attempt to translate Eastern insights into Western terms. This effort has not, for me, been merely theoretical. In my years living in an ashram in India and since, I have struggled existentially, as a spiritual seeker and as a poet, with the tensions, both creative and painful, of attempting to absorb and assimilate, as a Westerner, necessarily partially and no doubt inadequately, aspects of a culture not my own. This book addresses, if often obliquely, the issue of translation in its myriad forms, often exposing the limitations of language itself—a subject that, further elaborated, will likewise be a recurrent concern of this text, the writing of which has been for me a process of discovery in which the speculative notions I discuss gradually unfolded and were refined. The exploration I have embarked upon reaches no definitive, categorical conclusions, and is indeed inimical to such conclusions. It remains, for me and I hope for the reader, a tentative, open-ended exploration. My intent is to engage the reader, to excite his or her imagination, to encourage him or her to follow paths that will inevitably, and thankfully, be different from those which I have traced here.

In sum, this book deals with a set of concerns that I think can be described with justice as loosely confederated, dynamically interrelated. It is the dynamic alone that can declare, with Whitman, "Unscrew the locks from their doors! Unscrew the doors themselves from their jambs!" I hope that at least some of what follows, though too politely, too pallidly, can contribute in some small, some very small way to an understanding of the great ongoing imaginative work of some of those whose vocation has been the unscrewing and unlocking of the doors that block the expression of man's and woman's unalienable energies.

I. Stevens / Abhinavagupta

1.
Abhinavagupta: A Metaphysical Cameo

1.

I mentioned in my introduction to this book to that I fear that by beginning it with a difficult to digest gobbet of metaphysics as propounded by a little-known school of Indian thought, I am doing neither myself nor a potential reader any favor. Indeed, such an opening gambit seems like beginning what will be a long campaign with a perhaps fatal strategic blunder. Alas, I see no way around this problem, as at various points in this text, and particularly in the essay on Stevens that follows, I will refer to different aspects of this metaphysical/aesthetic system. It is one of many schools of mystical thought that I will briefly touch upon in this text. The good news is that whenever in the text I refer to an instance where the arcane terminology of the system in question arises, I will redefine that term; in the chapters that follow, my main concern is with the exploration of particular, mostly Western poets, largely on their own terms. I would hope that the reader, in what immediately follows, will remain content simply, as in a kind of flyover, to get a general sense of the terrain that it covers.

Many years ago I spent over a decade living in the ashram of my Guru or spiritual preceptor. His teachings were based on the nondual Shaivism of Kashmir, ultimately systematized by the great sage Abhinavagupta (950-1016 CE) which henceforth, I shall, not being a scholar, irresponsibly, for the sake of brevity, refer to as Kashmir Shaivism, or simply, more egregiously, as Shaivism.

In this chapter in particular, I will deal briefly with Abhinavagupta's metaphysics and then with his aesthetics. I hope thereby to set the stage for a virtual, admittedly unlikely, but hopefully generative and suggestive meeting between Abhinavagupta and Stevens, the great American Modernist poet, whom I have read, reread, and revered for over forty years.

The two foundational texts of Kashmir Shaivism, said to have been revealed to a sage named Vasagupta, are the *Shiva Sutras* and the *Spanda Karikas*. As Kashmir Shaivism developed, two main lines of preceptors and schools, the Pratyabhijna Shastra and the Spanda Shastra, commented on these texts. Kashmir Shaivism assimilated as well the teachings and practices of other Tantric groups with which it had been associated. It was Abhinavagupta who, in his voluminous philosophical works, including commentaries on previous authors in his lineage, drew together all of the related strands of Kashmir Shaivism and wove them together into a fully coherent philosophical system. His *Tantraloka*, a kind of *summa*, is a vast, systematic, compendious philosophical account of Kashmir Shaivism as well as of the significance of its various practices and rituals.

Abhinavagupta's two long treatises on aesthetics, the *Locana* and *Abhinavabharati*, have had from the outset a widespread, almost hegemonic influence and prestige in India. He soon came to be revered as the canonical Indian author on aesthetics, a position he holds to this day. Oddly, however, Abhinavagupta's philosophical works were, until the relatively recent work of scholars, both Eastern and Western, largely forgotten.

2.

On the face of it, it is preposterous to attempt to meaningfully suggest anything about the metaphysics and aesthetics of Kashmir Shaivism in the span of a few pages. A more expanded version of this chapter appears in my book *Providence*, and thus this chapter is a précis of an already inadequate précis. I hope it will be less egregiously inadequate if I limit my discussion to two questions: what is the nature of the Absolute, or Supreme Consciousness, and what is the relationship of that Consciousness to the phenomenal world?

Vedanta, the leading orthodox school of Indian spirituality, posits Brahman as a changeless, inactive being-absolute, utterly devoid of positive attributes. According to Kashmir Shaivism, the ultimate reality is Shiva, the transcendent light of Consciousness, the shimmering of pure awareness. And yet, at the same time, Shiva is ever inextricably one with Shakti, his divine consort, his conscious energy and power, through which Shiva is not only aware but is reflexively aware of Himself as Shiva.

It is through a primordial vibration of Shakti within Shiva, called *spanda*, that all things are constantly being created, flashing forth into manifestation, while simultaneously being resorbed into the transcendent state of Shiva. While spanda is beyond the realm of time or space, it can be conceived metaphorically as a simultaneous inward and outward vibration of Shakti, oscillating at a speed so infinitely rapid that it seems not to be oscillating at all. The inward vibration of spanda is the reflexive power of Shakti through which Shiva recognizes himself as Shiva. The outward vibration is the first stirring of Shakti's creative power, through which she unfolds multiple realms of appearance, including our own.

Shaivism ascribes five fundamental acts to Shiva, those of creation, sustenance, dissolution, concealment, and grace. The renowned, much reproduced, figure of the *Nataraj* portrays the dance of Shiva, his constant "enactment" of these five powers. We have seen that Shiva, through Shakti, in the form of spanda, constantly creates and dissolves the world or worlds of manifestation, enacting his powers of creation and of destruction or dissolution. At the same time, as the transcendent ground of all, he constantly sustains the universe. Through his power of concealment, Shiva, through his free will, veils his true nature, giving rise to "limited agents" who erroneously view the world of appearance as separate from them, as entities frozen in an external world of time and space. This power of concealment or contraction is effectuated by Shakti in the form of Maya, which is not considered, as in Vedanta, an independent principle which, when superimposed upon the absolute, gives rise to an illusory world of appearances. In Kashmir Shaivism, Maya Shakti is rather that aspect of Shakti through which, as a part of his divine play, Shiva willingly conceals himself. By means of her five *kanchukas* or veils, Maya Shakti appears to limit Consciousness with respect to agency; to knowledge; to fullness, or self-satisfaction, or bliss; to time; and to space, causation, and form. Finally, through his power of grace or revelation, Shiva, often acting through enlightened masters, grants to "contracted agents" a full awareness of their unlimited nature as one with Shiva, through which they regain their divine powers of omnipotence, omniscience, and bliss, and their freedom from time, space, and causality.

Thus Shiva, working through Shakti, enacts a constant play of concealment and revelation, contraction and expansion. These powers, like his powers of creation and destruction, each inextricably entail the other. All things arise and subside, are concealed or revealed, within Shiva, who is the transcendent ground of all. Somewhat counter-intuitively, at least, I suspect, to most Westerners, Shiva's creative power, through Shakti, to manifest multiple worlds involves his voluntary contraction. Conversely, again counter-intuitively, the process of dissolution, likewise abetted by Shakti, involves His increasing expansion. The worlds and the experiencers of these worlds thus created, ranging from the most subtle to the most gross, exist entirely within Shiva. Shiva is the container, all else the contained. As creation unfolds and the process of contraction continues, each phase is contained by the phase prior to it, and contains the phase succeeding it. Each level of Consciousness is both the container and the contained, and thus all are essentially homologous. As Shiva and Shakti continually both create and resorb all worlds, each level is a kind of crossroads in which both the creative/contractive and the destructive/expansive phases of Shiva and Shakti are continually at play. Everything from the fully expanded state of Lord Shiva to an apparently inert, lifeless stone is both pervaded and constituted by Consciousness, and is nothing other than Consciousness. Thus even apparently inert objects are not inert but alive.

All phenomena, according to Kashmir Shaivism, whether subjects or objects, and at whatever level of creation, are projected by Consciousness within Consciousness and are themselves forms of Consciousness. There is nothing that is not Consciousness. There is nothing that is not Shiva; therefore I, too, am Shiva. With respect to the phenomenal world of appearances, it is precisely this attitude, this awareness, that must be practiced. In Shaivism, though the reality of autonomous objects existing in an extended external space is denied, the phenomenal world of appearances is not considered illusory. Appearances are considered real *as appearances,* as the flashing forth of divine Consciousness in all its glory and freedom. Not only through deep, contemplative meditation, but also through recognizing and relishing sensory experience as one with the highest Lord, a spiritual adept comes to identify with Shiva himself and with Shakti as his active power.

Supreme Consciousness, according to the Pratyabhijna Shastra, is always linked with an agent and with action. At the highest level the agent is Shiva. He has the unbridled freedom to create and resorb, through Shakti, innumerable worlds, and possesses unfettered powers of will, knowledge, and action. At more contracted levels of creation, the primary format of agent and action still holds, but in increasingly restricted forms; for example, in the form of the bound individual, one whose power of agency, whose field of action, and whose knowledge or power of perception are all relatively restricted and circumscribed. We, too, of course, are such agents, but through the power of Shakti we identify more and more with Shiva; our freedom and power as agents—and the scope of the world or worlds in which we act—grow increasingly expansive.

Through the reflexive power of Shakti, Shiva is always aware of himself as Shiva, as the supreme agent. Shaivism calls this awareness I-consciousness. A seeker draws closer to full I-consciousness through the practice of inner absorption in meditation and by practicing witness consciousness. Through identification with the witness of thoughts rather than with thoughts themselves, the seeker is less likely to be impulsively carried away by his thoughts, to forfeit his self-mastery and self-possession. Through cultivating I-consciousness, he is cultivating the awareness of Shiva himself. However, just as Shiva becomes aware of himself only through the reflexive, inward-turning power of Shakti, so it is only through the power of Shakti that the I-consciousness of the seeker blossoms into the full recognition *I am Shiva* that is tantamount to the state of liberation. Such self-recognition is called by Kashmir Shaivism *pratyabhijna*, and it is a key doctrine of the school. Ultimately, one does not become Shiva. One recognizes, whether gradually or suddenly, that one has been Shiva all along.

With respect to the practices which it propounds, Kashmir Shaivism is aligned with the Tantric inclination to see the microcosm, man, as one with the macrocosm. In Shaivism it is usually as a result of initiation by the Guru—through whom the Lord's power of grace is channeled—that an adept's Kundalini Shakti is awakened. This energy is regarded as one, though operating in the microcosm of the human body, with Chit Shakti, with the power of the Lord himself. Thus, as the Kundalini unfolds in meditation, piercing increasingly higher *chakras*, or centers of energy, it leads the seeker to experience, in meditation, higher and higher levels of the macrocosm. Eventually his or her energy merges with Shiva in the *sahasrar*, the crown chakra at the top of the head, and the seeker becomes established in the awareness *I am Shiva*. At this point the microcosm and macrocosm merge, becoming one and the same, and the liberated being enjoys the same unrestricted freedom as Shiva himself.

The enlightened spiritual teacher, upon fully realizing and coming into alignment with himself, fully realizes and comes into alignment with, in a sense indeed becomes one with, both the phenomenal world and with others, particularly and ultimately with the genuine, committed spiritual seeker or disciple. This does not, however, mean, as some suppose, that the seeker's identity is annihilated and subsumed by the identity of the Guru. Quite to the contrary. Just as the Guru assimilates the disciple to himself, so he assimilates himself to the disciple. He recognizes, acknowledges, respects, indeed celebrates the otherness of the disciple. He tends to have an uncanny intuitive sense of the essential nature of the disciple both as it is in itself and as it expresses itself in a myriad of characteristic ways. The Guru does not liberate, translate (or further limit or bind) the disciple into becoming an effaced, egoless clone of himself. Rather, he liberates the disciple, empowers him to translate himself, in a way that taxes his creativity to the utmost, into becoming the truest, most characteristic, most unique and fulfilled version of himself. Some imagine that to be a disciple is to be something like an indentured servant of the Guru. Again, something like the reverse is true. The Guru, who is a selfless servant of God, is also the selfless, and often tireless, servant of the disciple, for whom he feels a kind of unconditional love.

What is true of the Guru is of course true of all genuine teachers of whatever kind, those usually unheralded figures who have the insight to see our potential, and the commitment and patience to help us to realize it, who often have a quietly decisive impact on or lives. False teachers, like abusive bosses, seek to aggrandize their own egos by making their students extensions of themselves. The work of the true teacher is to ultimately render him or herself obsolete, to glory in the student's eventual independence and autonomy. Those who have been the beneficiaries of such teachers tend, in turn, in whatever field of endeavor, to serve as mentors, as selfless servants, to their younger colleagues, thus perpetuating a kind of virtuous cycle.

Shaivism's four *upayas*, or sets of spiritual practices, range from the relatively gross to the most subtle, from outward rituals to the most inward states of awareness. A seeker performs the set of practices enjoined by the particular upaya appropriate to his or her level of spiritual growth. In all cases it is the expansion of Shakti's power that leads the seeker to the ultimate recognition of himself as one with Shiva.

It is beyond the scope of this brief excursus to delve into these various practices. I will simply note that those most prominently enjoined by Shaivite texts involve attending closely to the liminal, whose definitions, gleaned both from the OED and the Merriam-Webster dictionary, are as follows:

1. Relating to the initial or transitional phase of a process.
2. Occupying a position at or on two sides if a threshold.
3. Relating to, or situated at, a sensory threshold.
4. Of, or relating to, an intermediate state, phase or condition. In between.

Spanda, the primordial stirring of Shakti within Shiva, moving inward and outward at the same time, seems to be a quintessentially liminal phenomenon. It is like the hinge by means of which the pendulum of Consciousness swings. The spiritual adept is encouraged to apprehend spanda by observing it as it manifests as the various phenomena of a world constantly pulsating with energy, and to seize upon spanda as the inward moving power of Shakti herself, the power through which Shiva becomes aware of himself as Shiva, and through which the adept, too, can become one with Shiva.

The initial phase of any experience or phenomenon is related to spanda, which can, for example, be experienced as the subtle stirring of Consciousness just before a thought arises in the mind, or as the sudden flashing forth of some great but heretofore unrealized insight or understanding. Similarly, attending to the space between any two thoughts, states, or phenomena is recommended by Shaivite texts as a means of developing an increasingly refined, expanded awareness that eventually merges with Shiva Himself. The seeker is encouraged, for example, to focus on the space between thoughts. And to focus, as well, on the space between the inner witness of thoughts, aligned with Shiva or Supreme Consciousness, and thoughts themselves. As this virtual, mental space increases, the seeker becomes ever freer from limiting thought constructs. In meditation, the seeker is taught to meditate on the point at which the exhaled breath turns inward, and at which the inward breath turns outward, juncture points that grow closer and closer as meditation deepens, until the two points merge as the breath is stilled. In this state the inner and the outer ultimately merge. The seeker is encouraged, as well, to focus on transitional states, such as the point between waking and sleeping, or on apparently external, temporal phenomena, such as sunrise or sunset, which, suspended between night and day, are considered particularly auspicious.

The fourth and highest upaya is called *anupaya*, which is the practice-less practice, the means that abjures all means. It blossoms directly into the state of realization. A hallmark of the great masters of Shaivism is that for them the bliss of inner absorption in meditation is no different from the bliss of enjoying, in the wakeful state, the play of their own Consciousness in its ever-changing forms. They experience unimpeded freedom in both realms. Whatever they choose to do or not to do, their awareness of being Shiva remains unbroken. They act in the so-called outer world with great spontaneity and with an almost improvisatory verve. According to Shaivism, this unfettered freedom, like the freedom of Consciousness itself, is considered the highest good, a good that can be attained not merely upon death but while still alive.

3.

Turning now to Abhinavagupta's aesthetics, which I will likewise address in a far too summary and reductive a fashion, I will be concentrating on three key terms, *pratibha, dhvani,* and *shanta rasa,* whose meaning and resonances I shall now attempt to unfold.

To begin with a central question: what, according to Abhinavagupta, is the nature of the imagination? It is the faculty in the poet or artist that envisages, foresees, what is not yet actual; in this case the poem that he is about to write or the painting he is about to create, which then is unfolded in the words and images of a more or less realized work of art. Here I would like to invoke the first of my three key terms, *pratibha,* which, in Abhinavagupta's metaphysics, is the recognitive insight that leads to the realization of oneness with Shiva. In his aesthetics, pratibha refers to the creative intuition that is essential to the unfolding of any great work of art. Pratibha, in its dual aspects as recognitive insight and creative intuition, is akin to the inward and outward vibration of spanda itself. In Abhinavagupta's aesthetics, pratibha corresponds to the initial stirring or vibration from which the universe arises. Creative intuition is immediate, timeless. Like Blake's Poetic Genius, it is a moment of creative, synthetic, precognitive intuition, which is then translated into the world of time and space.

To use drama as our example, first the written text, then the performance itself unfolds, in a kind of centrifugal expansion of Shakti. Absorbed in the spectacle before him, the spectator, via a kind of centripetal motion, takes in the performance. If he is a sensitive, experienced spectator, or literally, in Abhinavagupta's words, a "same-hearted" spectator, something like the pratibha through which the poet created the play will begin to stir, to resonate, within him. It is as though through the same creative intuition he becomes the co-author of the play, an experience that will continue to grow stronger the more that spectator reads a given play or attends performances of it. Pratibha aligns both the author and the spectator with Shiva, the primordial creator Himself. The vibrating heart of both the poet and the same-hearted spectator, through the medium of the play, resonate as one, and both resonate with the Heart of Shiva. It is worth pointing out in this context that the word *Heart*, in Kashmiri Shaivite metaphysics, is one of several technical terms denoting the Absolute.

What is true of the drama also holds true of poems. Assuming that some form of pratibha, of creative intuition, is unfolded in the poem itself, it will have, again, the power to quicken the creative intuition of the reader. This is one reason the reading of poetry, for many poets, has so essential a role in inspiring the creation of it.

In connection with both spanda and pratibha, several words with similar roots denoting a kind of quivering light are also frequently invoked, recalling Shiva's nature as that of light, of a pure, luminous awareness, a light that begins to oscillate, to stir, as the movement toward creation begins. Certain great works of art have about them a kind of incandescent, transparent aura, their words or notes or brush strokes quickened, dynamic, alive with the light of creative intuition.

At this point it might be useful to explore the workings of pratibha, the creative intuition from which a given work arises and which the same-hearted reader comes to share, by looking at a well-known sonnet by Rilke in which the text that the speaker of the poem, as it were, reads, is not a verbal text but a physical icon which, though not articulated in words, has been lovingly and passionately articulated by the sculptor's hand.

Archaic Torso of Apollo

We cannot know his legendary head
with eyes like ripening fruit. And yet his torso
is still suffused with brilliance from inside,
like a lamp, in which his gaze, now turned to low

gleams in all its power. Otherwise
the curved breast could not dazzle you so, nor could
a smile run through the placid hips and thighs
to the dark center where procreation flared.

Otherwise, this stone would seem defaced
beneath the translucent cascade of the shoulders
And would not glisten like a wild beast's fur:

would not, from all the borders of itself,
burst like a star: for here there is no place
that does see you. You must change your life.

From one point of view the torso is a mere block of inanimate matter. And yet we recall that, according Shaivism, every level of Consciousness from that of Shiva himself to apparently inert stone is fully alive with Consciousness, is in fact nothing but that Consciousness. Immediately, in reading Rilke's poem, we are met with a suffusing, permeating glow that seems so often to accompany works of art that arise from a particularly powerful creative intuition. Images of light abound in the poem. The torso is suffused with brilliance from inside, as though lit by a lamp, a lamp that gleams in all its power. The torso dazzles, leads the eye to the only dark place in the poem, the place of procreation. Yet even this darkness is represented as flaring. Thereafter come references to translucence, to glistening. Finally, the torso bursts from all its borders like a star.

Immediately thereafter come the lines, "for here there is no place /that does not see you." The torso sees through every pore of its body, or rather from every molecule of its stone. It is as though the torso's gaze has become more powerful by not having vision localized in the now-absent head. As a result of not being localized in the head, (thought of in the West as the seat of the ego), as though not being identified with some nominal subject, the nature of Consciousness as a kind of non-localized awareness that is prior to and precipitates both subject and object is revealed. The poet and the torso are simultaneously gazing upon each other. Each is with respect to the other both subject and object; it is as though subject and object are interchangeable; the simple paradigm of conscious subject vs. unconscious object breaks down. Indeed, as the torso is capable of seeing not only from the eyes but from the whole body, it is a more powerful subject, a more powerful seer, than the poem's speaker.

From whence does the extraordinary radiance of the torso, its overwhelming gaze, arise? Is it invested in the torso by the poet/speaker? Presumably not, for how then would we account for the presence in the torso of a gaze more luminous than the poet's own, that almost overwhelms him? It seems that the role of the speaker/poet is to be a same-hearted spectator, to be open enough to internalize the radiance of the torso, to let it speak to him.

Was the poem's radiance invested in it by its sculptor? Is it his extraordinarily powerful gaze, the vision, both literal and figurative, through which he articulated the torso, suffusing it with light, that still has the power, undiminished by time, to speak with an uncanny immediacy to the spectator? Quite likely. But from whence did the sculptor receive the power to articulate the stone, to release from within it a kind of inner life and radiant light? Not, presumably, from his ego, but from the powerfully luminous, synthetic, creative intuition that is pratibha, which is here so intense that it assumes the form of an almost apocalyptic revelation. The same-hearted viewer is capable of receiving this revelation, a revelation in which an apparently inanimate, inarticulate stone torso confronts the spectator with the stark command: "You must change your life."

What has happened here? The speaker's intense vision, his pratibha both as a speaker/creator and as a same-hearted spectator, has resonated so powerfully with the pratibha, the creative intuition of the artist, here a sculptor, that a mere block of stone becomes completely and humanly alive, has itself become a seer capable of peering into the depths of the speaker's soul. Not only the poem's speaker and the torso's sculptor, but the sculpture itself—an object that has been miraculously transformed into a subject—all participate in pratibha, in the creative intuition that is itself an instance of the even greater creative power of Shiva himself.

And yet something still remains in doubt. As the very last line of the poem, the response to the command, "You must change your life," seems to be directed to us as readers as well. We are perusing Rilke's poem just as he has perused the contours of the sculpture. Will we, our own creative intuition awakened, become same-hearted readers of Rilke's poem just as he became a same-hearted viewer of the torso? Will we be quickened into a more creative and conscious life? The poem's last line remains an open question, one that only we can answer.

Another key term in Abhinavagupta's aesthetics, one which he borrows from previous theories of aesthetics but develops further, is *dhvani*, which can be loosely translated as the power of suggestion or evocation. Indian court poetry had typically focused on the elaborate use of ingenious figures of speech, decoratively reworked into ever more complex formal patterns. But Abhinavagupta recognized that even the most dazzling of such poets are mere technicians, however brilliant. In great poetry something different is happening.

That something is dhvani, an evocative and suggestive power that cannot be found locally, in any one part of a poem or drama. Its glow suffuses all. As such it is essentially fluid, dynamic, hard to pin down. Dhvani works by indirection. It is like Dickinson's truth that is told "slant." We feel the presence of dhvani in a poem, but cannot precisely account for how it operates. Nor can we paraphrase what it suggests.

Poet technicians have mastered, through hard work, a skill. Poets whose works are suffused by dhvani are blessed with a kind of innate genius, a divine gift. What cannot be framed by ordinary speech can be suggested, evoked, indirectly given voice to, by dhvani. Wallace Stevens once described poetry as the "hum of thoughts evaded in the mind." That hum, like the sound, the resonance of *Aum*, the vibration that inheres in all words, in all speech, but which no word can name, is perhaps the origin and essence of dhvani.

The Absolute preeminently, above all, is that which cannot be denoted or fixed by names. It is beyond the sphere of logic. Language can never fully apprehend or comprehend the absolute. Dhvani is like the long, sonic gesture of a sentence that, though beautiful in itself, always points beyond itself to the aura of something ineffable, something that words can never reach nor grasp directly, but which the inspired speech of the poet can intimate.

Finally, there is yet another vital way, perhaps the most significant, that art works can grant access to the experience of the divine. Here I must invoke the *rasas*, or predominant feeling tones or moods, which drama, the paradigmatic poetic art form for Abhinavagupta as for Aristotle, is designed to evoke.

There is in Indian aesthetics a clear distinction between the *feelings* evoked by rasas and the *emotions* which one experiences in everyday life. As presented in the theater, feelings as opposed to emotions are not aroused by contingent, mundane events. They arise in a context in which the contingent gives way to a realm in which the laws of time and space are temporarily suspended. The rasas, as feelings, not emotions, are not particulars but universals and as such grant access to that which is universal. It is because the rasas are universals that the spectator can respond to them with the combination of absorption yet detachment that is characteristic of a meditative state.

Additionally, among Abhinavagupta's key contributions to aesthetics was the inclusion of a ninth rasa, *shanta rasa*, at the center of the circle of the other eight rasas he postulated. Shanta rasa refers essentially to a kind of peace analogous to that which one might experience in deep meditation or in a state of liberation. According to Abhinavagupta, shanta rasa underlies all the other rasas, and is always experienced, by a sensitive or reader or spectator, as their substrate. That is why, for example, when leaving a performance of *King Lear*, in which the rasas of horror, disgust, and madness predominate, one is not in the throes of an agitated state, but is instead ensconced in the aura of a quiet, contemplative state that takes some time, as one exits the theater and re-enters mundane life, to be dispelled. A deep experience of shanta rasa entails an experience of peace and bliss that is analogous to, and partakes of, the peace that passeth understanding, the astonishing and indescribable bliss, of Lord Shiva himself. According to the Aristotelean model, such a state might be construed, with some justice, to be indicative of catharsis, of the exhaustion of emotion. But perhaps even the state of being drained of emotion as ordinarily understood leads to a state that underlies all mere emotion.

Thus all works of art, when masterfully realized, contribute—as effectively as ritual, and more pleasingly than philosophical speculation—to the spiritual attainment of spectators, auditors, or readers, granting them a foretaste of the creativity, bliss, and the peace of the divine. And thus Abhinavagupta's aesthetic theory is an integral part of his metaphysics.

2.
Stevens/Abhinavagupta

1.

Yet again: I am no scholar. I am no scholar of Sanskrit. I am not scholar of Indian aesthetics. I am not a scholar of any kind. I am something more unofficial, a poet. I have long, very long, been a student, an aging ephebe, of Wallace Stevens, but I find much of his best work impossible to paraphrase, much less to definitively and finally comprehend. I find it, often, uncanny, baffling. What follows, then, is the spawn of a marriage of ignorance with incomprehension. Nonetheless, I do not disown it. This thing of strangeness I acknowledge mine. In much of it, improbably, I feel I am getting at something of importance at least to me, although, in the spirit of Stevens, perhaps never quite getting there —presuming, perhaps erroneously, that there is indeed a *there* to get to. I am proffering this hopefully not altogether tasteless fruit of my labor not with hubris but with at least a semblance of humility. And so, to begin...

I thought it might be interesting, or rather resonant and suggestive, to examine three of the key terms of Abhinavagupta's aesthetics outlined previously—pratibha, dhvani, and shanta rasa—and to assess their possible relevance to a modern, or specifically a Modernist, American poet, Wallace Stevens. I will begin my discussion of Stevens with an exploration of dhvani; I shall refer to the notion of pratibha throughout, and shall conclude with a discussion of shanta rasa. I will also occasionally refer to the metaphysics of Kashmir Shaivism as propounded by Abhinavagupta, as his metaphysics and his aesthetics are unusually closely aligned. My treatment of Stevens will be at times quite granular, and might seem to veer from these three central terms, but I continually have them in mind, and consistently and frequently return to them.

The distinction between the dazzlingly rhetorical, elaborately patterned Sanskrit court poetry, with its emphasis on tropes (the more far flung rather better) and highly elaborate formal patterning, and poems instinct with dhvani, or what might reductively be called the power of suggestion, seems particularly germane to the generation of American poets who succeeded Stevens, so I will begin, as a kind of prelude, by briefly addressing this generation.

The New Criticism, prevalent during the middle years of the past century, with its imperative of close reading, of parsing poems as autonomous structures, with its extreme, fastidious focus on delineating and examining the operation of various kinds of tropes, with its valorization of formal unity, of the proper adjustment of parts to the whole, was ubiquitous and impossible to ignore. The prominent poets of this generation produced work that reflected high ambition, talent, and discipline. They tended to have a somewhat scholarly bent, and to be thoroughly conversant with the long histories not only of English literature, but often of various other poetic traditions as well.

But for all its virtues, the kind of poetry valued by the New Critics can be seen as in some ways similar to Sanskrit court poetry. The lesser poems of the poets writing in accord with the New Critical program can seem afflicted by a kind of arid intellectual virtuosity. Something essential seems to be missing from many of their poems—again, something like dhvani, the suffusing, permeating glow of a non-paraphrasable suggestiveness that can elevate a poem from an exercise in talent to an expression of genius, a word I follow Abhinavagupta in using despite knowing full well how discredited it has become. Of course dhvani, and the talent, discipline, and skill developed by poets over a period of years, are not mutually exclusive. Quite to the contrary. At some point, for a few poets, years of study and practice culminate in a kind of critical mass, and a breakthrough into writing poems suffused by dhvani occurs. Skill and talent, albeit coupled with inspiration, are still required for translating that inspiration into poetic form.

Whatever one thinks of them, the Beats were among the first to prick the academic bubble of the New Criticism, which was in any event ripe for bursting. Both *Howl* and *On the Road,* written during long, uninterrupted, drug-fueled seizures of what can only be called a kind of inspiration, with their free, improvisatory flow, with their unique, distinctive rhythmic signatures, seem suffused by dhvani. Sadly, neither Ginsberg nor Kerouac ever again wrote works of equal power, with the possible, heart-breaking exception of Ginsberg's *Kaddish.*

As a result of a rather unlikely joint reading with Ginsburg, Robert Lowell was impressed by, and perhaps envious of, the immediacy of impact that Ginsberg's poetry had on their shared audience. After having adopted Catholicism with a manic fervor, quite militantly expressed in his second book, *Lord Weary's Castle*, Lowell's religious enthusiasm waned. By the time of his encounter with Ginsberg, he was ready to abandon his highly wrought, marmoreal, densely agglutinated lyrics, rife with both classical and Christian allusions, and to feel his way toward a more relaxed, personal style, leading ultimately to his book *Life Studies,* which sent a minor shock wave through the world of academic poetry. Eventually, many poets raised under the aegis of the New Criticism—Berryman, Roethke, Merwin, Wright, and Plath, to name but a few—experienced breakthroughs in which they found their voice, a now highly suspect metaphor, but one which nonetheless suggests a real change from poems reflecting a hard-won skill and competence, allied with talent, to poems charged with a distinctive expressive force, allied with both talent and inspiration.

The metaphor of finding one's voice would cause no problem to any Indian philosopher. India has been, and remains, a preeminently oral culture. Scriptures were transmitted orally and memorized. Most were later written down, but many have been lost. Words or teachings imparted from a teacher to a disciple, to a far greater degree than written words, are considered instinct with the energy of the teacher's spiritual attainment. The greater the attainment and spiritual power of the teacher, the greater will be the efficacy and power of his words. Similarly, according to Abhinavagupta, the greater the attainment of the poet, the more he is in touch with pratibha, the power of creative intuition, the greater will be the suggestive power, the dhvani, that his poems will convey.

It is important to remember that, for Abhinavagupta, words and the syllables of which there are comprised are forms of Shakti, of her power, her potency. They, and the poems in which they are employed, can be more or less alive, more or less suggestive, depending on the degree of creative energy amassed by and available to the poet at the time of their making. That is why, according to Abhinavagupta, only poets of genius, inspired poets—again, words now thoroughly debunked in the West—not mere technicians, however talented, can create poems suffused by dhvani.

Western theories of semiotics or of aesthetics lack any sense that language, and poetry in particular, can have a non-discursive, very real potency, power, energy. This sense of the potency of language is something that has long been taken for granted in Indian culture. Brahmans who were steeped in the studies of the Vedas, for example, were not concerned with analyzing the meaning of Vedic verses, which were at any rate so obscure as to defeat such analysis, but were rather concerned both with memorizing Vedic chants and learning how to properly recite them with perfect pronunciation, pitch, tone, and rhythm. These chants were considered storehouses of effective energy and power, and to chant them incorrectly was not only to squander this power, but also to create a rip or tear in the fabric of the cosmos. There is no similar sense in Western poetics that poems are in any more than merely metaphorical way fields of energy, some more potent than others, and that what one receives in reading a poem is not merely fine shades of discursive or connotative meaning, but again, in some quite real and discernible, though difficult to define or characterize way, the quality and degree of the energy that the poet himself has invested in his poem.

Perhaps the only recent Western poet/theorist who can help us here is Charles Olson, who writes, in his essay "Projective Verse":

> A poem is energy transferred from where the poet got it, …by way of the poem itself to, all the way over to, the reader. …Then the poem itself must, at all points, be a high-energy construct and, at all points, an energy-discharge.

What is required to produce such verse is, according to Olson, "a change beyond, and larger than, the technical." Poems possessed of high energy, of dhvani, are "at all points" high-energy constructs. I emphasize "at all points" here because, according to Abhinavagupta, the effect of dhvani is nonlocal, suffuses, at all points, entire poems. Such poems discharge a high degree of energy that the reader absorbs and, if he is a same-hearted reader, presumably feels quickened and inspired by. I do not think it too far-fetched to liken this transfer of energy, though in a different, specifically poetic context, to a highly evolved spiritual teacher's oral transmission of empowered words to a receptive disciple.

W. H. Auden famously wrote that "poetry makes nothing happen." Even if Auden was implicitly referring to the impotence of poetry in the political sphere, his aphorism, deliberately and provocatively left unqualified, is one with which I strongly disagree. Leaving poetry aside, the simplest, apparently least charged words that we speak to each other have some more than merely discursive impact on us, in some way directly affect our own energy fields, assuming, as I do, that we, like poems, also have energy fields, what Tantrism calls our subtle bodies. Words are quanta of energy. When they are deployed in poems as parts of a larger context, a high-energy construct that exploits their full range of possible meanings and shades of affect, their power is amplified. More importantly, when a poet is in touch with pratibha, with creative intuition, his words will be instinct with the power that is their source. While retaining their discursive meanings, the words of an inspired poet affect us more immediately and directly than is usual with words that are deployed by merely competent, or indeed even by more than merely competent, poet/technicians.

Until fairly recently—though there is never total consensus regarding any one poet or poem—there has not, in general, been an unwillingness on the part of critics to make value judgements that distinguish between merely technically accomplished poems and poems whose force fields, to use my terms, are unusually strong and suggestive. One of the main reasons we read poetry rather than, say, philosophy, is to feel the quickening, enlivening linguistic energy that poems impart. Whatever ideas such poems entertain are either a small bonus or, except in egregious cases such as Pound and Eliot, a minor (or major) embarrassment. Poems are not inert marks on a page to be faithfully transcribed by a passive mind seeking some stable meaning or meanings. They are embodiments of energy. When that linguistic energy is strong enough, charged enough, it becomes what Abhinavagupta calls *dhvani*, and when it is absorbed by the sensitive, receptive reader it awakens in him something like the pratibha, the creative intuition, that has given rise to it.

2.

I will now, at last, turn to the poetry of Wallace Stevens, born too early to have been much affected by the New Criticism, a poet whose work, at least superficially, could scarcely be more different from Olson's, and which, though formal and often abstract, seems to me to be thoroughly suffused by dhvani. I will begin by focusing primarily on one of his late long poems, "Esthetique du Mal."

For a long time the most read and anthologized of Stevens' longer poems was "Sunday Morning," an elegant, extended lyric in eight stanzas of equal length clearly inspired by Keats' odes, which doubtless attained its privileged status by lending itself perhaps too easily to paraphrase. His later long poems written in unrhymed tercets, particularly "Notes Toward a Supreme Fiction," intermittently lend themselves to paraphrase, while at the same time assiduously resisting it. "Esthetique du Mal," written not in tercets but in verse paragraphs of varying lengths, seems to me the long poem of Stevens that most successfully, most uncannily, resists paraphrase.

In 1944, in an issue of the *Kenyon Review* read by Stevens, the poet/critic John Crowe Ransom questioned what possible relevance poetry could have in the face of the overwhelming, exigent reality of World War II. The issue also contained a touching letter by a young soldier on active duty, mentioning Stevens as a poet whom he had in the past admired. The soldier questioned what role poetry could possibly have in mitigating pain, and specifically, whether poetry could address the primary imperative facing soldiers, the struggle quite simply to survive. Ransom's query, but particularly the soldier's letter, prompted the writing of "Esthetique du Mal."

At the time that the poem was written, the furious battles on the Italian front had just drawn to a close. At the same time, Vesuvius had begun to erupt, burying the ruins of Pompeii under a foot of ash. The opening section of "Esthetique du Mal" seems to refer to a soldier in Italy, perhaps on temporary leave. He is alternately writing home, reading paragraphs on the sublime, and watching smoke arise from a rumbling Vesuvius, the terrifying eruption of which is a classic (or hackneyed) trope of the sublime cribbed from the earliest writer on that topic, Longinus. The soldier/reader/ observer/listener/scribe is clearly something of an aesthete. He is perhaps the kind of soldier that Stevens imagines he might have been had he been engaged in the war. The soldier watches as "...sultriest fulgurations, flickering, / Cast corners in the glass." These lines sound almost parodic in their exquisiteness, but the rest of the section clearly changes register and takes on a more somber tone. Immediately after these extravagantly flicking consonants a more sober discussion of pain in its various modes ensues. "Pain / audible at noon, pain torturing itself, / Pain killing pain on the very point of pain." Finally we are told simply that "pain is human." The volcano, trembling in another ether, is likened to a human body at the end of life. The soldier/scribe can describe the terror of the sound of the volcano's groaning because it is human.

Thus, as the poem begins, with its contemplation of pain, death, and a fearful sublime, we are at least on the periphery of the physical and emotional reality of the still raging war.

However, as the poem progresses, Stevens scarcely addresses the brute realities of the war at all. Instead, he makes a kind of end run around them. "Esthetique du Mal" is no less abstract than any of Stevens' other major late long poems, and yet the language of many of its fifteen cantos, compared to his long poems in tercets, or in couplets, feels relatively lush, and more tonally varied, not only varied within each canto, but often within each of its verse paragraphs, themselves uncharacteristically, uniquely (with respect to Stevens' long poems) variable in length.

And yet the relevance of this richness and suppleness of tone to the horrors of war seems at best tangential. Indeed, the strategy of "Esthetique du Mal" with regard to its ostensible subject is one of indirection, which is also a characteristic of Stevens' poetic enterprise as a whole. Two of Stevens' well known dicta are relevant here. The first is that "poetry must evade the intelligence almost successfully." The second, in a slightly different context, speaks of poetry as "the hum of thoughts evaded in the mind." It is his faithfulness to the first dictum that often makes Stevens' poetry so difficult, at times nearly impossible, to paraphrase. The second, the reference to a kind of hum that evades thought altogether, seems to me to be a brilliant evocation of the role that a poem's sound plays in contributing to what Abhinavagupta called dhvani. There is, in fact, a kind of pervasive hum, always felt but difficult if not impossible to analyze, associated with an uncanny suggestiveness, in Stevens' best poetry. Finally, Stevens, in touching on subtle phenomena of sound, whether in the form of poetic speech or music, tends at the same time to refer to them as entailing a kind of numinous transparency or glow.

All of these characteristics—indirection; resistance to paraphrase; an uncanny, difficult to analyze, power of suggestiveness; the all-suffusing resonance of a linguistic energy beyond thought, not merely appearing locally, as is the case with tropes and figures of speech, but throughout entire poems; the convergence of sound and light as language raised to a higher power—are redolent of dhvani. As is the notion to which I have earlier alluded, that imaginative genius and inspiration, not talent or skill alone, are capable off producing such subtle yet powerful effects.

3.

Having pronounced "Esthetique du Mal" beyond paraphrase, I will not here attempt to paraphrase it. However it might, at a minimum, be worthwhile to glean some sense of what Stevens means by "mal," which inevitably calls to mind Baudelaire's "Fleurs du Mal." Stevens' mal targets neither the peculiar psychic malaise of a Baudelaire nor the metaphysical evil once sanctioned by a Satan whom Stevens declares, or re-declares, dead in a later section of the poem. Perhaps mal refers to the universal human experience of pain addressed in the poem's opening canto. Perhaps it can be seen as arising from desire or craving which, when inevitably thwarted, is a source of that pain. Pain can refer either to physical pain or to mental/emotional pain, which are not airtight categories, but are often related. Both are inevitably aspects of the experience of being human.

Pain can also be seen, as in Buddhism, as arising from desire or craving, including the desire to avoid pain, which, when inevitably thwarted, is a source of that pain. It is not only our habitual attraction to the pleasing, but our almost instinctive revulsion to that which we register as painful or repulsive, that limit us. The notion that pain can arise from our attempts not to feel it, or from our tendency to succumb to the ministrations of a false consolation, whether self-administered or misguidedly offered by others, is one that I will explore in a later context.

Implicit in all of these sources of pain is the role that the mind plays in them. It is the mind that registers and reacts to physical pain, and it is also the mind that desires or craves, and suffers mental/emotional suffering when its desires are thwarted. In particular, it is the mind's rote habitual, instinctive, and above all unconscious responses to phenomena both inner and outer that limit our freedom and give rise to suffering. The imagination, which is intrinsically luminous and dynamic, is the enemy to all that that is unconsciously fixed and frozen by the predictably and blindly reactive lower order functions of the mind.

However, in what follows I will focus more narrowly on the rational mind as a locus of what Stevens calls mal in "Esthetique du Mal." When divorced from realities beyond its purview, the rational mind, which is not merely unconscious, but which often in fact is a well-honed instrument, can become particularly virulent. I am referring, for example, to the imperious mind of the purely analytical philosopher who "disposes the world in categories, thus," who insists on freezing and reifying, and thereby distorting, that which is always in flux, and to the monomaniacal mind of a revolutionary/logician who walks by a beautiful lake but, cut off from any grounding in the physical world or in his own body, is too preoccupied by thought to see it. Mal finds a place in the minds of logical lunatics of whatever stripe whose "extreme of logic becomes illogical," whether those who reify and deaden the world, who murder to dissect, or those whose unchecked cogitations lead to all manner of spurious and destructive ideologies. This targeting of the excesses of the specifically rational mind is characteristic of Stevens' post-Romantic brand of Modernism.

More generally and fundamentally, mal is a function of the mind's singular capacity for negation, which can metamorphose into a virulent negativity from which "fault falls out on everything." Seeing the world as a kind of secular hell, such a mind feels unconsciously driven to keep recreating that hell. The mind, in its destructive aspect, is a kind of evil genius. It is

> That evil, that evil in the self, from which
> In desperate hallow, rugged gesture, fault
> Falls out on everything: the genius of
> The mind, which is our being, wrong and wrong,
> The genius of the body, which is our world,
> Spent in the false engagements of the mind…

Self, mind, our being, body, world are all homologous here, and all participate in mal, but with mind, as the only reiterated term in the series, and the last, having pride of place. What, then, if anything, can save us from this evil? Not God, who is now as good as dead. Not Satan, who no longer allows us to evade our responsibility for evil. Certainly not the unaided mind itself. However, lest one despair, perhaps there is a residual angel who can provide a provisional cure, or at least a palliative. That angel is for Stevens the "necessary angel" of the imagination. Stevens wrote a great deal about the imagination, particularly about its role in resisting what he calls "the pressure of reality."

Stevens' formulation of imagination as that which is in conflict with the pressure of reality (in his most extreme formulation, "a violence from within meeting a violence from without") increasingly gives way to a recognition that the relationship between these two poles is complementary rather than antagonistic. The imagination, writ large, becomes the dynamism that generates the interplay between these poles, one of which Stevens still calls the imagination. Each necessarily entails the other. The interplay between the imagination and reality involves the swinging of a pendulum toward one pole, then toward the other, a movement that does not end with a final apocalyptic victory of either, but proffers many kinds of possible accommodation, however tenuous, between the two.

In his poem "Of Modern Poetry," Stevens says of the mind: "It can never be satisfied…never." Its manifold desires and cravings can never ultimately be fulfilled. When neither allied with the imagination nor chastened by the pressure of reality, the mind, particularly the coldly rational mind, orphaned and autonomous, can become not only insatiable but violently destructive. However, when allied with the imagination and responsive to the pressures of reality, including physical reality, which in turn includes the reality of the body, the mind can become a sublimely creative rather than a destructive force. Its intrinsic insatiability can goad the imagination to seek ever new solutions to ever new problems.

The final canto of "Esthetique du Mal" famously commences with a reference to the poverty of not living in the physical world, a poverty in which desire cannot be realized and becomes impossible to tell from despair. A few lines later Stevens asks: "One might have thought of sight, but who could think /of what it see, for all the ill it sees?" This almost plaintive question is a kind of culmination of all of the references to the destructiveness of the mind in the course of the poem. We seem still to be subsumed by mal.

But then the pendulum swings. The poem concludes, in a typical shift of tonal register, with a powerful affirmation.

> And out of what one sees and hears, and out
> Of what one feels, who could have thought to make
> So many selves, so many sensuous worlds,

> As if the air, the mid-day air, was swarming
> With the metaphysical changes that occur,
> Merely in living as and where we live.

This is one of Stevens' evocations of a kind of happy or more than merely happy moment of balance and accommodation in the relationship between the imagination and the pressure of reality. The very thought that just a few lines ago had such a destructive connotation now, when linked with the imagination, and crucially with the poet as maker, creates a wondrous swarm of metaphysical changes, as well as a plethora of changing versions of the self and of the sensuous worlds it inhabits. It is as though simply by living, moment to moment, as and where we live, we too, as imaginative makers, can create subtle, ever new versions of the ourselves and of our world, versions in which self, mind, being, body, and world are aligned. The mind above all, working with the imagination, grounded in reality, including the reality of the physical body, contributes to this constant process of enthralling transformation whose serial transfigurations "Esthetique du Mal" itself, with its constant transitions, subtle or abrupt, each flowing seamlessly into the next, seems to embody.

4.

But enough of the weak paraphrase I promised to foreswear. Stevens' poems, with their frequent poetic rather than philosophical use of abstraction, with their feints at making propositional statements, with their serial entertaining of hypotheses, can tempt us to produce such paraphrases, which they then inevitably evade, revealing our glosses as both inadequate and superfluous. In "Esthetique du Mal," the experiential reality of the sensuous yet metaphysical changes, the generative transformations, to which its conclusion discursively refers, is not primarily conveyed by whatever provisional ideas the poem may propose. Rather, the feeling of such metaphysical changes is conveyed by the resonant, luminous, ever changing, all suffusing sonic energy of Stevens' language itself, by its suggestive force. What is suggested by dhvani, as already noted, eludes easy definition, cannot be paraphrased or directly categorized.

There are a number of passages in "Esthetique du Mal," including the following, in which Stevens addresses aural phenomena, and in doing so reflexively refers to the elusive nature of sound as it works in "Esthetique du Mal" itself.

> When B. sat down at the piano and made
> A transparence in which we heard music, made music,
> In which we heard transparent sounds, did he play
> All sorts of notes? Or did he play only one
> In an ecstasy of its associates,
> Variations in the tones of a single sound,
> The last, or sounds so single they seemed one?

Clearly we are not listening here to Ludwig Richter, the pianist as turbulent shlemiel in Stevens' poem "Chaos in Motion and Not in Motion," of whom it is said, in lines that resonate directly with several in the closing canto of "Esthetique du Mal," he "has lost the whole in which he is contained, / Knows desire without an object of desire." Instead, D is obviously a version of Stevens, and his questions are rhetorical, unanswerable. Often when Stevens presents a set of apparently alternative hypotheses, frequently in the form of metaphors, about a given phenomenon, they are all, the law of noncontradiction notwithstanding, in some sense true or valid. Taken singly or together, all of the alternatives which Stevens proposes are aspects of dhvani, which is productive of "ecstasy," an ecstasy that a same-hearted listener can share, and that does not, despite its etymological roots, stand aloof from the whole of which it is a part, but is contained by it.

Stevens' uses of the words "transparent" or "transparence" hint at the almost luminous aura that opens a space in which the music can be heard. That same transparency creates a clearing in which words can be heard. The coincidence of sound and light, hearing and sight, is in Stevens, as it was for Coleridge ("a sound in light, a light like power in sound"), a sign of language working at its highest power, at its most suggestive. Vision, too, when not paralyzed by fixation, is fluid, protean, and what it sees, in Stevens' magisterial "The Idea of Order at Key West," is like the ghostly light reflected in the waters of the harbor. Stevens writes, in "Notes Toward a Supreme Fiction," of the world when imaginatively seen: "It must be visible or invisible / invisible or visible or both, / a seeing and unseeing in the eye." Taken singly or together, these hypotheses, the law of noncontradiction again notwithstanding, are again equally valid.

Stevens is a poet who, as has oft been noted, qualifies himself and then qualifies his qualifications. Often, he will present a series of phrases that entail multiple substitutions of one of the terms. The gently comparative term "as" rather than the more obvious "like" is also a constant feature of Stevens' poetry. In "An Ordinary Evening In New Haven," Stevens writes of "the intricate evasions of as," where one feels the word intricate might well be standing in for infinite. This tendency to endlessly qualify and compare suggests the Stevens who views ideas and things from multiple perspectives, seldom, if ever, categorically, definitively, fixing on one. It also suggests, again, that Stevens' poetry progresses, by means of serial evasions, by a constant indirection that nonetheless finds direction out.

The imagination apprehends the world it construes in glimpses—isolated, glancing, fugitive, partial—gleaned from a source that is itself mysterious, not fully knowable. The in fact unreasonable demand of reason that reality, after being put through its consecutive, preordained syllogistic paces, be made fully comprehensible, forecloses the imagination's intuitive intimations into the life of things. Keats wrote of Coleridge that he would "let go by a fine isolated verisimilitude caught from the Penetralium of mystery from being incapable of remaining in half knowledge." What is caught from the penetralium of mystery and might otherwise go by are glimpses

(Stevens calls them "quarter colors of half things") of a dynamic process that reason too often seeks to freeze, categorize, and reify.

The movement of Stevens' poetry tends to be accretive, additive (a trait he shares with Whitman) and circular or cyclical, with frequent iterations and reiterations, repetitions of the almost-same set in apposition to each other, affording us not only incremental changes of meaning but also, just as importantly, "the pleasure of merely circulating."

Stevens' poems do not progress by means of complex analogies or metaphors whose terms, as in Donne, unfold with an ineluctable logic. We do not feel that Stevens' poems are pressing, by means of argument, toward some definitive conclusion. Rather, they often progress through a process, sometimes restless and relentless, sometimes leisurely and playful, of increasing metaphorical refinement and acuity. The most frequent of several terms that Stevens often uses as interchangeable with metaphor is "resemblance." Goaded by the desire to generate finer resemblances, metaphors that more successfully suggest whatever imaginative truth he wishes to approach, Stevens often moves through a series of analogous resemblances, resulting in a profusion of metaphors and of metaphorical transformations, that do, at times, progress toward something close to a definitive formulation.

Above all, Stevens' poetry keeps moving, constantly if variably moving. Indeed, sometimes it seems as if it could keep ringing its changes endlessly, ever in motion yet ever somehow the same. "This endlessly elaborating poem," Stevens writes, as if all of his poems were one poem, "displays the theory of poetry." Yes, intricately imbricated, yet infinitely ramifying.

Stevens' "Notes Toward a Supreme Fiction," his poetical summa, contains an implicit account of his poetics. It is arranged in three sections of equal length, each of them titled with imperatives that together epitomize the qualities that Stevens deemed essential attributes of the supreme fiction that is poetry. They are: "It Must Be Abstract." "It Must Change." "It Must Give Pleasure." Though "Esthetique du Mal" is frequently abstract, and though it certainly gives pleasure, I think that it is written primarily under the aegis of "it must change."

Again, from the point of view of dhvani, the play of Stevens' consciousness as he entertains ideas, moving fluidly from one hypothesis, briefly held, to another—sometimes considering each as in some sense valid, sometimes progressing toward greater acuity through a process of increasing metaphorical refinement—and the sometimes abrupt, discontinuous changes of tonal register engendered by this play, all of which are seamlessly assimilated to the tone of a poem as a whole—communicates, suggests far more than whatever paraphrasable ideas his poems throw off like the froth, the spray, the spindrift from a wave that is constantly moving.

According to Olson, for energy-constructs replete with dhvani, with suggestive force, a practical question remains: how are poems to be written so as to communicate that energy to the reader? Olson's answer is: "ONE PERCEPTION MUST LEAD IMMEDIATELY AND DIRECTLY TO ANOTHER PERCEPTION..."

> At all points...get on with it, keep moving, keep in, speed, the nerves, their speed, the perceptions, theirs, the acts., the split second acts, the whole business, keep it moving as fast as you can...USE, USE, USE the process at all points.

Olson, somewhat dogmatically, emphasizes percepts, actions, and proprioception, the sense of the body's orientation in space, as most germane to his notion of "composition by field." Note the spatial "at all points" rather than the temporal "at every moment." Nonetheless, Stevens communicates the energy that is dhvani by likewise moving with an extraordinary rapidity not only from perception to perception, but from image to image, from phrase to phrase, from hypothesis to hypothesis, and so on. Stevens certainly, in his own way, keeps things moving. From moment to moment.

"Not to have," writes Stevens, "is the beginning of desire. To have what is not is its ancient cycle." The extraordinary, labile movement of Stevens' language is also the movement of desire. Just as the mind is insatiable, labile, so is desire, and thinking and feeling, thinking and desiring, are allied to an unusual degree in Stevens. Just as Stevens resists alighting on any one idea, on any one hypothesis, on any one meaning, so he resists seeking out and attaching himself to any one object, or any one possible fulfillment of desire. Rather, he keeps desire on the move, leaping from provisional fulfillment to provisional fulfillment, while discriminating, like an epicure, between ever more subtle nuances of feeling. This continual moment of desire in itself is for Stevens the fulfillment of desire, the source of the continual pleasure, one of the three main demands, as we have just seen, to which poetry must be responsive.

Stevens' desire is peculiarly unattached, uninvested either in the concrete particulars of the objective world, so beloved by William Carlos Williams, or in some human beloved, or in some realm of fixed, categorical abstract ideas or ideals. It is neither mimetic nor allegorical. As stated in "Of Modern Poetry," Stevens has no interest in descending toward the former nor rising toward the latter. Desire in Stevens' poetry is invested in prolongation of desire as provisionally satisfied by the linguistic formulations of poetry itself, of words referring to, making manifold connections with, other words in a kind of lateral movement within the mind and at the level of the mind.

Occasionally, however, there are consummate moments, particularly blessed intervals, pauses, within a movement that is itself blessed. In "Of Modern Poetry," the actor/poet is "a metaphysician in the dark," twanging a wiry string whose sounds pass through a sudden rightness, "wholly containing the mind," and presumably wholly contained by it as well, producing fortuitous passages that vibrate with the something approaching the "unalterable vibration," not an unalterable meaning, that the poet seeks but is destined never to find. Such passages are charged with an energy that resonates only with itself, that spins on its own axis, that has no meaning extraneous to it. They are redolent with, suffused by, dhvani. They are like mantras or like strings of mantras, skeins of a language that seem instinct with their own peculiar power, their own evocative, undefinable charge. The metaphysician twanging his single string is no Kant or Hegel. At fortunate moments, however, his humble instruments evokes metaphysical changes akin to those that sometimes occur to us by creatively living as and where we live.

I have mentioned that paying attention to the liminal, to the in-between, as well as to the initial phase of any phenomenon, is one of the most crucial spiritual practices enjoined by Shaivism. The characteristics of Stevens' poetry mentioned earlier, its tendency to rapidly substitute one term for another; to serially qualify its qualifications; to present a series of analogies or metaphors that more closely approach, but never definitively arrive at, some existential truth; to indulge, often using the word "as," in promiscuously proliferating comparisons; to play with ideas, never finally settling on one; to improvise constant transformations, variations on a theme, that lead to no definitive end, but offer a kind of pleasure that is an end in itself—all can enthrall us as readers, and yet can at the same time induce in us the feeling that the ground is too rapidly shifting beneath our feet, that we can find no toehold in the poem. The moment that we are aware that one movement in the poem has arisen, it has already passed us by, and we are on to the next movement. We are constantly, as readers, in between these arisings and subsidings, as though in some interstitial space, always abiding in the moment, the interval, between one phase or phrase and the next. The multiple transformations in Stevens' poems can occur with a vertiginous rapidity. It can almost seem as the poem is beginning again, repeating some always initial phase, with every line. And that we must begin again, as novices, along with it. It is thus highly apt that the first word of "Notes Toward a Supreme Fiction" is the strong imperative "Begin." We seldom have the feeling that we have mastered Stevens' poems or have command over them, but must, if we are to appreciate them at all, to some degrees, surrender to them, allowing them to perform their occult operations upon us.

The play of substitutions, of comparisons, of qualifications, of constant transformations in Stevens' poetry, need not be seen as endless deferrals of a fictional presence that is in reality an absence, but can equally be seen, as Shaivism sees them, as expressions of an overflowing presence dynamically unfolding itself, manifesting itself, in and as the world. What are we surrendering to when we surrender to these ever changing spaces of liminal transformation in Stevens' poetry? There is a reason why Shaivism enjoins paying attention to the liminal, to spaces between. They grant us "portals," (a key word of Stevens, used in such strikingly different poems as "Peter Quince at the Clavier," "The Anecdote of the Jar," and "The Idea of Order at Key West") from the conditioned to the unconditioned and the unconditional, to the blissful, or, to use Stevens' preferred term, the ecstatic experience of Consciousness itself. Attending to the liminal has the subtle yet powerful effect of transforming and expanding our state of awareness. The gaiety of Stevens' language, with its gliding and giddying play of transfigurations and transitions, with its pervasive liminality, discloses, opens up, suggests multiple possibilities. Yet through all the changes that "Esthetique du Mal" rings, its characteristic luminous hum, still more suggestive, remains a constant.

"Esthetique du Mal" is a linguistic tour de force that highlights the nature of its language. Again, as Shaivism reminds us, words are not inert. They, and the phonemes that comprise them, are specific quanta of energy, each with a specific charge. Indeed, the structure of the universe, according to Abhinavagupta, is linguistic in nature. Shakti contains an inherent linguistic potency, which unfolds itself in the form of various worlds, from the most subtle to the most gross. She articulates, in levels of speech, again from the most subtle to the most gross, the lineaments of these worlds, and establishes the nature of the subjects who dwell in them. The inherent potency or energetic charge of the phonemes of which words are comprised, as well as the notion of the several levels of speech, will be addressed in more detail in the second part of this book.

The inspired poet, in touch, through pratibha or creative intuition, with the higher levels of speech, manifests imaginative worlds, virtual, parallel universes, that are free of the usual constraints of time and space. These worlds are both real and unreal, and are not bound by the laws of mundane reality. By imaginatively engaging with them, by becoming absorbed in them, we ourselves enter into a space of relative freedom, and are empowered, like the poet, to create our own, ever-changing imaginative worlds, and to envisage a self that includes, moment by moment, various versions of the self and of the reality, sensuous or otherwise, that it at once inhabits, experiences, and creates. Stevens' poems are such subtle, luminous spaces of enhanced freedom, a freedom in which we, as readers and listeners, our own imaginations quickened, can participate, reveling in virtual worlds of which we are the co-creators.

I should note in this connection that playing off against the quicksilver, shape-shifting movement of Stevens' poetry, there is often something not only kinetic but kinesiological and gestural about his poems, gestural in the sense that many of the lines and passages in his poems do not point beyond themselves to any obvious external/sensuous nor internal/mental-ideational referents. The poet as "noble rider" pronounces phrases that call attention to themselves as phrases, and that enthrall us by the uncanny beauty of their sound and syntax. They are like gestures in those forms of modern dance in which movement itself, emerging, unfolding, in fluid transition, from moment to moment, rather than illustrating some narrative or conceptual content, is highlighted. This liminal, always in transition, series of movements, or of poses briefly held, which the dancers' bodies have learned by heart, and the patterns that they form in space, can, like Stevens' language, have an uncanny, difficult to account for, nobility and suggestiveness.

Much ink has been spilt on the question of whether or not Stevens was a philosophical poet. Certainly he plays with philosophical terms and counters, but he does not deploy those terms as most philosophers do. Interestingly, the philosopher with whom Stevens clearly feels the most kinship is Nietzsche, who was unique among Western philosophers in his willingness, indeed on his insistence, on gleefully, lightly, playing with such terms. Western philosophers in general are more interested in the categorical, in the fixed, in the accurately denotative rather than the connotative. Stevens is not a philosophical thinker in his poems. Rather, he is concerned, like a meditator, with closely observing his thoughts, with tracking, then almost simultaneously recording, the process of thinking itself. He is not concerned with the fixed and categorical, but with the essentially dynamic nature of both the imagination and reality. In his essay "The Noble Rider and the Sound of Poetry," Stevens, after a long series of preliminary minutiae, finally describes nobility as a force, a force something like that of a wave, a force apart from, and yet the source of and never finally exhausted by its possible manifestations, which vary from age to age. At the close of "An Ordinary Evening in New Haven," Stevens writes, "It is not in the premise that reality / is a solid. It may be a shade that traverses / A dust, a force that traverses a shade." It is the job of the poet to unfix the categorical, to put once frozen terms back into a revivifying circulation, and to rescue long dormant ones.

Finally, there is a conspicuous element of play in Stevens' poetry, including the playing with ideas to which I have just alluded. As it happens, play, free play, the play of Consciousness, is at the core of Kashmir Shaivism. Shiva is constantly engaged in the five acts referred to in the preceding chapter , those of creation, destruction, sustenance, concealment and grace. As part of his divine *lila* or cosmic play, Shiva appears to contract himself, concealing his true nature, creating "limited agents" and the phenomenal worlds in which they operate, and at the same time, through grace, to reveal his true nature to such agents, resulting in the expansion of their awareness, and ultimately to the experience of union with Shiva. Just as creation and destruction, on which I shall have more to say later, are constantly enacted by Shiva through Shakti, so analogously are the play of concealment and revelation, revelation and concealment, each of which, like creation and destruction, inextricably entails the other. The enlightened seer delights in observing this constant play of revelation and concealment as it manifests in the phenomenal world, realizing that it is a playful expression of Shiva Himself. In reading Stevens' poetry, I would suggest we experience something very like this play of concealment and revelation. What we think we gave grasped eludes us; what we think has eluded us we suddenly grasp—a process that keeps reiterating itself, that is at once the source of constant frustration and of constant pleasure. Perhaps above all, at least in one of his most characteristic modes, Stevens is a playful poet/creator, an inveterate tease, endlessly seductive, who always remains just beyond our grasp.

5.

In 1945 Stevens was asked to write a poem to be read at a ceremony honoring *Phi Beta Kappa* seniors graduating from Harvard. The poem he wrote was "Description Without Place." By tradition the *Phi Beta Kappa* poem was supposed to be brief and to address some particularly urgent reality, such as a war, that the graduates were likely to be confronting. "Description Without Place" addresses the war even more obliquely than does "Esthetique du Mal." It is also notably more abstract, so much so that its motto might be "no thing but in ideas," the reversal of Williams' famous prescription, "no idea but in things." Indeed, Williams, who had always, improbably, considered Stevens a kind of ally fighting under the same banner, intensely disliked the poem, and reacted to it as though it was a kind of personal betrayal.

"Description Without Place" returns to many of the questions raised by "Esthetique du Mal." In section 7, Stevens imagines Nietzsche, who is presumably the antithesis of the kind of revolutionary/logician unable to see the lake in "Esthetique du Mal," closely observing the changes of color and form reflected on the surface of a pool in Basel, a surface that when observed by the philosopher discloses great depths. This passage is a kind of visual analogue of the sounds of B's piano music in the passage I have previously quoted; in this case light, no longer the mere hint of light alluded to by the term transparency, falling on the surface of the pool, becomes the medium in and through which constant, subtle, quite literally fluid transformations of form and color both occur and can be observed. While observed by the philosopher who, like those listening to the sounds of the notes of the piano, is rapt in reverie, the ever-changing forms which he beholds shine with "an innate grandiose, an innate light." This light, again, is redolent of dhvani, which is experienced not only as a sonic phenomenon but as a suffusing glow.

In observing the movement of the much mottled, colored forms, Nietzsche is also observing his own thoughts, his own mind, and it is the light of his own solar consciousness that not only merely colors but gilders, makes golden, the pool.

> Nietzsche in Basel studied the deep pool
> Of these discolorations, mastering
>
> The moving and the moving of their forms
> In the much-mottled motions of blank time.
>
> His revery was the deepness of the pool,
> The very pool, his thought the colored forms,
>
> The eccentric souvenirs of human shapes
> Wrapped in their seemings, crowd on curious crowd,

> In a kind of total affluence, all first,
> All final, colors subjected in revery
>
> To an innate grandiose, an innate light,
> The sun of Nietzsche gildering the pool...

Nietzsche is clearly the inspiration behind the critique in "Esthetique du Mal" of Christianity and its "too, too human God, self-pity's kin / and uncourageous genesis," which supposedly further weakens those whose spirit lacks the requisite nobility and grandiosity to deal with reality as it is. But this weak discursive meaning, all too paraphrasable, is what I have described as a kind of propositional feint in Stevens. What really interested Stevens, and what interests us in Stevens, is not his ideas, borrowed or otherwise, but the dynamic play of the mind among ideas, and the linguistic power through which that play is enacted. Likewise, Stevens was primarily interested in the Nietzsche who was, like him, a master rhetorician, one who also delighted in indirection, whose fluid, protean discourse, often presented in brief quasi-autonomous passages that have something like the quality of prose poems, gaily and defiantly refuse to be pinned down, resisting easy paraphrase. Such passages are characterized by constant subtle transitions, changes both in theme and tonal register. It was the Nietzsche whose work, like Stevens' own, was suffused with dhvani, with an inexhaustible power of suggestion, whom Stevens admired.

However, the next couplet after passages cited above enacts, somewhat disturbingly, one of the shifts of tonal register to which I have referred. After we have been told that Nietzsche's words evoke "a kind of total affluence, all first, all final," come, immediately dispelling any notion of finality, the lines:

> Yes: gildering the swarm-like manias
> In perpetual revolution, round and round.

We are reminded that when colors first appear in the poem they are called "discolorations," and are described as much "mottled," hardly honorific terms. We are reminded, too, that the moving colors are also referred to as "eccentric souvenirs of human shapes, crowd on curious crowd," that become the "swarm-like manias" in the lines just quoted. One wonders if there is a suggestion that Nietzsche's manic, sometimes unbalanced rhetoric may in fact have had dangerous consequences, and not only for Nietzsche. Indeed, it has often been suggested, unfairly, that the tenor of his rhetoric, and some of his strongly held ideas, the notion of the Overman among them, may have prepared the way for the mass movement, the "swarm-like manias," that became Nazism, with Hitler a far less attractive master of rhetoric than Nietzsche. Under such despotic regimes, human beings are objectified, becoming mere horrific, "eccentric souvenirs of human shapes," spectral reminders of the no-longer fully human.

We do not have to imagine Stevens subscribing to the vulgar notion of Nietzsche as a harbinger and progenitor of fascism to sense that Stevens had some misgivings about him. In this context the odd word *gildering* appears in a different light, or *as* a different light. It suggests not the pure luminosity and transparency of the spirit, let alone the light of the actual sun, but something painted to give the appearance of being gold. Perhaps Nietzsche's rhetoric, though undoubtedly brilliant, also has this unwholesome gildering quality. Perhaps it is painting over something disturbing, unhealthy, unbalanced in Nietzsche himself, who was in real life as much an invalid as an Overman.

The "swarm-like manias" that are in "perpetual revolution, round and round" cannot help but recall not only Nietzsche's bleak doctrine of the eternal recurrence of the same, but more importantly the specter of political revolution. And indeed the lines directly following the couplet I have been discussing introduce us to what becomes a long contemplation of Lenin, yet another logical lunatic sojourning uncomfortably, feeling entirely out of place, by a lake, in what is clearly a reprise of the similar scene in "Esthetique du Mal." We shift abruptly yet somehow seamlessly from a discussion of Nietzsche to a discussion of Lenin. Though this shift perhaps primarily emphasizes the contrast between the two, one also senses that, conjured up in such close proximity, they are alike in being thinkers for whom, in different ways, the mind is dangerously paramount.

The two lines I have just quoted suggest a kind of alternative hypothesis about Nietzsche. But they do not erase or supplant the initial hypothesis of Nietzsche as a masterful rhetorician toward whom Stevens felt imaginatively drawn, and whom he admired as a kind of kindred spirit. Rather, as I have suggested above, both hypotheses can be held as in some sense true. Stevens is not simply reversing himself and judging Nietzsche in an entirely harsh light. Again, the kind of shift in tonal and thematic register enacted by this couplet occurs with frequency not only in "Esthetique du Mal" but in Stevens' poetry as a whole.

6.

All well and good, but a central question remains: does the poem satisfactorily respond to Ransom's request for poems that confront the brutal reality of war, or to the soldier's touching letter in the *Kenyon Review* asking what possible relevance poetry can have for the soldier whose chief and sometimes sole imperative is to survive? This letter, more than Ransom's request, inspired Stevens to write "Esthetique du Mal."

Stevens was far from being a hermit. He was deeply, if privately, engrossed in the politics of his time. The fact that he did not address the political in his poems led to some indictments, mostly by leftist critics during the thirties, of Stevens as a mere aesthete callously indifferent to the plight of others. Stevens was sufficiently stung by this criticism to have written a long poem, "Owls' Clover," in response to it. He soon judged this poem a failure. Years later, in "Esthetique du Mal," he returned to his typical strategy of indirection.

In the midst of the war years, Stevens wrote about the horrific pressure of a reality against which the imagination must somehow struggle: "I am thinking about life in a state of violence... physically violent for our friends, and still more violent for our enemies, and spiritually violent, it may be said, for everyone else."

Stevens did not believe that the poet had a political, social, or even an ethical role to discharge. Nonetheless, he believed that the poet, who could hardly do much to counter physical violence, could nonetheless address the spiritual violence from which all suffered. He wrote, with respect to those overwhelmed by the violence of the real, "I think it is the poet's function to make his imagination theirs and that he fulfills himself only as he sees the light of his imagination become the light in the minds of others."

The association of the imagination with light, with light as a positive force, is typical of Stevens. He believed that the light of the imagination, glowing in the mind of others, could help to offset, for them, the burden of the real, could offer a kind of spiritual consolation. He believed, quite simply, that the role of poetry is to "help us to lead our lives."

What could a lawyer and actuary in his sixties living in the suburbs of Hartford, who also happened to be a poet, have honestly and honorably done to address the Second World War, a reality whose pressure must have felt both distant and overwhelming? Should he have produced something topical, something more along the lines of what Ransom probably hoped for and expected? One can only imagine how baffled Ransom must have been when he received Stevens' poem. No. Stevens chose instead, like Keats, to try to make something beautiful and sublime even in the face of a surrounding chaos and ugliness. There is the risk in this strategy, this response, of seeming oblivious and callow, callous to the reality of suffering, a risk of which Keats, and doubtless Stevens, was very much aware.

There are passages in "Esthetique du Mal" that exemplify the downside of the risk I have just described, that are strangely tone deaf. I have mentioned that "Esthetique du Mal" scarcely addresses the brute realities of the war. Indeed, it scarcely addresses war at all, with two exceptions, and it is in these instances that the poet sounds most off key.

The first is the much maligned section 7, that begins with the line "How red the rose that is that is the soldier's wound," a line that many have found offensively trivializing and sentimental. It seems to me, however, that the greater issue here is that Stevens' poetry, despite his avowed distaste for Romantic idealisms, at times proposes its own idealisms, can give voice to an abstractive, universalizing, idealizing tendency that does not always serve him well.

> How red the rose that is the soldier's wound,
> The wounds of many soldiers, the wounds of all
> The soldiers that have fallen, red in blood,
> The soldier of time grown deathless in great size.

Here the individual soldier becomes one of many soldiers who together becomes one abstract, idealized, universal type of the soldier as hero who is "deathless," immune to the vicissitudes of mortality. Of "time's red soldier deathless on his bed," Stevens avers, "No part of him was ever part of death." The consolation that Stevens proffers here seems both premature and reductive. The universal type too easily eclipses the painful reality of the individual. As I will discuss later, Stevens elsewhere similarly proposes, though sometimes with considerable imaginative force, a kind of abstract, universal major man who epitomizes all men, and who, as thinker of the first idea, authors a supreme fiction, which will replace the consolations of a god who is now dead to us, who no longer inspires our imaginative assent.

The poem's second instance of tone deafness occurs in stanza 11, which begins:

> Life is a bitter aspic. We are not
> At the center of a diamond. At dawn,
> The paratroopers fall and as they fall
> They mow the lawn.

In the first two lines, comprised of two perhaps too-witty aphorisms or *apercus*, Stevens seems to be chiding his just mentioned tendency toward a universalizing idealism, his longing for an "impossible possible philosopher's man / who in a million diamonds sums us up." The reference to the paratroopers seems almost flippant, as does an ensuing reference to "poor dishonest people," and the ringing of bells in a village steeple that is identified with the ringing of bells in a vessel that "sinks / in waves of people," and that quite possibly memorialize an actual shipwreck. Here we are on a home front that is identified with a war that now seems almost, inappropriately, banal. The falling paratroopers are even said to "mow the lawn." A more quotidian domestic chore can scarcely be imagined.

The passage culminates with the lines "Children of poverty, natives of malheur / the gaiety of language is our seignor." Here we are again reminded of Nietzsche and his valorization of gaiety and of his "gay science," particularly as embodied in words that seem to be those of an Overman who defiantly laughs at human suffering, including his own. One cannot help but wonder if this gaiety of language speaks to that suffering in anything other than a dismissive way. Here Stevens, with an assist from Nietzsche, seems to ally himself with a thoroughly disabused tough-mindedness, the obverse of the idealisms mentioned above.

Neither of these tendencies, that toward an abstract, universalizing idealism nor that toward a ruthless, putatively tough-minded realism are successfully imaginatively realized in these passages in "Esthetique du Mal"—nor, indeed, wherever they occasionally crop up elsewhere in Stevens' oeuvre. Both feel inapposite, unconvincing, and the second courts suggesting a kind of callousness that the poem as a whole successfully avoids.

Nonetheless, despite these local imperfections or flaws, it seems to me that in "Esthetique du Mal" Stevens has done the one thing—other than complacently maintaining an unresponsive and unproductive silence—that he could have plausibly and convincingly done, given his temperament and the nature of his gifts as a poet, to address the pressure of the reality of the war. He has written an ultimately affirmative poem that shimmers and is suffused with dhvani, a subtle suggestiveness that refines the consciousness of the reader while opening it to myriad nuances of feeling.

7.

Finally, it remains for me to regard "Esthetique du Mal" under the aegis of the sublime, with which the poem not only expressly concerns itself but which it also, more importantly, exemplifies. I have already suggested, perhaps too speculatively, that that in the poem's first canto the ubiquitous pronoun *he*, the most common of Stevens' substitutions for the little used *I*, refers to an American soldier on leave from battle, reading a book on the sublime while watching the eruption of Vesuvius. I have assumed that he is reading Longinus, the first authority on the sublime, in whose brief treatise on the subject the eruption of volcanoes is a preeminent trope. For virtually all Western philosophers, however, and for poets, like Stevens, who have any interest in philosophy, Kant has of course long since displaced Longinus as the great authority on the sublime. For Kant the experience of the sublime is an overwhelming experience of awe, of vastness, even of a kind of infinitude, such as that occasioned by contemplating some awe-inspiring natural phenomena like the alpine vistas beloved by the Romantics. Through this experience of awe and immensity, which can be frightening as well as exhilarating, the ego is temporarily overcome, itself assuming a kind of vastness and expansiveness as the result of which the self experiences that which transcends it.

In the first canto in "Esthetique du Mal," Stevens writes that "pain is human." Pain is specifically human because human consciousness, unlike that man's fellow inhabitants of the earth, is also self-consciousness, and because it is not only aware of the present but is also the custodian of the past, both individual and collective, and the guarantor of the future. Of the protagonist of the first canto, Stevens writes, "He could describe the terror of the sound because sound was ancient." Were it not for our consciousness, which is the sole custodian of the past, "Vesuvius might consume / In solid fire the utmost earth and know / No pain." Similarly, a crucial part of man's awareness of the future is his knowledge of death. Thus, for him "The volcano trembled in another ether /As the body trembles at the end of life."

Because man's self-consciousness, according to virtually all mystical traditions, is limited, and his apprehension of the world partial and distorted, he is subject to feelings of attachment and aversion that result in psychic pain. As alone, isolated, in his experience of self-consciousness, man, particularly modern man, is liable, also, to feel doubly estranged, separate both from the phenomenal world and from whatever it is that transcends it.

In his beautiful poem "Less and Less Human, O Savage Spirit," Stevens writes, "It is the human that is the alien / The human that has no cousin in the moon." Man's self-consciousness, and particularly the experience of pain that is more than merely physical, sets man apart from nature and from his fellow inhabitants of the earth, but also, more importantly, from the experience of transcendence. Typically, when in pain, we wish for God to ratify that pain, to intervene in our affairs, to save us. We look, or used to look, toward a "too, too human God" who "out of sympathy has made himself a man," and who affirms as well as mitigates our own pitiable condition. When we pray, we pray for something, for some specific outcome. We are like those football players who thank God after a victory, as though God has an interest, a stake, in who wins a game. In asking God to ratify our pain we are asking him to ratify a kind of delusion, to validate a chimera, an hallucination, one that alas feels all to real, but which in fact is a function of limited self-consciousness, of our ego. We want Him, like Job's comforters, to offer us a kind of false consolation. But were God, in fact, to ratify our pain, to confirm us in it, we would remain cut off from the possibility of the experience of transcendence that alone has the potential to transform our experience of pain, that alone can save us.

In the second canto of "Esthetique du Mal" the *he* to whom the poem continually refers is lying on his balcony at night surrounded by blooming acacias, in what we first assume is a kind is a kind of idyllic scene. In Stevens' poetic oeuvre, night, moonlight, and the sound of birds is a recurrent symbolic triad that typically signifies the imagination at its warmest and most benignant, as a force by means of which the world draws near to us. Such is not the case here. The protagonist, whose sleep is "afflicted," who perhaps suffers from insomnia, listens to the song of birds, which is represented as "too dark, too far," too distant.

>   ...Warblings became
>   Too dark, too far, too much the accents of
>   Afflicted sleep, too much the syllables
>   That would form themselves, in time, and communicate
>   The intelligence of his despair...

Afflicted, distressed, the would-be protagonist projects his pain even upon the innocent warbling of birds. He conceives of the inarticulate notes of their song as *syllables*, which will form, in time, words that will communicate to him the "intelligence of his despair," and thereby confirm him in it. Language itself, operating through the mind and the obsessive thoughts to which it is prone, traps us in our own projections, projections from which we are unable to escape. The mind, once again, is the primary locus, the native ground, of *mal* considered either as pain or more broadly as a kind of habitual psychic disaffection and malaise.

At this point, however, the canto takes a striking turn.

> The moon rose up as if it had escaped
> His meditation. It evaded his mind.
> It was part of a supremacy always
> Above him. The moon was always free from him,
> As night was free from him...
>
> It is pain that is indifferent to the sky.
>   ...It does not regard
> This freedom, this supremacy, and in
> Its own hallucinations never sees
> How that which rejects it saves it in the end.

Again, it is "the human that is the alien / the human that has no cousin in the moon." A more commonplace formulation would regard the sky as indifferent to us, but Stevens insists that it is we who, particularly when mired in pain, are indifferent to the sky. The moon, rising up, "evades" the mind, our limited self-consciousness, our too-rigid ego, from which, as we have seen, "fault falls out on everything." It is blessedly free from us as night is free from us. It becomes part of a "supremacy" that is "always above us," part of the transcendent zone of the sublime. It is crucial that this zone remain transcendent, a transcendence whose very nature is "freedom" and which, if we could permit ourselves to experience it, might free us from the hallucinations of the limited selfhood and the pain that accrues from them. Instead the mind, typically, "does not regard this freedom, this supremacy and in / its own hallucination never sees / How that which rejects it saves it in the end."

The mind, beset by hallucinations, and by the primary hallucination of what Blake calls the Selfhood, by its limited, distorted experience of the world, rejects the experience of sublimity. For Stevens, the sublime is that zone of transcendence always above us, which alone, but only when we reject that Selfhood, only when we reject the limitations of the mind and the manifold ways in which those limitations cause us to suffer, has the capacity to save us. It is crucial that the transcendent, the realm of a supremacy remains always above us, apart from us, refuses to participate in the intelligence of our despair. It is also crucial that this zone be accessible and open to us, if not continuously, then in moments that have the power to profoundly alter our perspective on our own experiences.

Stevens, of course, owes much to Kant's conception of the sublime as that through which we transcend the quotidian experience of the ego, through which we are, as it were, rapt out of ourselves. Stevens' sublime, however, is not a mere concept subsumed under the category of the aesthetic, denoting a particular psychic phenomenon, but is a transcendent dimension that is actual, even sacred, that is still available to us, even though populated by no personal God. When we choose to regard this dimension rather than remaining blind to it, when we open our hearts to it even or especially in the midst of our pain, without demanding that we be consoled or that our condition be altered, we establish connection with a transcendence that has the power if not to heal us, then at least, again, to profoundly alter our state. Of course, we cannot dwell perpetually in a sublime whose very nature is to evade us. We can, however, catch glimpses of the supremacy always above us, and of the possibility of freedom which it continually holds forth.

I have said that "Esthetique du Mal" is evasive, performs a kind of end-run around the issue of actual human pain and suffering. Seen, however, from this slightly different persecutive, the poem, in its discussions of sublimity, and more importantly, as itself uncanny, ineffable, as itself sublime, in fact *does* address our pain. As we surrender ourselves to and participate in its sublimity which, as we have seen, entails a kind of freedom, specifically from the pain-inducing distortions of the ego, we are released, if only temporarily, from that pain. Thus the poem, again, helps us to lead our lives.

We need not of course deny ourselves all forms of consolation. We need only to abandon the false consolation of a God who has abandoned us, and to whom we can no longer grant our assent. The ravishingly ecstatic canto 5 of "Esthetique du Mal" begins, "Softly let all true sympathizers come." It is not only the usually fleeting experience of the sublime, but also the simple and uniquely human experience of love, and chiefly of our love for one another, that can mitigate the depredations of the isolated ego. As the heart in pain can be healed by opening up to the sublime, to the transcendent, so it can be healed by opening up to others. Thus its double estrangement, both from the transcendent and from the phenomenal world, can at least partially be mitigated.

Though rejecting a God who is "self-pity's kin," the speaker ecstatically embraces the community of those who are his genuine kin, who are "true sympathizers," whether by birth or as chosen by him as his own.

> Softly let all true sympathizers come,
> Without the inventions of sorrow or the sob
> Beyond invention. Within what we permit,
> Within the actual, the warm, the near,
> So great a unity, that it is bliss,
> Ties us to those we love. For this familiar,
> This brother even in the father's eye,
> This brother half-spoken in the mother's throat,
> And these regalia, these things disclosed,
> These nebulous brilliancies in the smallest look
> Of the being's deepest darling, we forego
> Lament...

Here Stevens, like Whitman, is a prophet of a kind of filial love. What a vast gulf separates this passage from Nietzsche, from his proud, defiant self-isolation, from his Olympian contempt for all but the most exalted of his species. And what a lie, too, this passage puts to any notion of Stevens as a fundamentally cold poet. Here Stevens suggests a kind of nondual vision not as achieved in isolation, but dialogically, through relationship to others. "So great a unity, that it is bliss, ties us to those we love." The filial, that which is brother to us, exists not in isolation, but as an image "even in the father's eye," and, touchingly, as words "half-spoken in the mother's throat"—as liminal words, words on the brink of articulation, potential words which correspond to spanda, to the primordial stirring of Consciousness immediately prior to the manifestation of words and the meanings to which they refer, and to the separation between subjects and objects extended in space. At this level of incipience unity still abides. Cleaving to it, we permit ourselves to experience a world that is actual and near, that discloses to us even the "nebulous brilliancies in the smallest look." Only later do we speak to ourselves or others in words that communicate "the intelligence of our despair."

8.
Stevens, though exquisitely sensitive to negations, was essentially a comic poet, in the most widely generic sense of the term, as was Whitman, despite the fact that he was exquisitely sensitive to human suffering. Neither, by temperament, had an instinct for the tragic as a genre, as is exemplified in Stevens' case by his abstract, detached gestures toward theoretically discussing the tragic in "Esthetique du Mal." Their lack of instinct for the tragic as a literary genre does not, of course, mean that either were oblivious to the actually tragic. Whitman volunteered in Union hospitals throughout the Civil War, an emotionally devastating experience that ruined his health but did nothing to break or alter his essentially affirmative spirit. For Stevens, as for Whitman, particularly in the midst of very real, all too real tragedy and despite it, imaginatively saying *yes* rather than *no* to experience is essential. For Stevens this is also the position of the realist, because it provides the only opportunity for new beginnings, beginnings which must be made even if they, too, in due course, will also inevitably come to entail tragedy.

> The mortal no
> Has its emptiness and tragic expirations.
> The tragedy, however, may have begun,
> Again, in the imagination's new beginning,
> In the yes of the realist spoken because he must
> Say yes, spoken because under every no
> Lay a passion for yes that had never been broken.

This *yes* is not that of a deluded idealist, but of the poet in whom the imagination and reality are aligned.

To whom is this *yes* spoken? Poems reach their readers not *en masse*, but one at a time. And lyric poems in particular have the capacity to create, or to suggest, a kind of intimacy with the reader, a bond that, particularly in the midst of difficult circumstances, difficult perhaps for both poet and reader, can grant a reprieve, if only temporarily, from feelings of alienation, or of despair. Stevens' poetry is singularly adept at establishing this kind of bond of intimacy with the reader, and has a number of strategies for doing so, strategies which I will now at least begin to explore.

There is yet another passage in "Esthetique du Mal" in which Stevens writes of sound, in this case the sound of the speech that ties us to those we love. The passage occurs in section 5, just after the previously cited passage on familiar and familial love. Stevens writes,

> Be near me, come closer, touch my hand, phrases
> Compounded of dear relation, spoken twice,
> Once by the lips, once by the services
> Of central sense, these minutiae mean more
> Than clouds, benevolences, distant heads.

The close, intimate, sensory communications of familial love obviate the need for the "clouds, benevolence, distant heads," for a fanciful heaven. And yet there is something else, something stranger transpiring here. It seems clear the "phrases / compounded of dear relation" refer to the phrases spoken to each other offstage by the hypothetical relatives and filial confreres Stevens has just invoked. And yet real relatives don't speak to each other in phrases compounded of relation, dear or otherwise. They just speak to each other. However, the phrases of Stevens as a poet can quite aptly be described as compounded of relation. The summoning of these phrases with the request that they touch his hand, the hand that writes his poems, a peculiar contact of the abstract with the organic and concrete, is subtly disconcerting. It seems as though Stevens, in a strange apostrophe, is beseeching his own phrases to draw near to him, to touch his hand, in order to establish a close, solitary, contemplative zone of intimacy with himself as he writes—an intimacy in which we as readers can participate. Perhaps it is something like this intimacy both with himself and with his audience to which Stevens is alluding in "Of Modern Poetry." He says of such poetry:

> ...It has
> To construct a new stage. It has to be on that stage
> And, like an insatiable actor, slowly and
> With meditation, speak words that in the ear,
> In the delicatest ear of the mind, repeat,

> Exactly, that which it wants to hear, at the sound
> Of which, an invisible audience listens,
> Not to the play, but to itself, expressed
> In an emotion as of two people, as of two
> Emotions becoming one.

It is often the case with Stevens that, feeling privy to his self-communing in the form of his poems, I do feel a peculiar intimacy with him, which is also an intimacy with myself. His self-reflection, the sound of it more than the sense, triggers a similar self-reflection on my part as invisible reader. For Stevens thinking and feeling, again, are unusually closely allied. By engaging in similar processes of self-reflection, writer and reader also come to share in two emotions that echo one. It is as though they become one in a shared space of intimacy.

Self-reflection and self-consciousness are transmuted, dissolved in the erotic process of becoming two people echoing one, a unity expressed by simple, unselfconscious action of a sort that is inherently satisfying, and in which, unburdened by thought or our limited and limiting self-consciousness, we lose and find ourselves. The writing and reading of a poem, like a "man skating, a woman dancing, a woman / combing," figures who appear at the end of "On Modern Poetry," are depictions of such unselfconscious actions, answerable to Stevens' imperative "It Must Give Pleasure."

According to Abhinavagupta, it is pratibha, creative intuition, that binds the poet, the reader, and the poem together, that is ultimately responsible for establishing a kind of zone of intimacy between them, a zone in which much of Stevens' poetry seems to take place.

To approach anew what Abhinavagupta means by pratibha, a key passage in Charles Olson's "Projective Verse," cited earlier, once again seems apposite:

> A poem is energy transferred from where the poet got it (he will have some several causations), by way of the poem itself to, all the way over to, the reader. Okay. Then the poem itself must, at all points, be a high-energy construct and, at all points, an energy-discharge.

In Olson's formulation, two questions remain unanswered, the question of from where the poem got the energy that it transfers to the reader, and of what the reader is to do with that energy when he or she receives it.

According to Abhinavagupta, pratibha, or the creative intuition of the poet, is instinct with the power of Consciousness itself, as is the poem that unfolds from it. The same-hearted reader, whose own pratibha, whose own creative intuition is awakened by the poem, participates in the poem so fully that he becomes in effect its co-creator. The creative intuition of the poet and of the reader are brought into close alignment, and both are aligned with the creative power of Consciousness itself.

Stevens writes in his essay "The Figure of the Youth as Virile Poet" that the poet helps us to live our lives, as we have seen, by making the light of his imagination our own. The power of Stevens' imagination to become one with, to merge with the light of the mind of the reader and thereby to activate the reader's imagination, creates a kind of close alignment between poet and reader, the shared resonance, the sense of intimacy between Stevens and his same-hearted readers that I have described. As we awaken, with the help of Stevens' poetry, to our own creative intuition, we become privy to the subtle disclosures of Consciousness, disclosures that sometimes have the sharpness of a flash of insight, sometimes the force of unprecedented revelations for which we as yet have no words.

When reading Whitman's poems in my own inner voice, as well as Keats', I feel as though they have the power to touch me impalpably from within, bridging the gulf of time that separates us. I often experience the same phenomenon when reading Stevens, a strange power for a poet whose temperament sometimes seems chilly.

In fact, however, the reticence and detachment, the aloofness in Stevens actually enhances and abets the same-hearted reader's feeling of intimacy with the poet and his poems. There is something in Stevens' reticence, as in Elizabeth Bishop's, that disarms us, that draws us in as readers, until we get glimpses of an affective state, a feeling that is intimately related to their reticence. This feeling seems somehow more impersonal, less attached to either memory or to objects, in Stevens than in Bishop.

By contrast, poems, even quite good ones, that too readily presume to subject us to the jackhammering *I* with its all too-pressing anxieties, worries, and concerns, often repel rather than encourage intimacy with the reader. This is true, for example, of the lesser, more histrionic poems of Lowell, Berryman, and Plath.

On the other hand, poets who too readily affect a kind of quasi-mystical dilation of the *I*, and who seem too consistently to be straining for an impersonal expansion of the self, can also leave us cold. Here I am thinking of the lesser poems of Hart Crane, Theodore Roethke, and Dylan Thomas, who were also of course capable—when not too conspicuously straining to produce grand effects—of producing rapturously beautiful poems.

Speaking more generally, there is always a danger that the lyrical *I*, particularly while in a sublime mode, will inadvertently preempt us, overwhelming our own tenuous *I*, or will seem to strive to supplant our own subjectivity with that of the poet. Such poems, at times, provoke our admiration while at the same time discouraging our full imaginative assent. All too often the lyric speaker, like a manipulative Hollywood director, has too overt designs on us, and as soon as these designs become apparent we are likely to resist them.

Keats specifically mentions Wordsworth as a poet who "has designs on us." Wordsworth was, of course, the prime exemplar of what Keats called the "egotistical sublime," a poetry that attaches all it surveys to the constantly supervening *I*, to the perhaps too stable identity of the poet. Assuming the tone of "a man speaking to men,"

Wordsworth too easily succumbs to a kind of pious didacticism. Keats claimed to have no fixed identity, as a result of which he was more readily able to identify with, to imaginatively participate in the life of whatever his senses perceived or his imagination called into being. Stevens, more detached, less prone to identification than Keats, nonetheless eschews, like Keats, the fixed identity of the lyric *I*. Neither Keats nor Stevens sound, in their poems, "like a man speaking to men," and neither succumb to didacticism. In Stevens, the first person is dispersed, becomes a diaspora of other persons, and operates under their assumed names.

It has been noted by Helen Vendler and others that the speaker of Stevens' poems seldom uses the aforementioned lyric *I*, deploying instead the pronouns *we, you, one*, and above all *he*, thus suggesting Stevens' detachment from these various iterations of the self, and perhaps from any fixed sense of the self in general. This practice is so unusual and novel that it is no mere idiosyncrasy; it suggests something central about Stevens' poetry. In place of the quotidian or sublime concerns of the overweening *I*, we are presented in Stevens' poems with what seem to be transcriptions of what has been taking place in a consciousness that is constantly engaged in witnessing and tracking itself. We have, then, glimpses of a consciousness that is detached from itself while at the same time observing itself. There is no overt *I* in this equation. This practice seems almost to exemplify what Shaivism calls witness consciousness, the abiding of the self in a pure awareness that remains unattached to the objects of that awareness. This detachment opens up a kind of liminal space between the witnessing consciousness and whatever inner and outer phenomena with which it is presented, or which it presents to itself. The larger and more consistently present this space becomes, the freer and more spontaneous, the less bound to internal and external constraints, consciousness becomes. Stevens has often written of the sense of liberation that his writing provided him, an exhilaration in which his same-hearted readers can participate.

The absence of an overt lyrical *I* in Stevens' poetry, and our at first subliminal sense, in reading it, of the detachment of an observing consciousness from the contents of that consciousness, encourages us, subliminally and over time, to detach ourselves from our own matchstick *I* as we read Stevens' poetry, to become one with his process of detached yet highly engaged observation of the linguistic contents of our minds. The poem becomes not the impersonal, but the more than merely personal ground on which poet and reader meet. Stevens' detachment becomes, again, paradoxically, not a detriment to intimacy, but an invitation to intimacy of a deeper kind.

Finally, there is something erotic in the process of reading Stevens' poetry, if by erotic we mean an enhanced sense of life, and have in mind something like two people, having finally having shed their constricting egos, meeting in a shared space of love or, in Stevens' preferred term, ecstasy—and perhaps, however briefly, becoming one with that love, with that ecstasy.

How can poetry help us lead our lives? In Stevens' case, by modeling for us unconstrained states of consciousness, deeper possibilities of intimacy, greater intimations of freedom—and also, as we shall soon see, starker, barer intimations of a mortality that, just as it always exerts its influence on life, always had a part, a vital part, in Stevens' poetry, one that naturally grew more prominent he grew older.

9.

In my discussion of Stevens' poetry, I have thus far dealt with the playful, exuberant, verbally extravagant, sometimes ecstatic Stevens who writes poems that will not be pinned down; that exult in the "paradise of meanings"; that valorize seeming, the world of appearances, more than that of being, and phenomenology over ontology; that seem as if they could go on forever, exemplifying the theory of poetry as endless elaboration.

It is important to stress that Stevens has, as it were, another theory of poetry, at first, particularly in *Harmonium*, a kind of minor chord to the major chord of his poems of endless elaboration, that by the time of his last poems itself becomes the predominant chord. I am referring to the pole in the poetry of Stevens that emphasizes the austere and the contemplative, that seeks to pare language and thought back to some bare fundament, to some essential condition for which there are no fully adequate words, in which the "paradise of meanings" gives way to a realm from which meaning itself is almost entirely banished as superfluous. This pole of Stevens' poetry operates by reduction rather than expansion. One can with justice call the two poles I am suggesting Stevens' winter vision and his summer vision, with justice because the changing seasons in New England do, in fact, have a richly symbolic value in Stevens' poetry. One of the earliest and still most powerful exemplars of Stevens' poems of winter is the extraordinary "The Snow Man," in which the speaker seems almost to dissolve into the winter landscape. His sole task is "not to think." At the same time, his senses are reduced to the barest listening, the simplest beholding, to pure awareness itself. Nothing himself, he "beholds / nothing that is not there and the nothing that is." In "Notes Toward a Supreme Fiction" Stevens speaks of a sun that is "washed in the remotest cleanliness of a heaven / that has expelled us and our images." To which I would add "our meanings."

Typically, and instructively, both Helen Vendler and Harold Bloom view the conclusion of "The Snow Man" as at best a kind of *Pyrrhic* victory, as a too severe reduction in which the prerogatives of the exuberantly figurative imagination are excessively and unnecessarily curtailed. Neither are comfortable with the "nothing" with which the poem concludes, Vendler in part because of her mistrust of anything that reeks of the mystical, Bloom because of his preference for the more expansive mythical mode of Stevens' "Tea at the Palaz of Hoon," which he regards as a salutary antitype of "The Snow Man." Their reaction reflects a tendency of critics to take "nothing" at face value as mere negation or nonbeing, as smacking too much of what is in fact a misunderstanding of the Buddhist void. The poem indeed enacts a kind of *via negativa*, a progressive process of ascesis whereby all of the attributes of the poem's protagonist are stripped away. What he thus experiences, however, is not mere a mere absence resulting from the encounter of a cypher with a cypher, but is rather the luminous, immediate apprehension of the real, as a result of which the real is freed of its "false compoundings" and appears in full radiance.

The meditative state so brilliantly suggested in "The Snow Man" is one devoutly to be wished for, not to be hedged about with reservations. The failure to understand this is a failure to understand the claim upon Stevens' imagination not only of the pole of the exuberantly figurative, but of the austere, stripped-down pole of the real.

Additionally, there are, of course, the ancillary seasons of autumn and spring, autumn as mainly leading into winter, spring as mainly leading into summer. Stevens' great late poem "The Auroras of Autumn," for example, with its severe abstractions, with its stripped down, solitary individual confronting an overwhelming sublime, with its parsing of different shades of white, from year to year, on the walls of an empty cabin by the sea, is a kind of first cousin to Stevens' winter vision.

One caveat: one must not be too literal about this seasonal scheme. Not all of the poems of Stevens' summer vision are set in summer, nor are all of the poems of winter vision set in winter. I have chosen these two terms because they are relatively less abstract and restrictive than the many analogous sets of terms I will shortly adumbrate.

It seems to me that the interplay between what I am calling his winter and summer visions is fundamental to Stevens' poetry. The poems of Stevens' summer vision, with their endless free play, in which the imagination seems to predominate, are reminiscent of Ovid, likewise a master of metamorphosis, whereas his meditative poems seem to approach, by way of ascesis, of a purging of the imagination, intellect, and speech itself, the pole of the real, a real that in these poems often has a kind of numinous glow.

I again want to stress that the notion that Stevens' poems of summer alone are imaginative, whereas his poems of winter have truck only with the real, is misleading. Stevens' imagination is essentially bipolar. It is at work every bit as much in the poems of winter as in those of summer. Thus the opposition between the imagination and reality or the pressure of reality, which was central for a long time to Stevens' theoretical discussion of poetry, along with the dualism which it implies, is belied by the dynamic, interdependent play of polar forces that continues unabated in his poetry.

Stevens' poems of summer are creative, endlessly proliferating, while those of winter are "de-creative," a term that Stevens borrowed from Simone Weil, paring themselves back towards the numinous source and end of creation. To provide a kind of perspective on these two poles, to see them slant, I will return, once again, to Abhinavagupta, but in this case to his metaphysics rather than to his aesthetics, an emphasis that I hope is justified by the fact that his metaphysics and his aesthetics are integrally aligned.

According to Shaivism, as you will recall, Shiva, who remains in a transcendent state, is inextricably one with Shakti. Shakti, in the form of *spanda*, a primordial stirring or vibration within Shiva, continually manifests, flashes forth, the world or worlds of phenomenal appearances while simultaneously resorbing them back into the indescribable plenum that is Shiva. What appear to be two different movements of consciousness are in fact one in the vibration of spanda, which is unconditioned by time or space. We, who are conditioned by both, experience this one energy as both manifesting itself and withdrawing itself. Stevens' summer and winter visions can be likened to these two movements, respectively.

In Stevens' summer vision, his consciousness, in its swift free play among phenomena and the ideas they suggest, never alighting for long on any one, exulting in change and the delight associated with it, endlessly both elaborating itself and reflecting on itself, is aligned with the creative movement of Consciousness. Through Shakti, Shiva's inherent potency, the manifold world of appearances constantly flashes forth, manifesting, moment by moment, the inexhaustible play of sensuous and mental phenomena. Stevens' protean language, in its kinetic energy, in its suggestive power, is instinct with and charged by the linguistic potency of Shakti, whose energy at once creates, articulates, and constitutes both the mental and sensory realms.

Stevens' winter vision, on the other hand, seems reflective of the resorbing motion of Consciousness in which the manifold world of appearances and ideas, and the speech by which they are constituted, are withdrawn, stage by stage, each more subtle than the last, toward some inconceivable, impossible to define pole of reality that has no place for us or for our images, a movement that entails both a reduction of the superfluous and an increasing abstraction and austerity of language, finally abjuring speech with its manifold meanings in favor of inarticulate sounds and the silence from which they arise, a movement that also approaches a sense of finality, completeness, and closure. Paradoxically, as we shall see, this movement of reduction and subtraction, of stripping or paring away both of language and of the sensory manifold in favor of the fundamental, the essential, also entails an expanded sense of self as Consciousness moves in the direction of an expansive, effulgent, impossible to define, indeed inconceivable source and end.

Stevens' poetry, like "the hermit in a poet's metaphors, /who comes and goes and comes and goes all day," keeps shuttling between the two poles, between his winter and summer visions, between the de-creative and the creative, between "early candor and its late plural," between "not to have and to have what is not," between the austerely abstract and abundantly, floridly particular, between a stripped-down use of language and an extravagant one, between the near end of meaning and multiple meanings, between the promise of finality and the endlessly open-ended, between being and seeming, between the ontological and the phenomenological, between the real and the apparent, between the inner world of the plenum or void and the outer world of appearance, between revelation and evasion or concealment, between the contemplative/meditative and the ecstatic. And so on.

Many other items could be placed on either side of these scales. And Stevens does full justice to both, while never finally alighting on or committing to either. To fully commit to either pole would be to lack the other, to be truly impoverished, as well as to be unbalanced. Stevens' winter and summer visions might erroneously be seen as the dialectical contraries through which his poetry progresses, but the movement of Stevens' poetry is not, again, dialectical or teleological, not tending toward some ultimate higher end. Rather, as previously mentioned, it is reiterative, accretive and additive, circular. The changes that Stevens delights in have nothing to do with the convulsive, dislocating Change past mere changing that is political revolution or spiritual apocalypse.

Stevens' delight, previously mentioned, in the circular, in the pleasure of merely circulating, is also a pleasure in the cyclical, primarily as manifested in nature by the cycle of the seasons. Stevens, like Blake, has no truck with the notional, abstract oppositions that are generated by logic. In nature there are no fixed opposites. Crucially, the relationship between Stevens' poles of winter and summer are between dual aspects of a continuum correlative with the bipolar nature of the imagination. "Winter and spring, cold copulars, embrace /and forth the particulars of rapture come." Again like Blake, Stevens is concerned with the particular, with the imagination as generative, not with sterile logical counters.

There is a long tradition in Western poetry and spirituality, often, as in Donne, derived from Neoplatonism, of positing a *conjunctio oppositorum*, a paradoxical uniting of opposites, at the heart of reality—as well as, according to Eliot, again with Donne in mind, of violently yoking together heterogenous images and ideas. Stevens, on the contrary, seldom has recourse to paradox, and the terms of his beloved resemblances require no violence to be yoked together, but rather tend to happily, gracefully, serially refine themselves, always mindful of stopping short of reaching "identity, the vanishing point of resemblance."

Much has been said about the almost endless series of what are usually called binary opposites in Stevens' poetry, so much so as to render any further discussion of them tedious, old hat. But the binary, both in computer programs and in poems, is the province of the logical either/or. Again, the apparent opposites in Stevens' poetry are not binary in the sense described above. They are not in the logical realm of the either/or. Rather, they are the complementary poles, mutually entailing each other, of a fluid continuum that naturally swings toward one pole, then toward the other. Stevens' imagination, essentially bipolar in nature, assiduously both generates and enacts, in its language, and tracks, both in its language and in the phenomenal world, this movement.

When one considers Stevens' body of work as a whole, in *Harmonium* the pendulum of the imagination swings predominantly toward what I have been calling his poems of summer. But again, as he grew older, facing mortality, it began, quite naturally, to swing more and more toward poems of winter. It is these poems to which I will now turn.

10.

The extraordinary first canto of "Notes Toward a Supreme Fiction" is for me the text that addresses the pole of Stevens' winter vision most directly. It is here quoted in full.

> Begin, ephebe, by perceiving the idea
> Of this invention, this invented world,
> The inconceivable idea of the sun.
>
> You must become an ignorant man again,
> And see the sun again with an ignorant eye
> And see it clearly in the idea of it.
>
> Never suppose the inventing mind as source
> Of this idea nor for that mind compose
> A voluminous master folded in his fire.
>
> How clean the sun when seen in its idea,
> Washed in the remotest cleanliness of a heaven
> That has expelled us and our images...
>
> The death of one god is the death of all.
> Let purple Phoebus lie in umber harvest,
> Let Phoebus slumber and die in autumn umber,
>
> Phoebus is dead, ephebe. But Phoebus was
> A name for something that never could be named.
> There was a project for the sun and is.
>
> There is a project for the sun. The sun
> Must bear no name, gold flourisher, but be
> In the difficulty of what it is to be.

As a prologue I want briefly to address the manner in which Stevens addresses us. We are *ephebes*, a Greek term for males in their late teenage years undergoing military training. Phoebus, the god whose very name connected us to him, is dead. We are now listening to Stevens, who, as though an elder entrusted with authority, is instructing us in a new discipline, imparting hard truths about the nature of a difficult reality that we must now confront. We are novices, in a sense novitiates, going through a rite of passage into an adult relationship with the world. Stevens' voice is magisterial. We, as readers, are metaphorically his students. I know of no other instance in Stevens where, without obvious irony, he assumes such an authoritative role toward the reader.

I will first address the idea in "the sun seen clearly in the idea of it" by indicating some of the things it is not. Crucially it is not the "first idea" referenced in subsequent cantos of "It Must Be Abstract." In these cantos Stevens reiterates his myth of the major man, a kind of abstract epitome of what it is to be most essentially, universally, and truly human. Having imagined this central man, Stevens imputes a fictional "first idea" to him. The central man, the thinker of the first idea, is a human abstraction invented by us, and he presides over an invented, fictional world.

But again, the first idea as thought by a fictional central or major man is not the same as the idea of the sun when seen clearly in the idea of it. The sun when seen in the idea of it is paradoxically "inconceivable." Its source is not the inventing mind, the imagination of man, nor is it the mind of God, a "voluminous master folded in his fire," who once assumed the name of Phoebus, of Apollo, the God of the sun. Phoebus, as well as the Christian God and his nemesis Satan, are dead. They are myths to which we can no longer give assent. Phoebus was merely the name of something that "never could be named," just as the idea of the sun cannot be conceived.

However, oddly, the "idea" of the sun can somehow be "perceived." Indeed, we are told to "begin" by perceiving it. What, then, is the nature of the sun when seen in the idea of it? The sun, so seen, appears clean, having been "washed in the remotest cleanliness of heaven." It has been cleansed by "expelling us and our images." Neither knowledge nor imagination can help us to perceive it. It as though we, too, must be scrubbed, washed clean. We must become "ignorant." Paradoxically, we must learn, be taught, to again become ignorant. Only as ignorant men can we again perceive what cannot be conceived. When the sun is perceived in the idea of it, it is no longer the metaphorical/mythical/divine sun, though it can still, apparently, be referred to with the harmless secular sobriquet "gold flourisher." Crucially, the sun when perceived in the idea of it is a percept, not a concept. Perhaps Stevens has gone back to the original Greek root of the word idea: *idein, to see*. To see the sun in the idea of it is to see it directly, as it is, is to see the sun as the sun, free of our mental and imaginative projections. The sun remains, of course, that which is illumined by its own light, and it is by that same light, after undergoing a kind of ascesis, that we will come again to clearly perceive it.

Later in this volume, in briefly discussing Chinese poetry influenced by both Taoism and Buddhism, and Japanese poetry influenced by Zen Buddhism, and again in a chapter of *Elective Affinities,* a book that is a kind of sequel to this one and dedicated to Stevens' erstwhile confrère William Carlos Williams, I will highlight what I call the poem of the pure percept. The poetic projects of Stevens and Williams in many ways can scarcely seem more different. It is here, however, with Stevens' valorizing of a pre-conceptual apprehension of reality, that those projects vitally converge.

The sun when seen in its idea is perceived directly, immediately. In many forms of meditative practice, the goal is to enter into a state free of thought and imagination, free of mental filters. In such a state a powerful kind of insight can occur. Things are seen with a preternatural clarity. Such perception is both direct and immediate, unmediated. This immediate, direct perception can grant access to a new knowledge of reality and a new experience of it. It is important to stress, by way of countering a common misunderstanding, that when we go back again, become ignorant again, we are not regressing to a primitive state but rather returning to the wellspring of being. We are being rejuvenated. We are beginning again. Again, it is no accident that "Notes" begins with the word *begin*. A word that is also an imperative, a kind of benevolent command.

The sun when "seen in the idea of it" is not merely inert, passive. Rather, just as there used to be a project, a specifically mythic and religious project, for the sun, it still retains a project, though changed to meet the spiritual demands of a secular era. The sun must "be in the difficulty of what it is to be." We, too, must be in the difficulty of what it is to be. We share the same project. This is what is being demanded of us. It is an ontological demand, a demand that we be. Stevens' meditative poetry moves toward the pole of being, not seeming. Ontology replaces phenomenology. Being is intimately related to the real, unlike Stevens' summer vision, the pole that exults in the play of the seeming, of endless elaborations and evasions where each term can seem analogous or homologous with the term that replaces it, and where the endlessly comparative reigns. The sun when seen in the idea of it is aligned not only with the pole of being but also, again, with that of the real. One arrives there, as we will see, by a series of divestitures. Divestitures of our powers of reason and imagination, even of our power of speech. Paradoxically, in our poverty, in our being washed clean, in our ignorance, our sense of ourselves becomes solar, is unexpectedly and blissfully expanded.

Stevens indeed wrote a number of meditative poems in which "to be without description of to be" more than suffices, in which an "early candor" is emphasized over its "late plural," "not to have" over "to have what is not," and in which reality, unmodified by the arrangements of the mind or the imagination, can come into its own.

We often confront, in Stevens' poems of winter, a reality that is "not our own and, much more, not ourselves," that is indifferent to our rage for order, for meaning or meanings. The sun when seen in the idea of it, an idea that has expelled us and our images, is celebrated by Stevens, as one pole, a necessary one, of human experience and of reality. In letting things simply be as they are, without the intrusion of thought or imagination—a letting go that seems simple enough, but that requires great discipline to achieve—we likewise allow ourselves to be as we are. The result, again, is a paradoxical enlargement of the self, and of its freedom, as well as an immediate sense of completeness, contentment, and wholeness.

Frequently, in these poems of contemplation, of being rather than seeming, human speech, the vehicle of reason, of a limiting knowledge, is banished along with our habitual selves, with "us and our images," and is replaced with inarticulate sounds. In "The Latest Freed Man," Stevens writes:

> To be without a description of to be,
> For a moment, on rising, at the edge of the bed, to be,
> To have the ant of the self changed to an ox
> With its organic boomings, to be changed
> From a doctor into an ox, before standing up...
> It was how he was free.

"To be without description of to be" here playfully results in a comic enlargement of self, in which an ant-like "doctor," which is a word cognate, in Stevens usage, with the usually positive words *scholar* and *rabbi*, becomes, on the edge of his bed as he is about to rise (ah, yet again the liminal), an ox who, rather than speaking, issues forth "organic boomings." The speaker, reduced to being an animal, which is at the most fundamental level what all of us are, is free, for a moment, from the intrusions of language, mind, and imagination, his stock in trade as a doctor, and experiences an immense increase in vigor, in sheer vitality. This formerly ant-like man, at the edge of his bed, poised to rise or beginning to rise, is likened to the sun, which itself is presumably also just beginning to rise.

In Stevens' contemplative poems the "intricate evasions of as," the endless play of meanings that in part are reflective of a desire that is never quite realized, are abandoned. Not to have, not to need, not to desire solacing speech can be a way, paradoxically, to a greater self possession, to a joyful realization, again, of one's own more than egoic self.

> ...there is an hour
> Filled with expressible bliss, in which I have
>
> No need, am happy, forget need's golden hand,
> Am satisfied without solacing majesty...
>
> There is a month, a year, there is a time
> In which majesty is a mirror of the self:
> I have not but I am and as I am, I am.

Not to have, need, or want, not requiring any recourse to any solacing majesty or to any speech proposing some supposedly divine comfort, is to become majestic oneself, and to have that majesty revealed both to oneself and others as in a mirror. In this exalted state of being, not seeming, the self is congruent with itself, realizes itself. The extraordinary line, "I have not but I am and as I am I am" is clearly a deliberate echoing of Yaweh's self-identification, "I am that I am," in the Talmud. It echoes as well the great Vedic pronouncement "I am That." Again, by embracing the winter vision of reduction, of not having, of not wanting, of rejecting the solacing majesty of speech, which in Stevens' summer vision endlessly elaborates itself, the speaker of the poem comes to a kind of exalted self-knowledge expressed in the pithiest possible terms.

Sometimes, in Stevens' meditative poems, the products of his winter vision, a more severe kind of reduction takes place. Often, as previously mentioned, human speech, the purveyor of meaning, is reduced to inhuman sounds, like the sound of the wind blowing in a bare place. There is often an approach toward finality, a final finding, and closure in these poems, even if the approach is toward a death that we are always, in fact, approaching. At the same time, this final finding entails the revelation of the thing itself—the holy grail of Williams' poetry in general, and of Stevens' when in a contemplative mode—not ideas about the thing. In the concluding lines of "The Course of a Particular,"

> The leaves cry. It is not the cry of divine attention,
> Nor the smoke-drift of puffed-out heroes, nor human cry.
> It is the cry of the leaves that do not transcend themselves,
>
> In the absence of fantasia, without meaning more
> Than they are in the final finding of the ear, in the thing
> Itself, until, at last, the cry concerns no one at all.

Blown autumn leaves stripped from their trees by the wind are a classic trope, from Virgil to Dante to Shelley's pestilence-stricken multitudes in "Ode To The West Wind" and beyond, for dying or newly dead souls. Here, the cry of leaves swept by the wind is "the cry of leaves that do not transcend themselves," a cry that is neither divine nor heroically human. It is not, in an interesting shift from sound to sight, the smoke drift of "puffed-out" heroes. At the time of death, according to the Greeks, the psyche leaves the body in a kind of puff of breath. The heroes here are described as puffed out, dead, not the more idiomatic puffed up, pridefully over-inflated, though I expect Stevens intended both connotations. In a heroic context, the smoke calls to mind funerary rites, either the cremation of the body, the common practice among Athenians, or the smoke arising from the cooking of sacrificial meat. But again, all such associations are brought up to be disowned, as instances of what the cry of the leaves might seem to refer to, but does not. And yet, spoken of as sounding a cry, the leaves are still being subtly personified, associated with the human and with human concerns, whereas fundamentally the sound of the leaves in no way transcends its nature as pure sound. In a telling and somewhat odd locution, the leaves do not mean more than they *mean*, but "more than they are." Again, there is an emphasis on ontology, of an approach to an ineffable state in which human meanings cannot trespass. The leaves and their apparent crying have no meaning beyond what they simply, existentially are as experienced by the final finding of a mortal ear, an ear that is in some sense concerned with them, still projects a last vestige of meaning on them. At this point, the point of final finding, we are close to the point at which, in "The Snow Man," in a similarly wind-swept winter scene, the speaker perceives "nothing that is not there/and the nothing that is." Apart from the final finding of the ear, human and mortal, the leaves, and the sounds associated with them, will "concern no one at all." At which point, perhaps at the moment of death, the cry of the leaves will finally and wholly no longer transcend itself, and the leaves will be nothing other than things in themselves—although, perhaps, there will be no one left to recognize this apotheosis.

At their finest, these poems of severe reduction, often confronting death or the fear of death, attain the status of the sublime. I am thinking here of Stevens' late long poem "The Rock," but particularly, again, of "The Auroras of Autumn."

At the inception of "The Auroras of Autumn," the speaker is standing by a deserted cabin, painted a faded and still fading white, on a beach. A cold wind, a wind we have met with many times before in Stevens' poetry, is blowing the sand across the floor and is chilling the beach outside. Darkness is gathering, though it has not yet fallen. Once again, we are suspended in a liminal moment. The speaker walks, turns "blankly" (recalling Emerson's magisterial dictum "the ruin or blank which we see when we look upon nature is in our own eye," which puns on *blanc*, the French word for white) and as he turns is confronted with a vision of the aurora borealis, the Northern Lights, with their spectacular colors.

> He observes how the north is always enlarging the change,
>
> With its frigid brilliancies, its blue-red sweeps
> And gusts of great enkindlings, its polar green,
> The color of ice and fire and solitude.

The solitary protagonist is confronted with the frigid brilliancies of blue and red, and with a polar green, not here, as is almost always the case with Stevens, a color connoting the fecundity of the earth, but the sterile color of "ice and fire and solitude." His radical aloneness in confronting an immense and awesome power of nature is a brilliant instance, again, of the Kantian sublime, in which the mind recoils on itself and experiences something "immenser than a poet's metaphors."

The ensuing cantos begin with the plaintive refrain, "Farewell to an idea," in which Stevens bids farewell to a number of nostalgias, remembered scenes, under the aegis of a gentle mother and benevolent, boisterous father.

In saying farewell to an idea, one is saying farewell to the thinker of the idea, returning to the stark, pre-conceptual confrontation of self and reality sketched, as I have pointed out, in the first canto of "Notes." In "The Auroras of Autumn," we come to a further, even more sublime and terrifying, recounting of the solitary subject's confrontation with the northern lights.

> ...He opens the door of his house
>
> On flames. The scholar of one candle sees
> An Arctic effulgence flaring on the frame
> Of everything that he is. And he feels afraid.

It is as though the protagonist, still solitary, now fearful, pitifully bearing his single candle, is confronting the imminence of his own death, a final reduction, just as at the end of "The Course of a Particular," human mortality is evoked. Here, however, the immensity of the arctic effulgence is so great as to suggest an apocalyptic conflagration. In referring, in the passage quoted earlier, to the lights as being the color of "fire and ice and solitude," Stevens may well have been echoing Frost's famous poem of apocalypse, "Fire and Ice."

But this apparently looming apocalypse proves to be a figment, or figure, of the protagonist's imagination. The poem draws inward at its end, in section 8, ends with a meditation on "innocence," on the innocent relationship of mother and child, of kinsman to kinsman, and moves thence to the notion of innocence as a pure principle, whose nature is its end, an innocence that does not reach beyond itself to some further fulfillment. Established in this principle, the speaker is able to look quite differently at the vividly flashing lights, recognizing, in effect, that the ruin or blank which we see while looking upon nature is, indeed, in our own eye.

> So, then, these lights are not a spell of light,
> A saying out of a cloud, but innocence.
> An innocence of the earth and no false sign
>
> Or symbol of malice. That we partake thereof,
> Lie down like children in this holiness,
> As if, awake, we lay in the quiet of sleep,
>
> As if the innocent mother sang in the dark...

Again, the lights have no meaning beyond themselves, are neither spells nor signs nor words/acts of a god speaking from a cloud, nor of some malevolent force, but simply are what they are, a part of the innocence of the blessedly unmeaning earth itself. An innocence in which the speaker participates, no longer single, no longer alone, but lying down like a child in the preverbal "holiness" of innocence while his mother sings to him in the dark. The word *holiness* also connotes of course, wholeness. Wholeness and completeness. It recalls, as well, Keats' reference, in a letter to his brother, of his certainty of the value of the "holiness of the heart's affection." The passage as a whole recalls the familial intimacy in the previously discussed section 5 of "Esthetique due Mal." As the poem's penultimate section begins, the aforementioned children, listening to the song of the mother, lie down together and

> ... of each other thought—in the idiom
> Of the work, in the idiom of an innocent earth,
> Not of the enigma of the guilty dream.

Once again it is we who project the enigma of a guilty dream upon the innocent earth, who see in the flashing of the Northern Lights the sign of some malevolent apocalypse. Again, here, astral lights, in this case the light waves, appear in the poem, but now they are humanized as the sublime gestures of an ecstatic actor:

> The stars are putting on their glittering belts.
> They throw around their shoulders cloaks that flash
> Like a great shadow's last embellishment.

In this section, which depicts perhaps the approach of death itself, that approach is not figured as terrifying, but, touchingly, in an echo of the passage in "Of Modern Poetry" in which Stevens' intimacy with the reader, and with himself, is described as like the emotion of two people becoming one, as like an encounter between two lovers.

> The rendezvous, when she came alone,
> By her coming became a freedom of the two,
> An isolation which only the two could share.

Finally, in a beautiful tercet in which the word *it* has no antecedent, is left ambiguous, and can refer perhaps to an encounter with death itself, or to some insight prior to death, or simply to some ultimate experience of intimacy itself, Stevens says:

> It may come tomorrow in the simplest word,
> Almost as part of innocence, almost,
> Almost as the tenderest and the truest part.

Whatever rendezvous is being referred to here, it is one with the simplest word of the poet, which in some sense calls it forth, and which is also Stevens' invocation of a kind of tenderness and intimacy in which we as readers, once again, as familial or familiar spirits, can share. Finally this ineffable encounter is this "tenderest and truest part"—or rather *almost* the truest part, as once again we have not yet reached some ultimate vanishing point of finality—of our experience of the world and of each other.

11.

Considerably after the mid-point of his career as a poet, Stevens increasingly concerned himself with the theoretical notion of a "major man," the "thinker of the first idea," who creates a "supreme fiction" that satisfies a need for belief in an age in which God and Satan have died. In my discussion of "Esthetique du Mal," I mentioned Stevens' abstractive, idealizing tendency, leading him, for example, to forego a discussion of actual soldiers in favor of the idea of an abstract, universal type of the soldier. Likewise, major man is depicted in "Notes Toward a Supreme Fiction," the poem in which Stevens most fully, if still glancingly, discusses the major man / first idea / supreme fiction complex, as a kind of abstract and universal type. Stevens writes, the "major abstraction is the idea of man / and major man is its exponent, abler / in the abstract and than in the singular." He is an abstraction somehow "blooded by thought." The problem, however, with this abstract, universal man is precisely that he is not blooded but bloodless. He is a kind of empty, imaginatively uninteresting, category. And so Stevens must turn to the "exponents," to particular figures instantiating the universal man, whom he has warned us in advance are even less able, less interesting, than the abstract universal itself.

The thinker of the first idea is figured in "Notes" as a "pensive giant prone in violet space," likely an allusion to the titans in the Greek creation myth. This giant bears the unlikely Scotch/Irish name of "the MacCullough." He is in fact merely the chief of many exponents, fictional incarnations of the major man in "It Must Be Abstract," the first section of "Notes," from the trio of artist, philosopher, and saint in its second canto to the chieftain, the rose rabbi, and the indigent old man in baggy pantaloons in its final canto.

The abstract universals in Stevens' theoretical triad major "man/first idea/supreme fiction" are instantiated, if at all, by these particulars, particulars that oddly diminish and trivialize our sense of the universals they should be buttressing. The proliferating fictional instances of major man lack inherent interest, and feel etiolated, pallid, deficient in imaginative vitality. I find it difficult to grant such minimally allegorical figures any kind of imaginative assent. Likewise, the first idea thought by the major man is devoid of any ideational content. It is the abstract "singular" from which a "late plural" develops, enabling the poem as a shuttling between the poles of unity and diversity. It is a kind of pallid recasting of the polarity of the imagination and reality. As for the "supreme fiction" itself, in response to his epistolary interlocutors, chief among them Hi Simmons, a longtime friend, Stevens is characteristically coy. Nonetheless, occasionally he entertains the nebulous idea of "the poem," perhaps some kind of ur poem, as the supreme fiction.

Stevens, who rejected Romantic idealisms, himself succumbs, in his notion of man, an abstract universal, as thinker of the first idea, to a peculiar form of subjective idealism. Stevens does not want to associate his first idea with a transcendental source, least of all with a deity who has been dismissed in advance as no longer viable, nor with an actual human being, like Christ or like the acknowledged realized masters of other spiritual traditions, who are considered to be microcosmic human embodiments of such a transcendent source. His solution is to conjure up major man as abstract and universal, a figure who thinks an idea that is likewise abstract, undefined. This idea is embodied not by a particular poem, but by a grand, synoptic supreme fiction which, though avowedly fictional, will also somehow command our belief, will baptize us in an immaculate beginning that is also an immaculate end.

It seems to me that the obvious inadequacy of this whole complex of ideas has been too little acknowledged. Few readers will be willing to grant imaginative assent to major man, an abstract universal, as a replacement for God, whether as transcendent or as once embodied by Christ, or to the first idea as a conceptually empty replacement for an embodied logos. They are still less likely to grant something like belief to a supreme fiction that is avowedly a fiction and that Stevens nowhere clearly defines.

"Notes Toward a Supreme Fiction" succeeds in spite of rather than because of broaching—fortunately, with characteristic levity and tact—Stevens' theoretical musings. Stevens' "Notes," after all, is just that, a collocation of notes, of provisional notions, that point toward possibilities not yet realized—if they are to be realized at all. Stevens continued to be coy and evasive in his discussion of the nature of his supreme fiction. This evasiveness, of course, can be seen as an expression of Stevens' distrust of the fixed, the categorical, the too easily defined. In this case, however, I suspect that there is an additional motive for Stevens' evasiveness.

When looked at from a slightly different perspective, the whole complex of ideas I have been discussing suddenly begins to make perfect sense. To put forth this thesis succinctly and directly: Stevens himself is the major man who thinks, or imagines, an original idea that proliferates into a number of original ideas. They blossom into a supreme fiction, not yet completed, to which Stevens gave the provisional title "The Whole of Harmonium," a fiction that is infinitely interconnected in its internal relations of part to whole and of part to part, and which succeeds, moreover, in granting a measure of imaginative satisfaction, and even of spiritual consolation, to those who can no longer grant their imaginative assent to the idea of God.

We suddenly have a concrete, coherent account of what hitherto had seemed merely, and unconvincingly, theoretical. Indeed, I find it impossible to imagine that it did not occur to Stevens that the evolving manuscript of what he had long quite grandly, provisionally entitled "The Whole of Harmonium" was the prospective, as yet incomplete, supreme fiction to which he referred. Nor do I imagine Stevens as too modest to think of himself as major man. Nor, for fear of seeming immodest, do I imagine him proffering the interpretation, too close to home, that I have just hazarded.

After "Notes," Stevens seldom revisits, in his poetry, the theoretical matters I have been discussing. Indeed, as I have pointed out, in the "Auroras of Autumn," Stevens keeps repeating, as the opening of several of the poem's first cantos, "farewell to an idea." Stevens, again, seems to be revisiting the nonconceptual idea, the kind of direct, intuitive confrontation with reality as percept, which I have fully discussed as exemplified in the very first canto of "Notes." Again, Stevens clearly distinguishes this idea from the first idea conceived by major man, which becomes the focus of the rest of "It Must Be Abstract." Indeed, the stark perceptual confrontation of the scholar of one candle with the Aurora Borealis is an extraordinarily powerful evocation of this immediate, unmediated, nonconceptual apprehension of reality, at first sublime and terrible, of which the first canto of "Notes" speaks, but which is more truly embodied in the immediate intimacy with which, in tenderest moments, we apprehend both the poet and each other.

Meanwhile, Stevens' exploration of the complementary polarities of experience, far from being replaced by a theory that after "Notes" found less currency in his poems, continued unabated, unobtrusively, like Whitman's noiseless, patient spider, to weave webs of its own.

12.

And yet, and yet... before abandoning altogether the subject of major man, I cannot overlook, as a kind of counter-example to the pallid figures in "Notes," "Asides on the Oboe," surely among the finest of Stevens' poems. It was written two years before "Notes," and perhaps before Stevens had worked out the scheme in which the major man, whether as abstract universal or associated with an instance such as the McCullough, becomes an unconvincing fiction in an unconvincing whole. It includes an early incarnation of the figure who will later become major man, here called the "central man"—a figure who, unlike the later iterations of major man, I find extraordinarily moving, and to whom I am more than willing to grant my imaginative assent. Somehow Stevens has so fully imaginatively realized this figure that it is almost as though he has conjured him into existence.

Occasionally a powerful, moving tone of insistence arises in Stevens' poetry, often involving a demand that what his imagination desires become, in some fashion, realized. In "Notes," section 3, verse 7, he writes:

> To discover winter and know it well, to find
> Not to impose, not to have reasoned at all,

> Out of nothing to have come on major weather,
>
> It is possible, possible, possible. It must
> Be possible. It must be that in time
> The real will from its false compounding come.

This tone in Stevens reflects his occasional desire for an imaginative apotheosis that is almost apocalyptic. In these lines, with their insistent repetition "It is possible, possible, possible. It must be possible," it is almost as though, like a god, Stevens is attempting to summon the real to appear out of its false compoundings, some of them doubtless his own. The repeated iterations of "it is possible" can be read as expressions of frustration, of desperation, of will, or of belief. Or of some mixture of all. Regardless, there are moments in Stevens' poetry where by force of will and belief, and through a kind of visionary intensity, what Stevens' imagination desires, like Adam's dream in Keats, does seem to be in some sense realized, and as a result to inspire our belief, our imaginative assent. In "Asides on the Oboe," which, with one brief ellipsis, follows, Stevens envisages the central man with this kind of visionary intensity.

Asides On The Oboe

> The prologues are over. It is a question, now,
> Of final belief. So, say that final belief
> Must be in a fiction. It is time to choose.
>
> I
> ...The philosophers' man alone still walks in dew,
> Still by the sea-side mutters milky lines
> Concerning an immaculate imagery.
> If you say on the hautboy man is not enough,
> Can never stand as a god, is ever wrong
> In the end, however naked, tall, there is still
> The impossible possible philosophers' man,
> The man who has had the time to think enough,
> The central man, the human globe, responsive
> As a mirror with a voice, the man of glass
> Who in a million diamonds sums us up.
>
> II
> He is the transparence of the place in which
> He is and in his poems we find peace.
> He sets the peddler's pie and cries in summer,

> The glass man, cold and numbered, dewily cries,
> "Thou art not August unless I make thee so."
> Clandestine steps upon imagined stairs
> Climb through the night, because his cuckoos call.
>
> III
> One year, death and war prevented the jasmine scent
> And the jasmine islands were bloody martyrdoms
> How was it then with the central man? Did we
> Find peace? We found the sum of men. We found,
> If we found the central evil, the central good.
> We buried the fallen without jasmine crowns.
> There was nothing he did not suffer, no; nor we.
>
> It was not as if the jasmine ever returned.
> But we and the diamond globe at last were one.
> We had always been partly one. It was as we came
> To see him, that we were wholly one, as we heard
> Him chanting for those buried with their blood,
> In the jasmine haunted forests, that we knew
> The glass man, without external reference.

We are told that "the prologues are over," that "it is time to choose." To borrow a concept from Christianity, it is as though *chronos*, the quotidian passage of time, has been replaced with *kairos*, the charged charismatic moment in which we are asked to choose, to declare ourselves with respect to matters of final belief. "Asides on the Oboe" was written in 1940, and once again the pressure of war, this time of impending war, has brought the moment to its crisis. Written two years before "Notes," it perhaps has the advantage of having been composed at a time before the "major man/ first thought/ supreme fiction" triad had been fully elaborated.

What is the nature of the central man with respect to whom we are ultimately being asked—no, told—to choose? The central man is "a man of glass / who in a million diamonds sums us up," and who is "the transparence of the place in which he is." The central man as macrocosm not only includes us but subsumes as well the no-longer external space in which both he and we dwell. Once again the word "transparence" occurs. He evokes a powerful luminosity which, moreover, is directly linked with sound by the extraordinary characterization of the man of glass as being "responsive as a mirror with a voice." The poem's title, too, suggests that the central man is equally a man of sound and of light. Once again the numinous coincidence of sound and light is suggestive of pratibha, the imagination working at something close to its highest pitch. The central man is depicted as a globe, a spherical figure who is complete, self-contained in the perfection of his form, and with whom we will eventually be wholly one. The central man "sums us up," with perhaps an etymological pun on the Latin word *sum* as *being*.

Put simply, the central man is man writ large, the macrocosm with respect to whom each of us are at first nearly, then wholly the microcosm. I have mentioned that an homology between the microcosm and the macrocosm, the human body and the cosmos, is at the very heart of Tantrism. Many of the practices enjoined by Kashmir Shaivism are aimed at granting the seeker a full, experiential realization of this homology. One's own body is considered to be one with the cosmos, and the cosmos, in return, is often considered as assuming the form of the human body, as the embodiment of a universal man, the vision of whom in meditation is considered the greatest of blessings.

In "Asides on the Oboe" it is when we see, see directly, the central man as he chants for the dead that we become wholly the microcosm, and that he becomes, for us, wholly the macrocosm. When we suffer, he suffers. Like us, he honors the dead. We are, finally, in an homologous relationship with him.

When we become wholly one with the central man we are becoming one both with ourselves and with a larger, more capacious version of ourselves—just as, in Stevens' poems of winter, through divestiture of self, we paradoxically experience a luminous, solar expansion of self. The central man, a perfect, luminous globe or sphere, is the container, and we are the contained. Stevens' vision of the central man is surprisingly similar to Blake's vision of the radiant, risen "cosmic man," Albion, in whom all men, when not deterred by a dark spirit of negation and denial, can participate, and to the meditative vision of a cosmic, universal man, radiating the light of Consciousness, that is said to be highly auspicious in Tantric texts.

When we are fully assimilated to, fully contained by, the central man, we have no external vantage point, no external reference, from which to view him. In "Of Modern Poetry" Stevens speaks of the ideal poem as completely containing the mind. The central man, the ideal man, "the impossible possible philosopher's man" who "in a million diamonds sums us up," contains not just our minds but our whole being. This containment involves no sense of claustrophobia, because each of us, as microcosm, is one with the macrocosm, is the central, universal man (who as a "globe of glass" recalls Emerson's ecstatic transparent eyeball, and the liberating, encompassing, revelatory vision associated with it—"I am nothing. I see all," another divestiture that grants an almost total widening of visionary scope). As one with the central man, the container of all, with respect to whom there is no outside and therefore no inside, we experience not claustrophobia but liberation from any limited identity. We share in his extraordinary luminosity, in his benign, almost divine, being.

Of course, Stevens' central man hews more closely to the tradition of secular humanism than does Blake's Albion or the universal man of Tantrism, but he is not without charisma. There is, again, the suggestion, unusual for Stevens, that he can "stand as a god," which at the very least means he can offer the believer in the supreme fiction some of the satisfaction—specifically a profound peace, or shanta rasa (about which more later)—that gods once offered their devotees. The central man is a figure whom Stevens, as a visionary poet, has so fully realized here, has so fully invested with radiance and charisma, that it is almost impossible for us to respond to him as a mere fiction.

Finally, what is the central man's relationship, what is our relationship, to war, to evil—the same question posed by "Esthetique du Mal"? Stevens' strategy here is less evasive, less indirect. When faced with the bloody martyrdom of war, the speaker of the poem asks "how was it then with the central man?" The central man, though englobed in glass, is, like us, a man. He is not an aloof, entirely abstract figure. He chants his mournful chants for the dead. He still sings his immaculate songs by the sea. In a humbler mode, he is still the confectioner of pies that he vigorously hawks. He is also still a dreamer climbing imagined stairs at night. It seems still to be with the central man as it has always been. He spans the full diapason or scale of human experience while remaining the epitome of that experience.

How is it for us? The central man stands as both an implicit reproof and an antidote to the despair and hopelessness we are prone to in difficult times, our sense that man is not enough, "is ever wrong in the end," can never stand as a god. It is as though in answer to these feelings that the central man is invoked, appears. He appears in the midst of war, of evil. In a time of war, "in his poems we find peace." Likewise, in a time of war we found, "if we found the central evil, the central good." The central man is the central good. It is he who compassionately chants, like a priest, dirges to the dead, assuming the role of a sanctified mourner. But he does not simply chant dirges. He still walks, cold and poetically numbered, in the early freshness of the morning dew. The central man as poet still by the seaside mutters "immaculate lines /concerning an immaculate imagery." In "Notes," Stevens writes that the poem… "satisfies belief / in an immaculate beginning / and sends us, winged by an unconscious will / toward an immaculate end." The poem as supreme fiction, like any religion or myth, satisfies belief. The word *immaculate*, of course, means not only unstained, pristine, but also without sin. The poem can restore us to the purity and innocence of an immaculate beginning, and sustain our belief in an immaculate end. The poet, at least with respect to his poetry, retains the freedom and sovereignty of a god whose decrees are paramount, are realized or not realized simply by being spoken or not spoken. He declares "thou art not August unless I make thee so," a declaration that punningly, playfully, can pertain either to man or to nature.

Thus the central man assumes the roles of priest, of poet, and of course, of philosopher, of the Emersonian human globe, of the man "who has had time enough to think." He may assume yet another role, perhaps, as we have seen, even standing as, or standing in for a god, an unusually radical suggestion for Stevens. In his very centrality the central man is the antithesis of the eccentric, unstable movement of evil. He is great in being the macrocosm with respect to whom we are the microcosm, but he is humble in being the central, the normal, the establisher of universal human norms. Is he proof against evil? Of course not. It is not as though the jasmine ever returned. Evil, and the irreparable losses it entails, will never disappear. But neither will the central man, the incarnation of a good, a nobility of spirit, a luminous light with a voice, with whom, at least in our imaginations, we can become wholly one.

I would like, as a point of privilege, as something more unofficial, still, than a poet, as a would-be spiritual adept, to speak of my more personal reaction, or reactions, to this poem. It was among the first of Stevens' poems that I read, a superb introduction. I was very moved by it. I have mentioned that I studied in India for many years with a teacher whom I considered to be a fully realized master (though I now doubt that there is any one state that one can click into, attaining enlightenment). I studied my teacher carefully. He seemed to me the epitome of what a human being, of what human consciousness, could become. A central man. When I read "Asides on the Oboe," it felt to me like an extraordinarily powerful and very moving depiction of my teacher. At that time I was not able to read the central man in any other way, certainly not as a fiction. I am sure Stevens was not consciously alluding to mystics or enlightened masters when he wrote the poem. But because it was written with such visionary force it suggested something very real and concrete to me. When poems are written with such imaginative energy, with such visionary and linguistic potency, they have the power to make what begins as a fiction end in reality, in a powerfully new realization, and/or in the expression of some profound existential, as opposed to propositional, truth. In such cases poems are indeed again, as Keats averred, like Adam's dream of Eve, which the dreamer awakens to find true. I cannot help but think that Stevens himself, composing the poems that would comprise his supreme fiction, knew that he was paradoxically getting at or trying to get at, to suggest, something essentially and universally human, some fundamental, existential human truth or truths, even if presented as fiction.

Finally, the poem is an extraordinary exemplar of Abhinavagupta's theory that shanta rasa, the feeling of a profound peace, underlies all the other rasas, even the most disturbing and terrifying ones. It is in the midst of the disturbing and terrifying reality of war that, in the poems of the central man, we find peace. The central man still walks in the freshness if the morning, still sings his immaculate songs, still remains the impossible possible philosopher's man. Other things may change; he remains the same. It is as though his imperturbability continuously underlies changeable phenomena, just as shanta rasa continuously underlies all other rasas. The central man is still a more than adequate figure with whom we can be wholly one, who is immaculate and without stain. He is still, in a time of central evil, the embodiment of a central good. He is a figure upon whom Stevens passionately insists, and whom he in some way wills into being. He is the insistent *yes* that must be affirmed against the depredations of the equally insistent *no*. "Asides on the Oboe," and the central man himself, directly communicate, embody the savor of shanta rasa which, according to Abhinavagupta, underlies all genuine works of art.

13.

In discussing shanta rasa, I will focus again primarily on Stevens' winter vision, as perhaps most beautifully exemplified by a series of his late, mostly short, lyrics, two of which I will later discuss at some length. First, however, I will glance in more generals terms at Stevens' relationship to the rasas, contrasting it with that of another great Modernist, Yeats.

Abhinavagupta postulates, as previously noted, nine primary rasas, which range along a scale from rage, disgust, and fear on the one hand, to love, beauty, wonder, and peace on the other. It is clear toward which range of the scale Stevens and his necessary angel habitually tend. Love, including erotic love or more commonly sublimation of it, beauty, a sense of wonder, and peace are the predominant rasas in Stevens' poetry. Occasional notes of fear related to the sublime, and perhaps to death, appear in Stevens' poems, particularly, for example, as in "The Auroras of Autumn." The rasa of the heroic appears in his poems about soldiers and about the hypothetical figure whom Stevens calls the central man or the major man, whom I have just discussed. There are also rare hints of disgust in his poems, often when dealing with the barren and imaginatively unassimilated parts of the American landscape, such as the slovenly wilderness of Tennessee in his "Anecdote of the Jar" and the smothering, dense natural world of the Carolinas in which Crispin's journey in the "Comedian as the Letter C" is becalmed, "all relation clippt." There are almost no instances of anger, rage, invective, or diatribe in Stevens' poetry. The rage for order invoked at the end of "The Idea of Order at Key West" hardly counts as rage.

There are of course poets whose work evinces a wider range of rasas than do those of Stevens. One need only think of Yeats, who also wrote poems that evoked love, including erotic love, beauty, and peace, but who wrote, too, more than his fair share of poems of blame, invective, and disgust that were often coupled with a kind of imperious, prideful high style (while experimenting, as in his "Crazy Jane" poems, with a low style as well). Heroism, again, is one of the rasas, and Yeats could be something of a hero worshipper, particularly, as in the case of Robert Gregory, when those heroes were aristocrats. Pride is one of the sub-rasas associated with heroism, and Yeats has no problem with vaunting rhetoric. Likewise, he was no stranger to disgust, particularly, in his waning years, to disgust at his own deteriorating body, and what he feared might be his deteriorating mental and sexual powers as well. There is the little matter of his experimental attempt to rejuvenate himself via simian gonads, which one hopes at least yielded a placebo effect. "The Circus Animals' Desertion" is perhaps Yeats' greatest poem of disgust and of frustration regarding his own possibly waning powers.

In his final years, he regarded even his approaching death with contempt and hauteur. He wrote his final, defiant poem, "The Black Tower" (the title says it all), just days before his death. He also wrote as his own epitaph:

> Cast a cold eye
> On life, on death
> Horsemen, pass by!

Toward the end of his end, Yeats enjoyed casting himself as a ruthlessly disabused realist. Nearing death, he conjures up, and identifies with, the cold-eyed, aristocratic horsemen of his own apocalypse, their features no doubt set in an Aryan sneer of cold command. How different this is from Keats' epitaph for himself, "Here lies one whose name was writ in water..."

Yeats' greater range of rasas does not make him a greater poet than Stevens. Quite simply, the two had very different temperaments and very different ways of being in the world. While Yeats was histrionic, flamboyant, always on stage, Stevens was reclusive, understated, and aloof. Yeats wrote a number of poems of a personal nature, most strikingly those tracking his relationship with Maude Gonne, but including a wide range of *dramatis personae*, incurring both praise and blame. Yeats' later poems in particular have a dramatic quality, often arising out of pressing, quite specific, personal and political contexts. One thinks, for example, of his poem "Easter, 1919," in which Yeats directly addresses both his personal and political reaction to a revolutionary uprising, many of whose leaders he knew and about whom he had strong feelings.

Auden famously eulogized Yeats, and his poem "September 1, 1939," written in the year of his death, is a clear allusion to Yeats' poem, and likewise combines the personal, with Auden situated in, and speaking out of, a particular time and place—"I sit in one of the dives / On Fifty-second Street / Uncertain and afraid"—with the political. Auden addresses both the low, dishonest decade that has just passed, in whose squalor, sitting in a cheap dive, he clearly feels personally implicated, and his forebodings of what is to come on the world stage.

By contrast, Stevens never mentions his personal life or personal situations in his poetry, which resolutely resists the confessional, nor did he assume a public role apart from several lectures delivered toward the end of his life. When he does address the political, as we have seen, his approach is oblique, indirect, not dramatic. The theory of rasas was propounded primarily with reference to drama in mind. Lyric poets whose work has a dramatic quality are likely to display a greater range of rasas than those lack that quality.

I think it important to reiterate that the rasas as they appear, whether in drama or poetry, are feelings, not mundane emotions. When we become absorbed in the worlds of drama and of lyric poetry, our mundane lives are temporarily suspended. We move in worlds of the imagination that are not bound by the usual restrictions of time and space. The feelings evoked in poems are the impersonal, universal essences of emotion, not ordinary emotions themselves. Hence the absorption in any rasa is absorption in the essence of all rasas. It was perhaps this that led Abhinavagupta to postulate one rasa, shanta rasa, at the center of, or underlying, all others. Shanta primarily connotes peace and tranquility, but it accommodates connotations of wonder and bliss as well. Thus to enter fully into any rasa is to enter fully into shanta rasa, and to enter fully into shanta rasa is to have a foretaste or glimpse of the peace and bliss of divine Consciousness.

Whereas Yeats viewed his advancing age with disgust, and viewed death with a disdainful defiance, Stevens seems to have approached both with a meditative or contemplative equanimity. The poems of Stevens' last years have, to use his word, an extraordinary transparency. It is as though all things have been pared back to their lucid and luminous essence. And that essence is akin to shanta rasa itself, which in much of Stevens' late poetry does not simply underlie all other rasas, but steps forth from its various affective compoundings, sheds all its guises, to become the predominant rasa in his poetry. Or, to mix metaphors, shanta rasa, normally like an invisible subterranean current that runs beneath all other rasas, now, as it were, has bubbled to the surface, forming a stream that is no longer occulted. Indeed, I cannot think of any poems that convey the essence of shanta rasa as powerfully and directly as do Stevens' late poems. I will refer to just two here. The first, "The House Was Quiet and the World Was Calm," presented in full below, is a poem that Stevens wrote in his sixties, with as yet no knowledge of his impending death.

THE HOUSE WAS QUIET AND THE WORLD WAS CALM

The house was quiet and the world was calm.
The reader became the book; and summer night

Was like the conscious being of the book.
The house was quiet and the world was calm.

The words were spoken as if there was no book,
Except that the reader leaned above the page,

Wanted to lean, wanted much most to be
The scholar to whom his book is true, to whom

The summer night is like the perfection of thought.
The house was quiet because it had to be.

The quiet was part of the meaning, part of the mind:
The access of perfection to the page.

And the world was calm. The truth in a calm world,
In which there is no other meaning, itself

> Is calm, itself is summer and night, itself
> Is the reader leaning late and reading there.

The house, quietness and calmness, the world, the reader leaning over the book, the summer night, conscious being, words spoken as if there were no book, the perfection of thought, the truth in which there is no other meaning, these are the primary terms, most of them repeated in slightly different contexts as the poem progresses, that comprise the poem. Such repetitions, as we have seen, are characteristic of Stevens, and often, as here, involve a kind circularity. The circular here, like circles themselves, suggests a feeling of completion, of wholeness. The primary terms mentioned above are homologous. Each participates in all of the others. And yet everything remains distinctly, luminously itself.

We are presented with a scene that is not simply a static scene like a world englobed in a ball of glass. In the second line of the poem, we are introduced to an uncharacterized reader. In his second appearance, in *medias res*, the reader is much more fully characterized. He is a scholar (always an honorific term in Stevens) leaning over his book. He is leaning as though in anticipation of something that he desires. Indeed, he not only wants, he "wants much most to be..." himself, the scholar to whom his book is true. Anticipation, longing, desire have not been banished from this scene of almost perfect peace. The reader appears toward the beginning, in the middle, and finally at the end of the poem, in its last line, in which he is referred to as not only leaning but also as leaning late. The reader, ultimately, is the final term in the series of terms in the poem. All that remains for the reader is that he recognize himself as the scholar for whom his book is true, as who he already is, to recognize himself as himself, as the final term in whose consciousness all the other terms— truth, conscious being, the perfection of thought beyond meaning, the words spoken as if there is no meaning, calmness or peace, the summer night, the world—will be realized if they are to be realized at all. In Shaivite terms nothing remains to be attained but *pratyabhijna*, self-recognition.

Failing that, though failure is not the right word here, if the reader is fated, in this calmest of scenes, to remain leaning over his book, to remain in a liminal state of rapt anticipation and longing, is his state any the less to be desired?

Finally, of course, we too are leaning over a book. We are reenacting, as readers, the role of the reader "leaning late and reading there." Will we, as same-hearted readers, recognize ourselves in this scene? Will we imaginatively participate in it, as all of the aspects of the scene, all of its terms, participate in each other? Will we resonate with the *pratibha*, the creative intuition—yes, with the genius of the poet—that gave rise to the poem, and thereby become its co-creators? If so, at the very least, we cannot help but experience shanta rasa, which seems to permeate and suffuse this astonishing poem.

Indeed, there seems to be some kind of essential homology between shanta rasa, the rasa that is inherent in and underlies all the others, and the non-local, all-suffusing, numinous suggestiveness that is *dhvani*—a suggestiveness which is, of course, equally present in both Stevens' austere poems of winter and his extravagant poems of summer. And which is also fully present in Yeats' poetry, despite his sometimes eccentric ideas, whether generated by Theosophy, by misinterpretations of Blake, or by the spirit channeling of his wife George, ideas which he held more seriously, even at times dogmatically, than Stevens held his. And which for most readers are simply beside the point, overridden by dhvani, by the pure rhythmic and tonal suggestiveness, the nondiscursive charisma and persuasiveness of Yeats' characteristic yet varying tone and sound. Analogously, with respect to shanta rasa, same-hearted readers of Yeats' "Among School Children," or even "The Black Tower," doubtless have access to much the same kind of deep satisfaction and pleasure experienced by same-hearted readers of Stevens' "The Rock."

As for some hypothetical reader, leaning late over Stevens' book, perhaps for him the flashing of the insight that is self-recognition will occur. For the rest of us, the longer, the more often, we linger over Stevens' words, even if that involves leaning late, whether in the lateness of our culture or late at night, the more, and the more powerfully we will remain in a state of rapt anticipation, awaiting all that the poem still has to disclose to us.

Before turning finally to the poem "Not Ideas About the Thing But the Thing Itself," one of Stevens' last poems, I want briefly to refer to one of the most luminous and exquisitely architectonic of Stevens' late poems, "To an Old Philosopher in Rome." The philosopher in question is George Santayana, who was Stevens' revered mentor while he was an undergraduate at Harvard. Santayana was a Catholic, and before his death he was granted sanctuary, as a kind of hospice resident, in a convent in Rome. In "To an Old Philosopher in Rome," Stevens imagines this experience to have been, for Santayana, an entirely appropriate and fulfilling final phase in a life that had been devoted to contemplation. Indeed, he imagines Santayana actively and alertly meditating on the life outside his window until the very end.

In "Esthetique du Mal," it is Santayana of whom Stevens is thinking when he writes:

>   ...it may be
> That in his Mediterranean cloister a man,
> Reclining, eased of desire, establishes
> The visible, a zone of blue and orange
> Veriscolorings, establishes a time
> To watch the fire-feinting sea and calls it good,
> The ultimate good, sure of a reality
> Of the longest meditation,...

Shortly before his death, Stevens converted to Catholicism, a move he had been pondering for some time. When it was clear that time was fast running out, he was baptized and took communion. Stevens' last days were also a fitting culmination of his life. And he, like Santayana, continued meditating to the last.

"Not Ideas About the Thing but the Thing Itself" is an extraordinary exemplar of what I have called Stevens' winter vision, although in this poem we are at the very end of winter, at the liminal moment when it is just beginning to turn into spring. The paradise of meaning has been reduced to a single scrawny cry—a cry that somehow feels as powerful, perhaps even more powerful, than the louder, manifold sounds of summer, and more significant than human speech. Evasion is not on the agenda here. Like many of Stevens luminous later poems, the barest of sounds also suggest the charged silence from which they have arisen. In "Not Ideas About the Thing but the Thing Itself" we may not be in paradise, but we are on equally sacred ground. The boundary between inner and outer, between dream and waking, has become so permeable that it is at first difficult to tell them apart, to determine from whence the scrawny cry has arisen. As the poet/speaker awakens, the cry no longer appears as such a meager thing, but as part of the colossal sun, a sun that is rising. The chorister's simple lower case "c," akin to the cry, is the anticipation of what will later be sung by a resounding choir. Anticipation is itself a joyful, liminal space. One senses that part of what the speaker anticipates is death, that the choral rings, still faraway, may never reach him. Perhaps he will experience them, after death, as sung by a heavenly choir.

Regardless, how touching it is that Stevens, still an explorer, still oriented toward the future, at the very end of one of his final poems, comes upon, is open to, a new knowledge of reality, one that is experienced in the still-living present…

NOT IDEAS ABOUT THE THING BUT THE THING ITSELF

> At the earliest ending of winter,
> In March, a scrawny cry from outside
> Seemed like a sound in his mind.
>
> He knew that he heard it,
> A bird's cry, at daylight or before,
> In the early March wind.
>
> The sun was rising at six,
> No longer a battered panache above snow…
> It would have been outside.
>
> It was not from the vast ventriloquism
> Of sleep's faded papier-mâché…

Some Segments of a River

The sun was coming from the outside.

That scrawny cry—it was
A chorister whose c preceded the choir.
It was part of the colossal sun,

Surrounded by its choral rings,
Still far away. It was like
A new knowledge of reality.

3.
The Sayable and the Unsayable in Mysticism and in Poetry

1.

A distinction has long been drawn between two broad terms applied to theology in general and to mystical theology in particular, the apophatic and the cataphatic. Apophatic mysticism is often referred to in the West as the *via negativa* or the negative way. God is held to be completely devoid of positive attributes, and can only be approached by the negation of all that is not God, which in practice entails renouncing as illusory not only the outer, objective world but all of the layers of our inner, subjective experience as well, until finally nothing is left but the experience of God. Cataphatic mysticism, on the other hand, is to varying degrees willing to ascribe at least some positive attributes to God.

Technically, according to prescribed academic practice, the terms apophatic and cataphatic refer only to what can or cannot be said about God, or the Absolute, or Supreme Consciousness, not about the relationship, or lack of it, between the divine and the created world. If one obediently restricts the discussion of the apophatic and cataphatic merely to an abstract discussion of what can and cannot be said or predicated of the divine, one is dealing with a simple binary structure, with what Blake would view as mere sterile, lifeless logical counters, not with genuine contraries. The negative and the positive are set up, or set themselves up, as opposites.

The negative is nowhere found in the natural world, the phenomenal world, and has its seat only in the mind. It is the most ingenious, scintillating, and seductive invention of logic. Like a child learning to say for "no" for the first time, one can simply slap the negative before anything positive, thereby nominally asserting the opposite of whatever it is one is negating.

In practice, however, things are more complicated. In negating something, one must also posit that which is negated. In negating, for example, goodness, beauty and love as attributes of God, one at the same time conjures them forth. If, in a parody of Mallarme, who used negative constructions more perhaps than any other poet, one were to declaim that no elephant does not gambol in a nonexistent sky, the listener would be left primarily with an imagined picture of a gravity-defying elephant ramping gleefully in the celestial ether, a picture that would perhaps be intensified further by being associated with the glamor of the negative. The assertion of something and the negating of it, far from producing genuine opposites, in fact completely mutually depend upon and entail each other. When closely examined, their distinction collapses, as is the case with all merely binary logical opposites, to a distinction without a difference. Moreover, the statement that God has no attributes is in fact every bit as positive as the statement that he has attributes—again, a distinction without a difference. If, however, one broadens one's focus and sees the apophatic and the cataphatic not merely as pertaining to abstract discussions of what can or cannot be said of God, to mere logical oppositions, but as involving the relationship, or lack of it, between God—or the Absolute, or Consciousness, or, as in the case of Buddhism, that which undermines all claims of a stable, independent reality—and the created world, then the distinction between them is no longer a distinction without a difference.

Perhaps the purest example, according to scholars, of apophatic mysticism is Vedanta, literally the end of the Vedas, as philosophically developed and systematized by the great sage Shankara (800 CE). In both Judaism and Christianity, there have been individual geniuses who have espoused some form of apophatic mysticism, though they have tended to be viewed with suspicion by orthodox theologians, and certainly have never coalesced into anything like a school. Vedanta, on the other hand, became for Brahmins, and still remains to this day, particularly for the educated elite, the preeminent religio/philosophical system in India. It is remarkable that what is essentially a mystical tradition has attained the status of a kind of orthodoxy.

While Shaivism espouses either an Ego Absolute or a Consciousness Absolute, the first embraced by the Pratyabhijna Shastra, the second by the Spanda Shastra, Vedanta espouses a Being Absolute. For Shankara, Brahman, pure being, alone is real, eternal, and immutable. The transitory world of appearances is essentially illusory. Brahman, beyond all predication, is seen as the radiant ground of all that exists, indeed as pure Existence itself, thereby distinguishing it from nonexistence, from the Buddhist notion of emptiness or the void. Being itself is not a predication, but is distinct from all predications as their necessary ground. Though it is ultimately true that nothing can be predicated of Brahman, this does not mean that Brahman itself is some kind of absolute negation; it has a positive reality, although one that cannot adequately be named.

What, then, is the relationship of Brahman to the phenomenal world? The manifest world is an illusory transformation of the real, immutably existing Brahman. This, of course, immediately gives rise to another question: how does such a transformation occur? Clearly it cannot occur as a negation or transformation of Brahman, which cannot undergo any change. Instead, the world of appearances is said to be falsely superimposed upon Brahman. To account for this superimposition, Shankara necessarily takes recourse to apparently positive principles other than Brahman, principles that are not themselves mere negations. Thus *avidya* and *maya*, primal ignorance and the cosmic power of illusion and delusion, are said together to bring about the superimposition that obscures the true nature of reality. These principles are at work both within the macrocosm, the cosmos as a whole, and within the microcosm, man. They can, however, be overcome when Atman, the individual soul, recognizes and experiences itself as being wholly one with Brahman.

Shankara's prescription for overcoming the illusion of the ego and of the world of illusory appearances, for realizing one's true self, the Atman that has become one with Brahman, is essentially, again, to follow a *via negativa*, to strip away the various levels or gradations of apparent reality—from the outer world of objects, of the physical body, and of the senses, to the so-called inner world of mind, the ego, and the reflective intellect—until one intuitively grasps the reality of Atman that is at their core, the reality of a selfhood that is annulled and ultimately subsumed and fulfilled by its complete identification with Brahman.

Kashmir Shaivism, on the other hand, as I have detailed at some length, sees the Absolute, Shiva, as one with Supreme Consciousness, as entirely transcendent while at the same time creating, and in fact constituting, the world or worlds of phenomenal appearances. From the Shaivite point of view, Vedanta's stripping of Brahman of all positive attributes and powers, and of all agency, seems a terrible and absurd limitation of the Absolute's freedom. Freedom, *svatantrya*, and the attainment of it, becoming one with a Consciousness whose very nature is freedom, is perhaps the paramount concern in Kashmir Shaivism.

And yet, finally, with respect to apophatic and cataphatic mysticism, and to Vedanta and Kashmir Shaivism in particular, there is a point at which, for all their striking differences, they converge. Both view the ultimate reality as wholly transcendent, undefinable, ungraspable by the terms of any language, whether positive or negative. It is as though Shankara and Abhinavagupta have been climbing from opposite sides of a mountain toward the same summit. Shankara did not, in the face of a transcendent reality about which he claimed nothing positive could be said, merely lapse into silence. He did the best he could to communicate, to suggest, using the flawed instrument of language, that which cannot be directly communicated. Abhinavagupta, when likewise trying to communicate the transcendent nature of the Absolute or Supreme Consciousness, faced precisely the same dilemma, and likewise did not remain silent. Both arrived at the same apparent impasse, and both took up the hopeless but at the same time productive task of attempting to say the unsayable, as is the case with all genuine mystics of whatever stripe, who are also destined to be teachers.

Wittgenstein famously said, in the last aphorism of the first section of his "Tractatus," "that of which we cannot speak we must pass over in silence." What we must pass over in silence is presumably everything that cannot logically be established to be the case, to be true or false. There is some debate as to whether the *we* in Wittgenstein's prohibition refers specifically to fellow logicians or more generally to all forms of discourse. There is some question, too, as to whether Wittgenstein, who was sympathetic to the ritual aspect of religions although decidedly not to the dogmas justified by their metaphysics, might in fact be referring to some numinous reality about which nothing can profitably be said, and which we must pass over in silence. Or perhaps, in yet another reading, Wittgenstein might have been saying that with regard to that about which we, as logicians, have nothing pertinent to say—whether some numinous realm, or simply broad swatches of human experience, from falling in love to what it feels like to ride a bicycle—we should have the tact not to venture as logicians, too reductively, to attempt to speak.

Anglo-American logical positivists, or at least its earliest one, were prone to adopt the apparently most tough minded (i.e., the narrowest) of these interpretations, regarding only that which is the case, and can be established as true or false, to be the sole proper ground not only of philosophy but sometimes, it seems, of discourse of any kind. All else, that with respect to which we cannot speak, is regarded, strictly speaking, as meaningless, a species of nonsense, and should therefore either be ignored or passed over in silence.

Regardless, if apophatic writer/seers, those who deny any positive attributes whatever to the divine, whether an early Christian like Pseudo-Dionysius the Areopagite, or a Neo-Platonist like Plotinus, or a Kabbalist like Isaac Luria, not to mention St. John of the Cross or Meister Ekhart, among many, many others, had followed what supposedly tough-minded logical positivists imagine to have been Wittgenstein's advice, some version of a prohibition, whether narrow or broad, against saying anything that cannot be logically established to be the case, the world would be much the poorer for it. And again, cataphatic writers like Abhinavagupta or Jnaneshwar, an Indian poet-saint to whom I will refer frequently in this text, ultimately face precisely the same impossible challenge when they try to characterize the transcendent nature of the Absolute. In his great philosophical poem the Amritanubhav, Jnaneshwar constantly, in what comes to seem almost like a running joke, refers to the utter uselessness of words in conveying the true nature of reality, while at the same time saying, saying playfully, almost as though with tongue in cheek, a number of brilliantly suggestive things about it.

Poets, particularly those with a speculative cast of mind, are liable at times to face a dilemma, to reach an impasse, similar in kind if not necessarily in degree to that faced by the mystics mentioned above. Some poets, again, restrict themselves primarily to the relatively safe precincts of the sayable. But as for merely saying the sayable, I as an erstwhile poet am tempted to say, let our logical positivists or engineers or economists or political scientists, or practitioners of any form of discourse in which accuracy of denotation is rightly a paramount concern, say that for us.

However, though tempted to make such an unequivocal assertion, I must in good conscience admit the obvious: that there are poets of genius whose self-appointed task is to say what is often said but "ne'er so well expressed," whose work does seem to lend itself to paraphrase, among whom are poets like Herrick or Ben Jonson or Herbert or Blake and his fellow Romantics' great arch-nemesis Pope, or sometimes Byron, or, closer to our own time, the later Auden whose Anglicanism was a kind of Gospel of common sense, who was the apostle of an urbane sanity, and whose late masterpiece "In Praise of Limestone," seemingly a dubious paean to the eternally beautiful boy, is more profoundly a hymn in praise of the glories of its own uniquely formal order. Similarly, Pope's "An Essay On Man" does, at first blush, seem a series of commonplaces rendered in verse, while a poem like "The Rape of the Lock" can seem merely trivial.

I would like to put forth a counter-intuitive notion—that such poems suffer more from paraphrase than those that more obviously resist it. Paraphrase completely misses the point of the poems that most seem to invite it. The interest in "The Essay on Man" or "The Rape of the Lock" or "Don Juan" or "In Praise of Limestone" is no more a function of their discursive meaning than is in the most apparently obscure and equivocal poem of Stevens. In the case of "The Essay on Man," commonplaces (that are or were not commonplace for no reason) are raised to a kind of higher power by the elegance, economy, inventiveness, and wit of their expression. "The Rape of the Lock," a mock epyllion or short epic, the chief example of which in English is Milton's "Paradise Regained," is a glorious excrescence whose exuberance lies in its superfluity, in its dazzling excess. At the same time, it indicts the triviality that it seems to embody. It lampoons, in particular, the effeminate fripperies and excesses of a court to which Pope's skill as a poet, ironically, had granted him entry.

"The Essay on Man" is decorous. "The Rape of the Lock" gleefully violates decorum. Both display Pope's masterful refinement of the heroic couplet. Pope, who was cruelly physically deformed and frequently wracked by pain, nonetheless wrote—in an act that can only be called, like his couplets, heroic—lines that are a miracle of balance and proportion. Though much imitated, he proved to be inimitable. He wrote not only specific poems, but a kind of poetry which, but for him, would have remained unsayable, or at any rate unsaid.

Nevertheless poets, and particularly the Romantic or Neo-romantic poets whom I address in thus book, insofar as they are poets, are prone to wandering (a kind of occupational hazard) into the unofficial no-man's-land between the sayable and the unsayable, and some, again, will be brave or foolhardy enough to attempt to press beyond it to the realm of the unsayable itself. Again, insofar as they are poets, the luxury of deciding to remain merely silent is not, contra positivist scruples, an option. Indeed, the poet's vocation as a poet demands that he not remain silent, and often that he speak in extremis as well as in other less problematic, less demanding, more existentially circumscribed situations.

The boundary between the sayable and the unsayable is not simply that between the earthly and the ineffable, the conditional and the absolute. It is encountered, too, in the aftermath of horrific circumstances like the holocaust, by poets who, like Paul Celan, courageously address that unspeakable horror, and for whom the boundary between the sayable and the unsayable no doubt also seemed almost impossible to bridge. In confronting an historical trauma that compromised his confidence in meaning itself, undermining and subverting the integrity of words, Celan sought, necessarily by means of homeopathically deploying those same words (and by choosing to write in German), to speak the unspeakable in poems whose broken language is itself all the more powerful for being scarcely articulate.

In attempting to capture and convey in words intense, essentially subjective states, such as extreme physical pain or spiritual elation, words falter, abashed at their inefficacy. Even in the attempt to convey the more quotidian landscapes, the flora and fauna of one's interior psychic state, words are also inevitably, to some degree, inadequate, and come up against the boundary between the sayable and the unsayable. One can begin to wonder, as a poet, about the incapacity of language in general to convey human experience of any kind, to become skeptical that experience can ever really be perspicuously translated from one person to another by means of words. The poet is always, in one form or another, confronting the limitations of language itself.

As I have mentioned in my "Few Words in Lieu of an Introduction," the intuitive apprehensions of the poet or of the mystic, if they are to be expressed at all, involve, broadly speaking, what I there called translation, as do the attempts of their listeners or readers to interpret their words. Poems that present interpretive difficulties highlight the limits of language, its resistance to acts of interpretation, which are also acts of translation.

But the difficulty of saying what cannot be said, of communicating the ultimately incommunicable, the difficulty of translation, is not, of course, the exclusive concern of mystics, poets, and readers of poetry. It is an essential part of our lives, of all of our lives. How poor, how impoverished is language in communicating our felt sense, the particular quality, of our experience to others. When Hamlet, in frustration with the tendentious pseudo-discourse of Polonius, dismisses his prattling with exasperation and disgust as mere words, words, words, he is also indicating, despite his own prodigious linguistic gifts, his suspicion of, his distrust in, the efficacy of language in general. Language, again, is peculiarly ill-suited to the task of conveying our internal, qualitative, affective states to others, or of divining, as Hamlet well knew, the internal, subjective states of others. Surely Shakespeare, himself the most prodigiously gifted of poets, was more aware than any other poet of what the Indian poet-saint Jnaneshwar called the inefficacy of speech. Much, and often that which is most essential, is inevitably lost in translation. And yet words, apart from silence, are the only tools, the often blunt instruments, that we have at our disposal.

Particularly when attempting to give voice to the furthest reaches, whether positive or negative, of human experience, the poet is likely to feel, like Shelley, that he has produced failure after dispiriting failure, and the sense of having lost his way as a poet is the consequence. Poets who choose, or are chosen, to attempt to push beyond the limits of the sayable, subject themselves, or are subjected, to a task that is taxing and solitary. It can wear the poet out, deplete his or her resources, to the point of exhaustion, while only rarely providing a compensatory nourishment or sustenance.

Those poets whose habitual tendency, whether Promethean or Faustian or simply bordering on the mystical, is to attempt, in Stevens' words, the accomplishment of an extremist in an exercise, risk, like Icarus, crashing and burning. The list of such casualties is a long one—Smart, Shelley, Holderlin, Nerval, Trakl, Celan, Crane, Mayakovsky, even, by poetic or philosophical license, Nietzsche, to name but a few.

From one point of view, including that of a number of critics, the attempt to say the unsayable is both presumptuous and foolhardy. Poets who decide to write, sometimes brilliantly, insightfully, within the bounds of the sayable, are of course also, as mentioned above, capable of producing estimable poems, even poems of genius, and are surely more sensible than their more venturesome confreres, who are likely, when not buttressed by strong familial or spiritual or societal bonds or simply by good genes, to come to grief. Wordsworth famously wrote, "Poets in our youth begin in gladness. / But thereof come in the end despondency and madness." And yet the failure of the life is not necessarily, in the case of such figures, the failure of the poetry, which one hopes will continue to have a robust life of its own.

Stevens' poetry continually flirts with the no-man's-land between the sayable and the unsayable. Stevens, however, unlike the tragic figures I have mentioned, seems to have had an essential sanity and hardiness, a sense of proportion and decorum, an engagement with the real world that anchored him, that prevented his poetical flights, finally, from becoming untethered, ungrounded, from haunting the boundaries not only between the conditioned and the unconditional, but between darkness and light, madness and sanity.

Stevens was no mystic. He did not attempt, like Holderlin or Shelley or Crane, or Trakl or other mostly tragic poetic figures without the benefit of spiritual discipline, to undertake a Promethean raid on the precincts of the mystically unsayable. For too many poets, this kind of thrust has devolved into a death wish, a feeling that only by breaching the bounds and limits of life itself can one enter such ardently longed for, unspeakable mystical precincts.

Stevens himself, in his late poems that flirt with silence but stop short of it by registering the residual inarticulate cries of windswept leaves in autumn or the muted cry of a scrawny bird at dawn in early March, seems to suggest that any final, apocalyptic revelation of the real, any knowledge of the unknowable, will only occur, if at all, at the moment of death or just beyond it, when *be* will be the finale of *seem*. This did not, of course, lead in Stevens' case to a death wish. That Stevens was not tempted to thrust the exquisitely adorned rapier of his language by main force into the penetralia of the mystically unsayable does not mean that Stevens was uninterested, in his own more temperate but still original way, in probing at and pushing against the limits of the unsayable, thereby expanding the limits of the sayable. Quite the contrary is the case. All poems, Stevens wrote, are experimental poems.

Stevens' negotiations between the sayable and the unsayable, and at times, more playfully, between sense and nonsense, are an integral aspect of his work. His project of evading the intelligence almost successfully, of engendering in his poems an inimitable music—whose bass note, often almost too low to hear, is the hum of thoughts evaded in the mind—constantly explores the boundaries between sayable and the unsayable, between what can and cannot be paraphrased. These ever-shifting boundaries and the ineffable territory they open up constitute, in a particularly pure way, the province-less province, the description without place, or the place that admits of no description that is Stevens' native land.

Stevens wrote that the poem is the cry of its occasion. Helen Vendler, along with Harold Bloom perhaps the most brilliant and devoted of Stevens' critics, interprets this phrase to mean that we can infer or imagine from Stevens' poems some prior set of circumstances resulting in the particular mood or psychic/emotional state of which they are the cry. I think Stevens is speaking much more literally here. The occasion of which the poem the cry is not something extraneous to or prior to the poem, but is the unique and unrepeatable occasion of the utterance of the poem itself as it unfolds as the constellation of words and sounds that comprise it, evoking some unique and unrepeatable adjustment between the imagination and reality that is likewise, for the poet qua poet, primarily realized in language, and is only secondarily, if at all, mimetic of a clear, internal prior intention or affective subjective state, or of a nature that is out there, extended in time and space, independent of a consciousness that is encoded by language.

The role of the mystic is to free his consciousness entirely of encryption by language until it is finally one with Consciousness itself. The more modest role of the poet is to deploy language itself, like a splinter removing another splinter—an operation of great delicacy, to paraphrase John Berryman, which the poet must perform upon himself— to unfix the habitual codes of language, codes that reify our sense of ourselves and of our world, and in so doing both to model and grant us access to freer, more unconstrained, more dynamic modes of awareness.

It has always fascinated me that Stevens tends, among the more abstract of poets, to be regarded as having endorsed Williams's motto, "no ideas but in things." Perhaps because of his preoccupation with the seasons and the weather, and his often avowed affection for particular places (better a hard rain in Hartford than a drizzle in Venice), Stevens is often regarded as a poet in close touch with nature—this despite the fact that his poems nowhere provide anything remotely like sustained depictions of any natural setting. Despite appearing to be concerned with place, often with Connecticut in particular, all of Stevens' poems are at a deeper level descriptions without place. If Stevens is a nature poet, then surely he is a poet not of *natura naturata* but of *natura naturans*, not of nature as a vista of mere statically external objects frozen in space, but of nature naturing, whose phenomenal objects are in a close but ever changing relationship to each other. To quote the extraordinarily last line of "Description Without Place," they are like "rubies reddened by rubies reddening."

Reality, Stevens wrote, is a force, not a presence. Again, for Stevens reality is an ever changing process, not a product—a process which is essentially fluid, dynamic, and can never without a kind of mental violence, as by an excessive use of reason, be fixed, pinned down. Stevens writes, in the concluding verse of "An Ordinary Evening in New Haven,"

> It is not in the premise that reality
> Is a solid. It may be a shade that traverses
> A dust, a force that traverses a shade.

And yet, of course, reality is no less real for not being a solid. It is perhaps more real for being correctly perceived, or conceived of, as a force. For Stevens, thought itself, or particularly poetic thought, is analogous to *natura naturans*. For the poet, thought realizes itself in the act of thinking freely and of recording that act, not in the act of freezing thought and producing or establishing the validity of some one thought or postulate above all others. This freedom, the free play of poetic thought, is experienced by the poet, Stevens says, as a kind of liberation.

The refusal to be pinned down is one of the cardinal principles or characteristics of Stevens' poetry. Stevens insisted that true poems cannot be adequately paraphrased, and that their meanings are thus necessarily at least to some degree equivocal. He notoriously chided Frost about his poems having paraphrasable themes. Indeed, one wonders what he would have made of the Yeats who in "The Circus Animals' Desertion" characterizes himself as frustratedly thrashing about in search of some theme—or of the Yeats who, remarkably, often first wrote prose glosses outlining the thematic content of some of his greatest poems, which he then, as it were, versified, with the unsurprising result that his poems, despite their sometimes disturbing, unsettling provocations, lend themselves to comfortingly stable thematic readings. But again, what is of interest in Yeats' poems lies not in their meanings, which are a hodgepodge of theosophy; of a clueless, dualistic misreading of Blake; of the seemingly endless channeling of his wife George; of his researches, along with his patroness Lady Gregory, into the vanishing lore of an idealized Volk; and finally of his typically Modernist, regressive, right-wing longing for the aristocratic values of an imagined past. Rather, it lies in the miraculous sea change that occurred when he translated his preliminary prose glosses into poems of an often numinous and unaccountable power.

Stevens, as we have seen, not only speaks of his poems as evading paraphrase, themes, stable readings, but also insists on the poem saying that which cannot be said—except in specific poems, whose meanings themselves are equivocal, ambiguous, unsayable except as poetry. Stevens wrote that the poem says what could not otherwise, by other means, be said, and what but for the poem would remain unsayable.

Stevens' cataphatic poems of summer revel in the intricate evasions of *as*. His poems of winter approach a reality that likewise evades the poet's grasp. Similarly, his various theoretical formulations of poetry determinedly avoid anything approaching fixed definitions. Stevens' widespread evasiveness, in his poetry, in his prose, and in his correspondence, far from being merely coy, is a principled determination not to definitively say what is not definitively sayable, but to say that which can be provisionally addressed by a poetry whose meanings, nonetheless, themselves remain equivocal or, in Stevens' preferred term, ambiguous, escaping easy paraphrase. Poems can only say what can be said in the form of particular poems themselves, and more generally by poetry itself, written by poets who, as opposed to philosophers, provide an unofficial view of reality in its ever changing guises. This realm of the unofficial and the equivocal and ambiguous is the native land of the poet, as opposed to those whose undeniably useful task and discipline it is to clarify the realm of what can be definitively said and is subject both to error and to deliberate distortion.

I want to emphasize, finally, that Stevens' propensity for writing difficult to paraphrase poetry is not some clever, fashionable strategy, some way for Stevens to aristocratically thumb his nose at the overmatched reader, the equivalent of one of our current bewildering array of meta-discourses. Far more is at stake. Again, for Stevens' reader, the loss of interpretive certainty entails a very real gain in interpretive freedom. And freedom, for Stevens as for Abhinavagupta, is of paramount value.

2.

In much of this chapter I have been trying, clumsily, by way of a series of detours and divagations, to speak of what I have glancingly called in the introduction of this book *translation*, with respect to which interpretation is a kind of subset, and of both the necessity and the inefficacy of language as a medium of translation. I have spoken of the attempts of both apophatic and cataphatic mystics, and of some brave, foolhardy poets, to say, to translate into language, what is by its very nature ineffable, including both the transcendent and the unspeakably traumatic. I have spoken of poets' attempts to translate into poetic language what can only be expressed as poetry, much of which by its very nature is untranslatable, resists paraphrase into terms other than its own. Those poems that are, on the other hand, amenable to paraphrase are never reducible to it, and are ironically in more danger of being falsified by it than are poems that more obviously evade it.

I have in previous chapters spoken of the reader's attempts, in turn, to translate, to interpret the poem. I have discussed the role of the same-hearted reader, who is tasked with intuitively interpreting the poem, with reforming and recreating it. I have perhaps insufficiently indicated that in so doing the same-hearted reader does not, as it were, simply recreate the poem verbatim, but rather appropriates and *transforms* it, thereby serving as a guarantor of its continued dynamism, of its renewed vitality. It is by means of its serial transformations, re-enacted by many sensitive, same-hearted readers over many years, that a poem keeps being propelled toward the horizon of its future.

When the poet himself has completed his poem he is in the same position as the reader. He has no privileged status as its interpreter. Any given interpretation or translation he may proffer of what he may imagine to be his own poem, but which upon completion is thoroughly out of his hands, will leave unrecognized, like all translations, even or especially to the poet, much that is untranslatable.

I have not yet mentioned what is a perhaps parenthetical but nonetheless important point, that the relationship of the poem and its reader cuts both ways, that the poem itself judges, interprets the interpreter, revealing his or her limitations and competencies, a point I explore further in my book *Elective Affinities*. This is why so often people speak of feeling intimidated by poetry.

Finally, we are all always engaged in translating, interpreting the words of others, a process that usually goes on smoothly enough, but often fails us when we most need it, when we attempt to express in language our own particularly intense qualitative, internal states, or when we try to divine through language the internal states of others. These difficulties can only be bypassed, in moments of rare insight, by what Abhinavagupta calls *pratibha*, a wordless, silent, synoptic intuition through which we can apprehend much of what we cannot translate or interpret. In seeking to alleviate, for example, the intense physical or emotional suffering of another, which seems by its very subjective, qualitative nature unknowable to us, we often take recourse to proffering profuse words of comfort, words which, like those of Job's comforters, are in some cases unconsciously intended to keep the suffering of the other at arm's length, to ensure that we not know and feel what we really do not wish to know or feel. It is often when we are silent, when we are simply being with the other, when we have given up the false project of trying to alleviate his or her pain, that some kind of insight or transmission occurs in which we catch a furtive glimpse of the sufferer's state, a transmission that the other also silently receives, in which he feels what he wishes to feel, which is in some way to feel acknowledged. Of course we cannot remain silent forever, but words that emerge from the background of this silence, a silence which can be cultivated, retain an added potency, an added power.

Though I have been speaking of the limitations of articulated language and of the inefficacy of speech, I will conclude by giving language its due. The peculiar potency and power of great poems, as well as their inexhaustibility and resistance to paraphrase, their exhilarating vitality, is a reflection of the inexhaustibility of language as the unbounded reservoir of potential energy that Shaivism calls *Matrika Shakti*, the mother or womb from which the subtle as yet unsounded array of all Sanskrit phonemes, each instinct with its own power, arises, only later to combine into the words of which language is comprised. I will address this topic more fully in a later chapter. Genuine poets are likely to be both more than usually aware of the limitations of spoken speech and the written word, while at the same time being more than usually aware of the vast potential energy that gives rise to language and works through it. They are more the awed servants of language than its masters.

II. An Ecstasy of Associations

1.
Detours and Divagations

1.

William Bevis' remarkable book *The Mind of Winter*, to which I confess myself greatly indebted, examines Stevens' poetry from the point of view of Buddhist texts. In some of what follows I take issue with him, but I would like to acknowledge that I have found his book to be exhilarating and revelatory. *The Mind of Winter* is one of the very few of the many books on Stevens that adds something new and vital to a by-now disproportionately garrulous conversation.

Bevis believes, both on the evidence of Stevens' poetry and from accounts of his life and habits, that Stevens had a kind of powerful, innate attraction to and propensity for experiencing meditative states. I find his arguments, culled from Stevens' biography, letters, and poems, convincing—as does, more importantly, Helen Vendler, along with Harold Bloom the most influential and insightful critic of Stevens, whose critical work in general exhibits an antipathy to the mystical. It is largely Stevens' openness to and experience of meditative/ecstatic states that connects him to his great predecessors Whitman and Emerson.

Bevis argues, again convincingly, that Stevens' poems of winter are consistently misread by his critics, are often regarded as puzzling failures of the imagination. Because they share in our culture's general distrust of and lack of familiarity with meditative experiences of self-loss, Bevis argues, Stevens' critics miss the experience of radiance, of clarity, of an expanded sense of being, of wholeness that are also, as I have detailed in the previous chapter "Stevens/Abhinavagupta," characteristic of Stevens' poems of winter, of de-creation, or of meditation/contemplation.

Bevis focuses primarily on Buddhist meditation and secondarily on Buddhist philosophical speculation as they pertain to Stevens' poetry. With respect to the former, he relies heavily on the *Visuddhimagga*, a brief fifth-century précis of the stages of meditative absorption that condenses and summarizes the voluminous discussions of meditation in much larger treatises in the canon of Theravada Buddhism. With respect to the latter, he references Nagarjuna, (although surprisingly, as we shall see, only glancingly), who is considered by many as not only great a saint but also the greatest of Buddhist logicians, and who is the founder of the Madhyamaka school of Mahayana Buddhism, commonly referred to as the "middle way."

The *Visuddhimagga* outlines a number of stages in the unfolding of spiritual practice, leading ultimately to the state of enlightenment. Bevis concentrates on the first four of these stages, as he regards the subsequent stages as refinements of the fourth. Bevis regards the first two of the stages outlined in *Visuddhimagga* as mere threshold states on the way to meditation, so I will concentrate, as does he, on the third and fourth stages. The third stage Bevis calls excited—or ecstatic—self-loss, a meditative state in which thought has ceased but feeling remains. In the final or contemplative stage, both thought and feeling vanish altogether. Bevis maps Stevens' meditative poems of winter onto the hierarchical structure thus outlined by the *Visuddhimagga*. Those of Stevens' poems that reflect the most intense experience of self-loss, the cessation of both thought and feeling, occupy a privileged space at the top of the hierarchy.

I confess to being suspicious of this hierarchical, typological mapping of Stevens' poetry, but I have even more reservations about Bevis' discussion of the four types of mysticism that precede it, which are also arranged hierarchically: the occult, the visionary, the ecstatic, and the meditative, the last of which refers to the meditative state as modeled by Buddhism, purged of any tint or taint of the blissful, of the visionary, or of the ecstatic.

The occult can be and should have been dismissed out of hand as not representing genuine mysticism in any way. The visionary and the ecstatic are characterized by Bevis with an eye to their second-class citizenship when compared with the truly quiescently meditative/contemplative. Bevis' account of the visionary is oddly literal-minded. It refers strictly to visual hallucinations. Bevis' prime exemplar of the visionary is the Blake who represents himself in the "Marriage of Heaven and Hell" as having conversed with Biblical prophets in his garden and who, when beholding the sun, sees not a "round disc the size of a guinea" but "an innumerable host of angels crying Holy, Holy is The Lord God Almighty!" Bevis overlooks the unruly, sardonic humor that animates "The Marriage of Heaven and Hell." He demotes or regresses Blake to the status of an eccentric and possibly mad crank from which Northrop Frye, and numerous scholars since, have rescued him.

Bevis calls the meditative state of excited self-loss—in which thought is suspended but feeling and emotion remain—the ecstatic. He claims that within our culture, the ecstatic "has stood for almost all mystic experiences, feelings of unity, of merging, of thrills on the mountain top, drug highs, orgasms," and further claims that most Western writers mistakenly deem all mystical experiences to be ecstatic. Once again, Bevis conjures the category of the ecstatic with an eye to dismissing it by comparison with what he calls contemplative experience. His prime exemplars of ecstatic self-loss, consistent with the decision to remain focused on our culture, on native ground, are Emerson and Whitman.

In truth, the visionary and the ecstatic often coincide. To move beyond our culture, St. Theresa of Avila is a paradigmatic exemplar of an ecstatic mystic. Her intense mystical visions, often involving a passionate communion with Christ, were regarded with considerable suspicion by the church for their at times almost sexually graphic portrayals of such union. There is something of the antinomian, something of the Tantric, about the ecstatic, something that tends to breach conventional norms. For example, the great Indian saint Ramakrishna, the most well-known and certainly the most influential Tantric guru of his time, underwent intense visionary experiences of the Divine Mother, saturated with a profound experience of divine love and bliss, which were a staple of his spiritual life, as was his tendency to routinely slip into anything-but-routine ecstatic states. Famously, Ramakrishna submitted himself to studying, as an obedient disciple, in what was a kind of sublime farce, with a master of Vedanta, under whose strict supervision he quickly progressed from *saguna samadhi*, meaning the contemplation of God with form or qualities, to *nirguna samadhi*, meaning the supposedly superior contemplation devoid of any trace of thought or feeling; moving from his ecstatic visions of the Divine Mother to the experience of the formless absolute—which should, from the point of view of his Vedantic preceptor, have ended the matter, except that Ramakrishna could not help but indulge himself in backsliding into ecstatic experiences of union with his beloved Divine Mother. For reasons that should be clear, he had no interest in extirpating the experience of divine love from his spiritual repertoire.

Why would one who has experienced the state of pure being, of Brahman in nirguna samadhi, or the experience of God without form—the Vedantic equivalent of Bevis' highest stage of tranquil, meditative self-loss—and who has become established in the awareness of the essential formlessness of things, wish, like a hoarder of nothingness, to restrict himself to that experience alone, rather than delighting as well in the full diapason or scale of possible meditative experiences—including, say, the rapture of the love of the Divine Mother, or the intimation of divinity in a blade of grass.

Tantric Hinduism, of which Kashmir Shaivism is perhaps the finest flower, and Tantric Buddhism, of which Tibetan Buddhism is perhaps the purest expression, both embrace ecstatic self-loss as one aspect of the highest mystical experience. As I will emphasize, however, Shaivism also embraces contemplative self-loss. The complete absorption of Shakti, and presumably of excited or ecstatic states, in Shiva, is a complementary aspect or pole of mystical experience. The same is true, again, of Tibetan Buddhism, which, like all forms of Mahayana Buddhism, stresses intense logical inquiry as complementary to the practice of meditation in the search for enlightenment. I have, of course, already discussed Kashmir Shaivism at considerable length, and it will remain my primary touchstone in what follows. Two other traditions, however,—Sufism, and what in Hinduism is known as Bhakti, or the path of divine love—embrace the experience of ecstatic self-loss with a particular poignancy and force, and should not go unmentioned here.

Sufism is, among the mystical traditions, perhaps the most steeped in ecstatic self-loss, in the rasa of divine love. Jalaluddin Rumi (twelfth century AD), both a poet and a saint, was a practitioner of Sufism, the mystical tradition indigenous to Islam. In Rumi's time, ecstatic mysticism flourished in the context of a Persian society that was highly cultured, in which intellectual study of all kinds was nurtured and encouraged. Rumi's poetry, revolving around the center of his spiritual life, an intense love of his Guru, Shams Tabrizi, draws upon, beneath its exquisitely and deceptively transparent surface, a deep well of learning and culture. His poetry, intrepidly, ingeniously, and seemingly inexhaustibly, describes the experience of cycling through experiences of ecstatic unity with his Guru and periods of separation characterized by the ache of an ardent longing, which was intensified by his Guru's death. This ache of longing itself becomes prized among the saints of Sufism—virtually all of whom were great poets—as much as or more than the bliss of union with the divine. Suffering, too, the experience of being refined and purified by the scalding fires of divine love, assumes a kind of exalted position in Sufism. Just as for the Vedantin, all layers of experience, both inner and outer, are stripped away before the experience of the divine as pure being remains, so for the Sufi, all of the layers of experience—sensory, mental, intellectual, and spiritual—are not so much consumed by the fire of divine love as, after having been subjected to its scalding crucible, assimilated to it—until nothing but that love itself, which in Sufism is the highest good, remains.

Rumi was an almost exact contemporary of Dante. These two titans of world literature have much in common. Both were extraordinarily learned. The Dante of the "Convivio," who temporarily abandoned Beatrice to flirt with lady philosophy, sought, like Rumi and his peers, to master all branches of knowledge. When Dante, abandoning the "Convivio," went on to embrace divine love, not knowledge, as the highest good, as the prime agent and mover of all things, he did so with no sacrifice of intellectual rigor. Similarly, in Rumi, as in his successor Hafiz, the embrace of ecstatic self-loss, of a mystical union with the divine in which love is the paramount value, is in one way opposed to but is in fact, rather, enhanced by a highly developed and refined intellect.

Hafiz, a near-contemporary of both Rumi and Dante, was born in the early part of the fourteenth century. Though slightly less well known in the West, his prestige in what was then Persia and what is now Iran outstrips even that of Rumi. There is a crux in the hagiography of Hafiz that also has quite startling parallels to Dante. As a young man, Hafiz caught sight of a young girl named Shakh-i-Nabat, who seemed, like Dante's Beatrice, the very embodiment of beauty, and overpoweringly and instantly ignited in him a kind of longing for a highly idealized and unattainable figure of the beloved. This obsession, which could find no other object worthy of it, would not abate. Shakh-i-

Nabat remained a central figure in his work, as did Beatrice—who, of course, plays a central role in both "La Vita Nuova" and the *Divine Comedy*—in that of Dante. A number of Hafiz's poems are addressed to Shakh-i-Nabat.

In pursuit of attaining his beloved, Hafiz kept a forty day and night vigil at the tomb of a venerated saint. Toward the end of this vigil, Hafiz was visited by the archangel Gabriel, who informed him that the beauty and the pangs of love ignited in him by his brief glimpse of she who seemed an incarnation of beauty would only be satisfied by the consummation of a love of a higher order, by the ultimate consummation of love as union with the divine, and that henceforth he should seek to devote his energies to the realization of this higher form of love. Not long after this visitation, he encountered Shams Al-din Shirazi, who was to become his Guru.

Though every bit as learned and cultivated as Rumi, Hafiz affected a more outlandish persona, sometimes that of a common drunk. His poems are known for satirically lambasting the pretentiousness of the orthodox. Like Li Po, the great Taoist Chinese poet whom I shall later briefly discuss, Hafiz was a celebrant of the intoxicating virtues of wine, though in the context of Sufism wine was also symbolically the elixir of divine love.

Persian poetry by the time of Hafiz had become densely symbolic. The literal always had potential links with the figurative/mystical. The vocabulary of carnal, erotic poetry, sometimes of an idealized and romantic kind, had fused so thoroughly with that of poems of spiritual ecstasy that it was difficult to know whether a given poem was primarily erotic with possible spiritual overtones, or primarily an account of ecstatic union with the divine expressed in erotic tropes. The boundary between the mystical and the erotic was ambiguous and porous. In general, however, the poetry of Hafiz traces an arc in which erotic love, though its carnal aspect is recognized, becomes increasingly idealized and Platonic, is seen as a stepping stone on the way to the experience of the mysteries of ecstatic union with the divine.

The relationship of Hafiz with his Guru was every bit as legendary as that of Rumi with Shams of Tabriz. Hafiz is said to have studied under Shams Al-Din Shirazi, a particularly hard taskmaster, for years. Shams, himself a well-known poet, also guided Hafiz in the development of his art. There were long stretches of time when Shams seemed cold, aloof, and disdainful of his disciple, who became increasingly desperate and impatient in his quest for the full realization of divine love. It was not until his early sixties, after having served and entreated his guru for forty years, that Hafiz was granted the experience of complete union with the divine and himself became a realized master. When his master died, however, Hafiz became as disconsolate upon his death as had Rumi upon the death of Shams Tabrizi. He spent his few remaining years haunting the shrine in which his Guru was buried. Even for the realized master, the ache of longing remained an integral corollary to the ecstasy of divine union.

A third great Sufi poet, Amir Khusrow, himself a near-contemporary of the triad of Rumi, Dante, and Hafiz, was born to a Sunni Muslim family that had been forced to flee Uzbekistan before it was overrun by Genghis Khan's invasion of Central Asia. His family had sought and been granted refuge by the sultan of Delhi. It was here that Khusrow was born in 1260 CE. A brilliant polymath, he received a first-class education. Though he wrote primarily in Persian, he was thoroughly conversant with Arabic, Sanskrit, and various Indian dialects. He eventually became a court poet in New Delhi, where the brilliance and technical mastery of his poems, some of which, famously, took the form of ingenious riddles or runes, was recognized. Khusrow was credited with melding Persian, Arabic, Turkish, and Indian strains of music into one of the great flowers of Sufi culture, an intensely driving, rhythmic musical form called *Qawwali* that incorporated and highlighted the chanting of complex poetic forms like the *ghazal*. Hearing a group of highly adept Sufi musicians perform Qawwali when they visited my Guru's ashram was one of the most transporting musical experiences of my life. Finally, Khusrow's relationship with his Guru Nizamuddin, like Rumi's with Shams Tabrizi and Hafiz' with Al-din of Shirazi, was legendary. He, too, was scorched by the fire of divine love and wrote poems steeped in its mysteries.

These great figures had not only striking points of contact, similarities with each other, but also with prominent aspects of other mystical traditions. With respect to their affinities with each other, all three were, at one time or another, court poets, though they were from time to time distanced from the court during periods in which the inherent antinomian tendency in Sufism was denounced and driven underground as heretical by the forces of orthodoxy. All, reflecting the highly advanced, cosmopolitan culture in which Sufism arose, were extraordinarily learned. All as court poets were expected to master an array of highly technical poetic forms that prized, in particular, the capacity to produce riddles, puns, and double entendres. At the same time, and above all, as we have seen, all were intense spiritual seekers who were guided by Gurus who were regarded as quite literally the embodiments of God in human form. They themselves, finally, were venerated both as saints and as poets.

The love and devotion of a disciple for a spiritual preceptor that is so prominent a feature of Sufism cuts across cultures. In Tibetan Buddhism, Milarepa's selfless love for his Guru Marpa, and the countless trials he uncomplainingly endured, has a central, legendary, exemplary status. The centrality of the sometimes fraught relationship between the Guru and the disciple is also essential to all forms of Tantric Hinduism, including, of course, Kashmir Shaivism. So, too, crucially, is the notion that the realized master is an embodiment of the Lord. In the West, the relationship of the true disciple of Christ, likewise conceived as a perfect embodiment of the divine, also comports with this basic paradigm.

My brief inventory of exemplars of excited self-loss, and in particular of the ecstasy of divine love, would be incomplete without reference to the long history of *bhakti,* of divine love of the devotee for God, that has constantly generated and regenerated itself within Hinduism, at times reaching an extraordinary intensity. In the Bhakti tradition, the divisions of caste were not recognized. The great poet-saints associated with this tradition—Namdev, Eknath, Tulsidas, Kabir, and many others—were not Brahmins. Nor were they learned. Their poems, called *abhangas*, written to be sung, are simple, direct, and accessible. They are less complex, less steeped in highly refined, classical forms, which presuppose a rigorous formal poetic/philosophical training, than the work of the great Sufi poet-saints, whose accessible, literal surfaces often partly conceal richly layered, occult allegorical meanings. Typically, though with prominent exceptions such as Jnaneshwar, whom I shall shortly examine at some length, Indian poet-saints were not philosophers or intellectuals but truly men and women of the people. Typically, abhangas are structured as a series of verses and refrains, the spiritual equivalent of the Western popular song.

More simply still, chanting the Lord's name, in the form of melodious chants called *kirtans*, which begin slowly, then are repeated, gradually more rapidly, until they reach a kind of ecstatic crescendo, before the whole cycle is repeated again, is an essential practice of Bhakti Yoga; long pilgrimages to the temple of the deity that involved continuous ecstatic chanting were the high point of every year. So too is the internal recitation of mantras like *Om Namah Shivaya* that both extoll and repeat the name of the Lord and are considered as instinct with his power as well as that of the Guru, one with God himself, who, in initiating the disciple, awakens the power of the name of the Lord within him.

The leitmotif, which I have noted in Rumi and his Sufi conferees, of the alternation between periods of blissful union with the divine beloved followed by periods of separation and profound longing, is common to other mystical traditions as well. Again, the experience of separation, of the profound, painful yet sweet longing for the divine beloved, typically comes to be valued by the Indian poet-saints as much as, or more than, the experience of ecstatic union itself.

2.

A question naturally arises here: why is Bevis so dismissive of the traditions involving ecstatic self-loss that I have briefly outlined above, traditions whose breadth and depth he seems reluctant to acknowledge? He scarcely touches upon Sufism or upon Tantric traditions, whether Hindu or Buddhist, except insofar as he tacitly dismisses them. It seems to me that Buddhism, with its tastefully tranquil self-loss, has come to seem more intellectually respectable, more palatable, in particular, than Hinduism, which is taken to exemplify primarily ecstatic self-loss. This is despite the fact that the primary philosophical/theological system in India, among the cultured elite, as previously mentioned, has been Vedanta, which clearly valorizes the meditative experience of tranquil self-loss. Buddhism, of course, itself emerged from an Indian culture that was already highly advanced in its exploration of logic, of grammar, and of various other non-ecstatic disciplines.

Again, in what I consider Bevis' distorted view, the only kind of mysticism that Western writers in general have properly acknowledged is that of ecstatic self-loss. However, if one thinks, for example, of the great Christian mystics Pseudo-Dionysus, St. John of the Cross, Meister Eckhart, or Thomas à Kempis, author of *The Cloud of Unknowing*, not to mention perhaps the greatest Jewish mystic/theologian Isaac Luria, who sketched out the lineaments of what would become the normative strain of Kabbalah, there have been many examples of Western mystics, both Jewish and Christian, who were fully acquainted with the meditative self-loss in which both thought and feeing are suspended, which Bevis associates with Buddhism.

One cannot help but acknowledge that there is something, for a certain kind of temperament, embarrassingly too much, at times even shameful and transgressive, about the manifest symptoms of ecstatic self-loss, particularly when associated with the antinomian strain of Tantra.

One need only think, again, of the mostly upper middle-class Brahmins who were the disciples of Ramakrishna, and of the bewilderment they initially felt when confronted with their Tantric master's extravagant raptures and outré ecstatic high jinks. In one particularly choice passage from the *Gospel According to Ramakrishna*, the Master expatiates upon the ecstasy that accompanies a good bowel movement. Clearly, for Ramakrishna, ecstasy can either come in through the front or go out through the back door; he makes no distinction between the two.

Those of a certain temperament, too, are allergic to prattle about mystical union and divine love, particularly in the form of the love of disciple for Guru, an allergy intensified by the near-epidemic of false Gurus who preyed upon Westerners during the peak of the now mostly defunct New Age. And of course, a few of us are old enough to recall bald, top-knotted Hari Krishnas roving through urban wastelands in packs, melodiously chanting the praises of Krishna and Rama.

I recall attending, while an undergraduate at Harvard, what was billed as a poetry reading by Allen Ginsberg. For at least twenty minutes, before a word of poetry was spoken, Ginsberg plugged away at a battered harmonium; deploying his rich and resonant baritone, he led his captive audience in chanting *Hare Krishna, Hare Rama*. I remember how annoyed I was by this silliness. I felt like a guest who was being rudely imposed upon by a willfully oblivious host. Ironically, however, only a few years later I would be living in an ashram where the chanting of hauntingly sweet ragas would be the culmination and highlight of my days.

Those who are drawn to the experience of ecstatic self-loss might ask of Bevis' extreme putative Buddhist advocates of contemplative self-loss why there is relatively little of the *rasa*, the relish, the juice of divine love in the more austere forms of Buddhism. True, there is in Buddhism the ubiquitous emphasis on *karuna* or compassion, but it is a form of love that tends toward the ethical (it is difficult to think of a more sublime example of the ethical than the Bodhisattva vow). It is more empathic than passionate, more self-possessed than rapturous, when compared to

Hindu Bhakti or to any form of love modeled on the relationship between lover and beloved. In fact, however, most schools of Buddhism leave ample scope for the affective and the ecstatic. Bodhisattvas themselves tend to be viewed as deities. And in Tibetan Buddhism in particular, there is a proliferation of gods and goddesses upon whose forms monks are required to rigorously concentrate.

Bevis' state or stage of tranquil, meditative self-loss, purged of all feeling as well as of thought, which he sees as the highest stage of meditation and clearly identifies with Buddhism, is suggestive and illuminating with respect to Stevens' more austere poems of winter, but clearly, it seems to me, it cannot account for Stevens' exuberant, free-wheeling, improvisatory, endlessly self-proliferating, charismatic, and often ecstatic poems of summer.

I would like, as a reminder, to note that one could easily enlist one pole of the Kashmiri Shaivite experience, that of profound inner absorption in meditation, as fundamentally homologous to, if not identical with, the experience of contemplative self-loss in Buddhist meditation as detailed in Bevis' chosen text, a kind of manual of Theravada Buddhism. The Madhyamaka school of Mahayana Buddhism, as we shall soon see, entails a position of epistemological and ontological uncertainty with respect to any ultimate characterization of reality. It seems that Vedanta's notion of reality as Brahman, as pure being—glimpsed in nirguna samadhi, in meditating upon the formless—corresponds more with the pole of the real that predominates in what I have been calling Stevens' poems of winter than does any radical questioning or undermining of the status of the real itself *as* real. Although particularly in Stevens' late meditations on death something like this kind of uncertainty quite naturally arises, it tends, in many of his poems of winter, to be balanced or subsumed by a kind of ontological glow, a resting in the radiance of something like pure being, a category not countenanced by most forms of Buddhism.

3.

Bevis' typology of meditative states is of little use to him with respect to Stevens' longer, more free-wheeling poems of summer, and so he turns, in discussing them, from Theravada to Mahayana Buddhism. Strangely, however, Bevis only briefly cites Nagarjuna, generally considered to be the greatest of Buddhist logicians, the founder of the hugely influential Madhyamaka school of Mahayana Buddhism, or the so-called middle way. Nagarjuna is said to have received from the Nagas, supernatural water snakes, the Prajnaparamita texts, which are a foundation of the Madhyamaka teachings. Among them is the pithy and highly influential *Heart Sutra*, according to which, famously, "form is emptiness, emptiness is form."

Most schools of Buddhism, along with meditative practice, emphasize logical inquiry, which is considered meditation's equal partner in bestowing *prajna*, or insight into the nature of reality. Despite my undeniable lack of talent in grappling with matters logical, I wrestled, years ago, with the angel of the *Mulamadhyamakakarika,* Nagarjuna's seminal work on logic. I committed myself, as though signing up for a kind of forced march, to reading it from beginning to end, which I then proceeded to do. I confess to having felt intellectually slain, defeated numerous time along the way. But that the reader be so slain is perhaps one of the intended consequences of the text. Though I cannot say that the angel of his great treatise blessed me, and admitting from the outset that Nagarjuna is operating in a region beyond my ken, I will nonetheless venture a few tentative words about his use of logic, a subject that Bevis addresses only glancingly.

That logic centers around a venerable series of operations called the *catushkoti*, which was hardly original to Nagarjuna, and which had in fact sprouted many centuries prior to his use of it from the venerable milieu of Indian logic. The operations of the logic are the following: with respect to any given x there are four possibilities, x is x; x is y; x is both x and y; x is neither x nor y. With respect to a number of apparent logical opposites—for example, with respect to existence and nonexistence—Nagarjuna runs through these permutations and finds none of them logically viable or supportable. Thus Nagarjuna, in effect, negates the whole series. This would seem to lead us merely to a place of extreme negation, to *sunyata*, or the void, as the ultimate reality, except that Nagarjuna has already negated nonexistence as well as existence. Moreover, the positive statement that reality is void, if run through the same set of operations, would likewise be found invalid.

What is Nagarjuna's solution? By what may seem like logical sleight of hand, he asserts that the true nature of reality lies between existence and nonexistence, a kind of ultimate liminal state. With respect to *nirvana*, or liberation, and *samsara,* or the apprehension of a quotidian reality resulting in remaining trapped in cycles of death and rebirth, another set of apparent opposites, the true nature of things again resides exclusively in neither. From one perspective, samsara and nirvana are one, while at the same time, from another perspective, they remain distinct. Both perspectives are in their own way valid, according to Nagarjuna; the phenomenal world is not merely, positively void. He has a less skeptical and negative regard for the phenomenal world than do some of his predecessors. This avoidance of extremes, too, is part of the middle way. What is experienced as the phenomenal world is not entirely nonexistent, but it is illusory. Lacking any real substrate, it is a fictional projection of the mind. These considerations lead to the Madhyamaka doctrine of two truths: one provisional, relative, knowable in the way that our everyday experience is knowable; the other absolute and unknowable. It seems that there is some equivocation, some loophole here, that allows, as it were, Nagarjuna not to have his cake, yet to eat it, too. But to put the matter less glibly, Nagarjuna is exemplifying what Henry James called the sign of the superior intellect in all of the spheres of its operation, artistic or otherwise—the capacity to entertain as equally valid, simultaneously and in some way implicated in each other, two apparently incompatible thoughts.

With respect to the appearances of the phenomenal world, for Nagarjuna, it cannot be said that they arise, nor that they subside, nor that they both arise and subside, nor that that they neither arise nor subside. The fundamental aim of this and other such exercises is more than merely intellectual; it is the existential realization that the appearances of this phenomenal world are without any epistemological foundation, have no real status as independent realities. Nonetheless, again, they have a kind of provisional, experiential reality.

Finally, according Nagarjuna, the apparent continuity of the appearances that comprise the phenomenal world is likewise illusory. Such appearances are in fact discontinuous, discrete. They are digital, binary, rather than analog, blinking, as it were, on and off, off and on. Micro-moment by micro-moment. They are like the beads of a necklace connected by no thread. For Shaivism, on the other hand, Consciousness is the continuous thread that temporally connects the ever-changing appearances of the world, which are in fact nothing but Consciousness, and without which we would know nothing at all.

It can seem, in particular in reading Nagarjuna's uncompromising logic, that he, like Stevens, is a master of evasion, that whatever position we feel we have reached is subject to yet another twist, another linguistic turn, another negation; that we are left with no final word, nothing positive to say about the nature of phenomena, which have no epistemological or ontological foundation. For this reason, Nagarjuna was for a time misguidedly championed by the minions of deconstruction, was seen to subvert the dreaded metaphysics of presence, even to endorse the notion there is no reality apart from the endlessly self-prolonging and self-proliferating operations of language itself.

Indeed, though Nagarjuna leaves us with no definitive final word, posits no transcendent logos, he in no way endorses or takes pleasure in the lateral drift of language, let alone of textual language, endlessly self-proliferating and endlessly self-deferring, as a tide with respect to which we have no choice but to be happily or resignedly carried away. On the contrary, it is through the illusions generated by language, through the endless flow of mentation, that one becomes subject to endless cycles of craving and suffering. Far from endorsing the pleasures of merely linguistically circulating, Buddhism seeks, above all, to abolish the suffering wrought by the words that pass through the mind, which cause the soul to circulate through life after pointlessly painful life.

Nagarjuna's logical operations are not endless. They take us, hopefully, to a point at which we realize, in a lightning strike of insight that Buddhism call prajna, that nothing, including ourselves, has any fixed, independent identity. Having reached this point, having freed ourselves of the depredations of language, particularly abstract, conceptual language, we can sever, cut through, the distortions of reality wrought by the mind, and their attendant suffering, at their very root. Buddhism drives toward cessation, not prolongation.

In Bevis' attempt to assimilate Stevens' long poems, his poems of summer, to a Buddhist model, he overemphasizes the discontinuous, the random in Stevens' long poems, seeing each transient passage as reflective of the discrete, intrinsically unrelated nature, according to Nagarjuna, of the momentary, atomistic appearances that arise and vanish like indifferent flotsam on the surface of the ocean of the phenomenal world.

But in reading Stevens' poems of summer, we exult in the continuous and continuously varying flow of language and its capacity to ring seemingly limitless changes that are instinct with their own kind of unaccountable suggestiveness. Stevens' poems of summer are improvisatory, not random. They are more Duke Ellington than John Cage. Stevens is not an avant-guard poet. Many of the so-called language poets, and other current exemplars of our current would-be avant-garde, adopt a number of arbitrary rules designed to generate randomness in their texts. Stevens would have had little interest in such procedures.

4.

Those who have truly assimilated the teachings of Nagarjuna see the things of this world, undistorted by thought constructs, as pure percepts, as fleeting instances of the ever-changing flux of phenomenal appearances. At the same time, of course, the experience of the pure percept entails a human perceiver, in whom the perceived often, perhaps always, evokes an affective response. In the case of the enlightened perceiver, that response is likely to be one of contemplative peace or of unalloyed joy ruled out of bounds by Blevins' doctrinaire account of contemplative self-loss.

In the exquisite first canto of Stevens' "Notes Toward a Supreme Fiction," discussed at some length in "Stevens/Abhinavagupta," Stevens seems to be advocating a poetics of the pure percept. Immediately thereafter, however, he posits a first idea and the thinker of that idea as that which generates the supreme fiction that is both the poem and the phenomenal world. He thus reverts to a version of the subjective idealism that, along with objective realism, is one of the two apparently opposed default modes that characterize much of Western thought and, by extension, of Western poetry, which tends to prefer the mode of subjective idealism, while various forms of analytic philosophy make the case for objective realism.

Chinese and Japanese poetry, on the other hand—to generalize while at the same time bearing in mind Blake's dictum that "to generalize is to be an idiot," a notion with which the poets, Li Po and Basho, (whom I am about to too-summarily discuss) would heartily concur—tends to be concrete rather than abstract and conceptual, to favor the pure percept over the discursive or the didactic. Such poems are not, however, either devoid of affect or of the potential to evoke affect in the reader. In other words, contra Bevis, even the most contemplative poems have at least a trace of the ecstatic.

The poem of the pure percept tends to be intuitive, condensed, pithy, and unelaborated. I have mentioned that for Abhinavagupta words are quanta, units of energy. How true this seems of the more condensed forms of Chinese and Japanese poetry—highly-charged quanta of linguistic energy emanating a potentially endless series of concentric ripples. The finest of such poems are among the most powerful examples of what Abhinavagupta calls dhvani, the peculiarly poetic power of suggestiveness. Like all great poems, they are inexhaustible; they keep generating in the reader new responses, new perspectives, new nuances of feeling.

The Chinese poet best known in the West is Li Po (eighth century CE) who still retains, in China, unsurpassed prestige. He lived and worked during the Tang Dynasty, a period in which the arts flourished. His poetry includes, in an extraordinary way, both the contemplative and the ecstatic.

Li Po was a poet steeped in tradition, a reviver of old forms. Apart from occasional verses, he favored two kinds of poems: pithy, highly condensed lyrics, and apparently simple but highly sophisticated adaptations of folk ballads. A famous extoller, in verse, of wine, of intoxication, and of beautiful women, he also wrote poems, some while hung over, whose delicacy and directness of perception are of unparalleled beauty and would put the poetry of any ascetic to shame. The following poem is still taught to Chinese schoolchildren to this day.

QUIET NIGHT THOUGHT

Moonlight beside my bed.
Perhaps frost on the ground.
Lift up my head and see the moon.
Lower my head and long for home.

Li Po was a highly charismatic figure. His personal impact on all who met him was immense. He was something of a vagabond and lived a life of great simplicity and spontaneity, traveling often, a life influenced by Taoism, of which I will have more to say later. Some of his ballads read as accounts of shamanic spirit journeys; shamanic trances, often aided by hallucinogens, involve both an ecstatic going out of oneself and an intense identification with some chosen object or spirit; they were not inimical to Taoism, but were characteristic of one strain in it, a strain analogous to Tantric schools in Hinduism and Buddhism. In his poetry, Li Po often assumed personae, consistent with his essentially ecstatic practice of self-evacuation and identification with others. Indeed, his use of intoxicants, chiefly wine, his fascination with Taoism, particularly with ascetics and their alchemical practices, and his shamanic spirit journeys, all point to Li Po, in one of his modes, as an exemplar of the ecstatic.

Ezra Pound was highly influential in introducing, or reintroducing, Chinese poetry to the West. Pound, famously, was the founder of imagism, which with typical didacticism he turned into a programmatic doctrine. Pound defined the image as "an intellectual and emotional complex in an instant of time." I have noted that in

Buddhism, the appearances of the phenomenal world switch on and off, arise and subside, in the briefest of moments, of instants, randomly flashing and fading. For Pound, the poem is or should be a succession of such moments, exemplary instances gleaned from the past or from the present, which can only be grasped concretely as pure percepts. What he refers to as intellectual here is properly not intellectual but *perceptual.* Abjuring all generalities and abstractions, the imagist poem is a "direct treatment of the thing whether subjective or objective"; it is an explicit rendering, be it of external nature or of emotions. Pound fails to mention how much remains implicit in such renderings. He also suggests that direct treatment of the thing and of emotions are allied but separate categories, whereas in Li Po's poetry, emotion arises out of the pure perception that evokes it. Regardless, imagism's indebtedness to Pound's study of Chinese poetry is clear.

In his volume *Cathay,* Pound translated a number of Chinese poems, some more successfully than others. The most successful of Pound's translations, which manages to work perfectly in English while taking only a few liberties with the text, is of Li Po's "The River-Merchant's Wife: A Letter," a poem in which the poet assumes the identity of a young girl awaiting the return of her beloved husband. In its simplicity and directness of speech, its unadorned purity of perception, it evokes a painfully poignant sense of the passage of time, as well as suggesting affective states, such as intense anticipation, anxiety, incipient dread, a deep longing, and the intensity of young love.

What may be implied by the poem, but is never directly stated, is that as the precisely, concretely delineated seasons and months pass, it becomes increasingly likely that the young bride's husband will never return to her.

The River-Merchant's Wife: A Letter

While my hair was still cut straight across my forehead
I played about the front gate, pulling flowers.
You came by on bamboo stilts, playing horse,
You walked about my seat, playing with blue plums.
And we went on living in the village of Chokan:
Two small people, without dislike or suspicion.

At fourteen I married My Lord you.
I never laughed, being bashful.
Lowering my head, I looked at the wall.
Called to, a thousand times, I never looked back,

At fifteen, I stopped scowling,
I desired my dust to be mingled with yours
Forever and forever and forever.
Why should I climb the look out?

> At sixteen you departed.
> You went into far Ku-to-yen, by the river of swirling eddies.
> And you have been gone five months.
> The monkeys make sorrowful noise overhead.
>
> You dragged your feet when you went out.
> By the gate now the moss is grown, the different mosses,
> Too deep to clear them away!
> The leaves fall early this autumn, in wind.
> The paired butterflies are already yellow with August
> Over the grass in the West Garden;
> They hurt me. I grow older.
> If you are coming down through the narrows of the river Kiang,
> Please let me know beforehand,
> And I will come out to meet you
> > As far as Cho-fu-sa.

The predominant emotion in the poem, or perhaps simply the one with which I most resonate, is longing. In discussing Bhakti Yoga, or the yoga of love and devotion, I have suggested that it has two phases: one in which the disciple or devotee feels the pangs of separation from the Guru or the deity, the other in which he or she feels the longed-for state of ecstatic communion; and I have noted that the phase of longing often becomes as prized as that of mystical union. I mentioned, too, that bhakti is morphologically similar to the experience of any human lover with respect to his or her beloved.

In the case of such lovers, of course, full ecstatic union can never be achieved, and the pangs of separation, whether physical, emotional, or spiritual, can be both protracted and painful. Longing, like aspiration, is a quintessentially liminal state in which one is acutely aware of the space between oneself and the longed-for other, between oneself and the desired goal. The young river merchant's bride, literally separated from her husband, suffers a state of protracted longing in which the wished-for reunion is continually deferred. With the passage of time, so carefully and concretely delineated in the poem, that longing becomes more intense.

Longing entails, like ecstasy, a kind of anticipatory going out of the self. The young bride's willingness to leave her home—not merely a place but a world, an almost sacred space, a *temenos*, which, like the passage of time, is lovingly, carefully, and again concretely delineated in the poem— and to meet her husband halfway is a literal expression of longing as ecstatic, as a feeling that pushes against the confines of the given. The young bride is finally determined to break free, if necessary, from the circle of her innocence, from home, with all of its connotations, and imagines herself, like her husband, undertaking what for her would doubtless be experienced as a daunting and perilous journey.

Li Po exhibits throughout the poem, to a remarkable degree, what Keats, as we shall see, called *negative capability*. Li Po's own identity goes out of itself and becomes one with the identity of the other, in this case a girl becoming a young woman, a figure whom he has imagined so powerfully that not for a moment do we doubt her existence.

I find Pound's rendition of Li Po deeply moving. Indeed, I regard it as among the finest poems that Pound wrote (or in this case, co-wrote). Nonetheless, Pound's translation, like all translations, has its shortcomings. "Forever and forever and forever" is an extraneous addition. The mingling of dust with dust is not in Chinese a funerary image. Such an image would be altogether too explicit for Li Po. Pound misses, too, what is clear in other versions—that the young bride's husband, in departing, has left footprints, traces of his former presence, in the grass, and that it is these imprints that the growing grasses obscure.

5.

I have already suggested, in discussing the limitations of language, and will directly address in the section called "Abhinavagupta and the Four Levels of Speech," that all human attempts to communicate subjective states through language are in effect translations that are never entirely successful. They are always approximate, in some sense, in which one metaphorically relates the state of the other to some presumably analogous, familiar state in oneself.

In actual translations from one language to another, this problem can be even more daunting, particularly so in the case of languages as radically different as Chinese and English, and even more so in the case of poetry. Chinese and Japanese poetry can seem, to the Westerner, to be maddeningly simple-minded, to leave too much out. And indeed too much, inevitably, *is* left out, is lost in translation. Conversely, Western poetry can seem to native Chinese speakers to include too much of the extraneous, as if the poet were attempting to conceal rather than reveal, like the grasses overgrowing the river merchant's footprints, the essence of what he ought to be attempting to suggest. In addition, too much in Western poetry can seem to be discursively spelled out, as though drawing unnecessary, explicit lines between points of a pattern that would have been better, more tellingly, left implicit.

The best known of Pound's imagist poems that are not translations is "In a Station of the Metro":

> The apparition of these faces in a crowd;
> Petals on a wet, black bough.

The poem, though striking in its own way, does not seem to me entirely successful. Of its two juxtaposed percepts, the second is more powerful and direct than the first.

The relationship between the two percepts is entirely visual, a simple form of association, an instance of what Coleridge would call, in a distinction that I shall discuss in a later chapter, fancy rather than imagination, and so the poem remains superficial, has little affective power.

Its stark juxtaposition of two pure percepts is characteristic of the haiku and other highly condensed Japanese forms. Indeed, the increasing interest in Chinese poetry in the early twentieth century was paralleled by an increasing interest in Japanese poetry and drama.

I will now turn as promised to a second figure relatively well known in the West, the Japanese poet Basho (seventeenth century CE), reputed to have been a practitioner of Zen Buddhism. Zen evolved from the Chinese Chan, a mainstream school of Mahayana Buddhism. The haiku, a form in which Basho was a pioneer and of which he was later acknowledged as a preeminent master, is perhaps the quintessential instance both of the poem as pure percept and of the poem as profoundly liminal. The haiku is devoid of the conceptual. It is concrete, not abstract. It emphasizes the particular and unique, not the general and typical. It allies itself with the moment, not with an artificially arranged succession of moments. It strictly adheres to what corresponds, in English, to three lines with a fixed 5/7/5 syllable count. In no way discursive, it gives form to flashes of insight. Those flashes occur in the empty, liminal space between the second and third lines, between two juxtaposed percepts. Emptiness is form, form is emptiness.

The enlightened Buddhist seer apprehends phenomenal appearances directly as pure percepts. Likewise, the poet of genius, free of conceptual distortions and their attendant attachments, sees with clarity and insight the emptiness in forms, but also the form in emptiness. He sees the uniquely characteristic if evanescent quality at the heart of all forms, what Zen Buddhists call their suchness. Through the poem, not only the suchness of the perceived but also the most refined and nuanced gradations of mood and feeling, which one ordinarily associates with the perceiver, are simultaneously evoked.

Pound's imagism and its doctrinaire program influenced a number of his lesser disciples, whose poems feel diluted, watered down. The typical imagist poem is no longer an instance of the poem of pure percept. Rather, it draws upon remembered images that are like flowers pressed between the pages of a book, faded simulacra of pure percepts, which are then artfully arranged. Imagism degenerated into a kind of sentimentality, of subjectivity disguised as objectivity. The poem of pure percept, on the other hand, dissolves both subject and object.

After the heyday of Pound's Orientalism and the depredations of imagism had passed, something like an efflorescence of the poem as pure perception occurred in the poetry of the great Modernist American William Carlos Williams, who unfortunately summed up his poetics in the confusing slogan "no ideas but in things." In haiku, as in the philosophy of Nagarjuna, there are no ideas, no things as separate self-subsisting entities. In no way, certainly, do ideas inhere in things.

Fortunately, Williams was as fine a poet as he was clumsy as an aesthetic theorist. Among the best of his poems are those that are, in fact, instances of the poetry of the pure percept. Williams, who was a fiercely and self-consciously American poet, came by these poems, as it were, naturally, not as a participant in a decadent and distorted revival of Chinese or Japanese aesthetics. Williams was a physician, specifically an obstetrician, and as such had a respect for the minute particularity of the things of this world. The best of his poems have the implicit affective power that I have suggested is often an attribute of the poem as pure percept. Unfortunately, it is beyond the scope of this chapter to discuss Williams' poetry at any length. I have, however, attended to Williams extensively in an essay in my book *Elective Affinities* called "Williams' Brave Descent." It with a close reading of what I consider perhaps the most moving of Williams' poems of the pure percept, or of slightly more than the pure percept, "On The Road To The Contagious Hospital," a poem that is embedded, along with other such brief poems, in the prose—part manifesto, part prose-poem—of Williams' breakthrough volume *Spring and All*.

Of course, not all poems by Buddhist authors are enlightened exercises in maximal minimalism. Basho, for example, was partial to long, collaborative poems that began with a haiku with its 5/7/5 pattern of syllabic verse, which was followed by a number of poems in a slightly different but equally brief 7/7 format. These were contributed by any number of other poets, resulting in an eminently improvisatory form that calls to mind the riffs of soloists in jazz bands. In these poems, potentially of great length, any number of contiguous epiphanic moments of pure perception, while essentially autonomous, could be strung together, thus combining the discontinuous with the continuous. During Basho's time, haiku were assimilated to larger collaborative structures such as those just described, structures that, like Stevens' poems of summer, accommodate not only the discontinuous but the continuous as well.

I remember, on the first day of the first poetry workshop that I ever took, being asked, along with my new confrères, to participate in what is a not-uncommon exercise. Whoever was designated to begin the exercise wrote two lines, then folded the page so that only the second line could be seen. The next poet write two lines in response, then likewise folded the page so that only his second line could be seen. This process continued until the last poet in the class had participated. The resultant poem, which entailed passages both surprisingly continuous and strikingly discontinuous, was read back to us by our teacher, interrupted by frequent outbursts of laughter. A lighthearted humor and what Keats called a fine surprise are likewise often a feature of Basho's poetry.

Only later were haiku predominantly written to stand alone as an autonomous genre. Even when standing alone, however, haiku, though devoid of thought constructs, are not merely instances, to return to Bevis' typology, of meditative, tranquil self-loss devoid of feeling, but are also epiphanic and ecstatic. Likewise, they are not merely poems as pure percepts; as acts of perception they implicitly include the perceiver and are suggestive, again, of the subtlest nuances of feeling, the subtlest of moods.

There were, of course, other ways in which brief, epiphanic poems could become parts of larger structures. Between stints as a teacher of poetry, Basho undertook long, dangerous journeys on foot into the interior of Japan, into wilderness areas populated only by roving outlaws banished from civil society. These journeys placed him in great peril. He could easily have died either at the hands of bandits or by failure to survive, unaided, in the wilderness. The closeness to death intensified Basho's experience of life and of nature. Basho's masterpiece, *Journey to the Northern Interior*, is the account of one such journey in which brief, epiphanic poems in various formats, including haiku, are embedded in a lengthy prose narrative.

A number of years ago, a friend of mine—a twentieth, now a twenty-first century American poet—undertook a long trek that led through and beyond the Lake District of England now associated with Wordsworth, who was, of course, himself in the habit of taking long treks. In my friend's backpack were only two books, *The Prelude* and *Journey to the Northern Interior*, which in the course of his trek he read for the first time. He became rapturously enamored with Basho's masterwork, which he later insisted I read—as a result of which now, years later, I am giving this doubtless wholly inadequate gloss of it.

Are all poems that touch, however lightly, upon the mystical, in some sense journeys to the interior, no one like any other but all bearing a kind of family resemblance? Are they all, however heterogenous, somehow parts of a larger structure, of an unofficial view of reality, that cuts across the boundaries of time and space?

Do all such journeys, like any risk worth taking, involve some element of danger?

6.

Though both the Madhyamaka school of Mahayana Buddhism and Kashmir Shaivism espouse the liminal, the in-between, and the nondual, the former, seeing the essential fact of human life as suffering tends, like Vedanta, to have a skeptical view of the reality of the world of appearances, and to question the value of engaging it.

Rather than simply reiterating the characteristic tenets of Kashmir Shaivism and its typically Tantric, relatively affirmative stance toward reality, I will discuss a philosophical/poetical text, far less well known than Nagarjuna's famous treatise or the poetry of Li Po or of Basho, that approaches nondualism from a Kashmiri Shaivite point of view.

I am speaking of the *Amritanubhav*, usually translated as *The Nectar of Self-Awareness*, by the great Maharashtran poet-saint Jnaneshwar (twelfth century CE). After completing *Jnaneshwari*, a lengthy verse commentary on the *Bhagavad Gita*, Jnaneshwar wandered for two years throughout Northern India where, scholars generally agree, he was exposed to Kashmir Shaivism. When he returned, his Guru asked him to compose an original work in verse form on his own state of nondual awareness. Much of the resultant work, the *Amritanubhav*, channels the insights of Kashmir Shaivism in a unique and compelling way. The *Amritanubhav,* remarkably, is equally effective as a philosophical text and a poem. In this, its only Western peer is Lucretius' *De Rerum Natura,* which feels, by comparison, pedantic and heavy-handed.

Astonishingly, scholars agree that Jnaneshwar wrote the *Amritanubhav* at the age of twenty-two. He seems to exemplify what Stevens called, in the title of one of his essays, "the figure of the youth as virile poet."

The *Amritanubhav* has come down to us as divided into ten chapters, which most scholars regard as the work of a later editor. Nonetheless, these chapter divisions are in their own way helpful. The first two chapters of the *Amritanubhav*, "Homage to Shiva and Shakti" and "Homage to Nivrittinath," are akin to its last two chapters, "The Secret of Natural Devotion" and "Blessings to the World." These chapters provide a kind of devotional frame to the text as a whole. Rather than engaging in logical argument, they are essentially exercises in praise of what Shaivism calls *anupaya*, the pathless path, exemplified in the first two chapters by the loving union of Shiva and Shakti, and then by grace-bestowing power of the Guru, the embodiment divine love. This pathless path of Consciousness as divine love is again taken up in the final two chapters of the *Amritanubhav*, which extol the actionless action, the "Secret of Natural Devotion," which is the hallmark of the being who has attained the state of liberation while still in the body. Such a state, according to Jnaneshwar, is our natural state, our birthright. It is instinct with the rasa, the relish, of joy and love that Jnaneshwar extends to the reader in the poem's final section, "Blessings to the World."

By far the largest portion of the poem, chapters three through seven, constitute a devastating, closely argued critique of Vedanta, particularly of its notions of knowledge and ignorance. At the same time, no longer referring to the highest state of pure, direct awareness in theistic or personal terms, Jnaneshwar instead refers more abstractly to an Ultimate Reality whose nature is that of Supreme Consciousness or pure awareness itself. This long medial section begins and ends with a challenge to Vedanta's view of knowledge and ignorance, and implicitly critiques *Jnana Yoga*, the way of knowledge— the very form of yoga of which Jnaneshwar was universally considered a master. Jnaneshwar ruthlessly deconstructs the idea that so-called knowledge, which is merely the notional opposite of so-called ignorance, can grant access to the experience of Consciousness or the Ultimate Reality.

Jnaneshwar, like several Sufi poets whom I have discussed, was almost exactly contemporaneous with Dante, whose *Divine Comedy* also reflects both a peerless intellect and a susceptibility to the suasion of a divine love that is ultimately regarded as moving all things. Like Dante, Jnaneshwar made the bold decision to write in the vernacular, in Marathi rather than in Sanskrit, with which he was thoroughly familiar. A Brahmin who renounced his status as a Brahmin, who wanted his work to be accessible to all, he is considered the founder, and still the finest flower, of Marathi literature, as Dante is of Italian literature.

Jnaneshwar invented a new stanza for all of his works, consisting of three rhymed lines, each comprised of four metric units, and a final unrhymed stanza consisting of two. This stanzaic form is almost impossibly compact, a point that is brought home when one looks at the various free verse translations of these stanzas, some of which tend to run on at some length. I think of Jnaneshwar's stanzas as benign hand grenades, exploding, particularly in the poem's middle chapters, not only the false, meaningless antinomy of knowledge and ignorance but many other shibboleths as well. At the poem's medial, central point, it challenges the classic Vedic notion of the Absolute as *Sat Chit Ananda*, or existence, consciousness, and bliss, with a particular emphasis on undermining the notion that existence, as the mere notional opposite of nonexistence, can in any way be said to characterize the ultimate reality. The poem also explodes, along the way, the view of the phenomenal world as an illusion engendered by Maya; any notion of Consciousness as embodied by a transcendent logos or primal word; the slavish adherence of prior Indian philosophical works to the authority of revealed texts; the requirement that such texts directly address *pramanas* and *prameyas*, the so-called valid means of proof, a demand which Jnaneshwar explicitly and gleefully flouts. And so on, and so on. Jnaneshwar's compact stanzas consistently blast conventional cant while at the same time illuminating the surrounding landscape, open to direct experience, that we share.

What are some of the other salient features of the *Amritanubhav*? Perhaps foremost in this context, in comparison with Buddhist poems that arise from analogous nondual apprehension of the structure of reality, or the concretely perceived and delineated poems of Basho, it does not contain, in its one hundred plus pages, a single percept, a single direct observation of the natural world.

In contrast to Nagarjuna's *Mulamadhyamakakarika*, the *Amritanubhav* is a supremely rhetorical performance, as self-aware as any postmodern poem about its status as a poem, foregrounding questions about the medium of language itself, and constantly reminding the reader of the woeful limitations of words, and particularly of the singular inefficacy of language to convey the natural state of enlightened consciousness that the reader, without knowing it, has already attained. When Jnaneshwar asks himself a pointed, rhetorical question—why, then, has he composed such an apparently useless text at all?—he gives an entirely characteristic, insouciant response: "for the pure joy of expounding." It is joy, not suffering, that is seen by Jnaneshwar as man's natural estate, as the birthright of all.

The *Amritanubhav*, though in fact, as noted, in large part a closely argued philosophical critique of Vedanta, is nothing if not playful, and despite its tight and elegant structure has an improvisatory feel. Indeed legend, instructive but likely apocryphal, has it that the *Amritanubhav* was delivered extemporaneously in the public square of Jnaneshwar's town of Alandi before a rapt audience of devotees. The poem, legend has it, was recorded by a scribe.

In thinking of Jnaneshwar, I think of the wonderful onomatopoeic term *sprezzatura*, coined during the Italian Renaissance, an laudatory term describing the qualities of those—often younger artists—who seem to produce masterful works of art easily, off-handedly, diffidently, exuberantly, jazzily, playfully, indeed perhaps ecstatically, as though with minimal effort, for the sheer joy of artistically propounding. Sprezzatura involves a kind of showing off raised to a higher power. The Western idea of the artist as genius and polymath has deep roots in the Renaissance. Jnaneshwar, saint/poet/philosopher/scholar, was nothing if not a genius and a polymath.

In our attempt to grasp the ineffable state of awareness out of which the poem *Amritanubhav* was written, we as readers frequently experience a state of almost vertiginous disorientation. Just when we feel we are grasping some key insight, it eludes us. The text continually reveals and conceals itself, conceals and reveals itself. Reading it is like simultaneously weaving and unweaving some sublime vestment. We are always, again, in the moment of the liminal, of the in-between, of beginning again. The poem is often bracingly ironic and humorous in tone. Jnaneshwar almost seems to assume the role of divine trickster—of being in on some cosmic joke which we, too, are in on without realizing it. Jnaneshwar mesmerizes and beguiles us, charms us, despite ourselves, into almost getting the joke, into catching glimpses of what should be and in fact is self-evident.

Nagarjuna uses and exhausts language to help us arrive at an experiential state of insight and clarity beyond logic, to arrive at or suggest the *madhya*, the liminal, the in-between, a state in which we realize than neither we nor the things of this world have any independent identity. Jnaneshwar gleefully, exuberantly, deploys both logic and the rhetorical language of metaphor while fully recognizing the limitations of language. Ultimately, in reading the *Amritanubhav*, one grasps that Jnaneshwar speaks from and out of a state of pure, unconditioned, and unconditional awareness. By occasionally letting go of the burden of attempting to understand the poem's argument, one becomes, however briefly, attuned to the state of awareness from which it arose.

Several of the attributes I have ascribed to the *Amritanubhav* are reminiscent of Stevens' endlessly elaborative, seemingly improvisational poems of summer. Like the *Amritanubhav*, Stevens' poems of summer are almost entirely devoid of pure percepts, of direct observations of the natural world. Stevens' poems, like the verses of the *Amritanubhav*, resist easy paraphrase, continually eluding us even as we imagine we are grasping them. Finally, I am convinced that Stevens, too, wrote for the pure joy of expounding, or rather perhaps of propounding, and would have found such a notion entirely congenial

More broadly, it seems to me that Shaivism's insistence on the identity of what Bevis calls the meditative and the ecstatic, with neither privileged over the other, with both given equal pride of place, provides a framework that illuminates Stevens' poems both of summer and of winter. Stevens' longer poems of summer repeatedly gather into provisional epiphanies that are then dispersed, a kind of alternate current that keeps playing itself out. One senses in Stevens' poems of summer that, as in Shaivism, and as in the *Amritanubhav*, there is always some kind of play between concealment and revelation, revelation and concealment, which is again not merely random, but rather is built into the structure of reality and of our experience of it

Nagarjuna's logical treatise, Basho's longer collaborative poems or longer narratives including poems, and Jnaneshwar's poetical/philosophical treatise, all, despite their differences, reflect a nondual state of awareness. None of them enforce Bevis' clear-cut distinction between contemplative self-loss, devoid of either thought or feeling, and ecstatic self-loss. Nor do Stevens' longer, improvisatory, ecstatic poems of summer, which accommodate both discontinuity and continuity, both contemplative and ecstatic moments.

7.

There remains a yet another work to discuss, an exemplar of a mystical tradition that, unlike Buddhism, is distinctively and indigenously Chinese. I am, of course, speaking of Taoism, and specifically of the *Tao Te Ching* of Lao Tzu, which is as beautiful and sublime a text as any I have thus far discussed. Though it is not technically poetry, it has the feel of poetry. I cannot even begin to do it justice here. I will restrict myself, instead, to two interrelated topics, the similarities and differences between Shaivism and Taoism, and the relevance of both to Stevens' poems of summer.

Much of what immediately follows involves a complex of ideas discussed at some length in "Stevens/Abhinavagupta." Among these is the idea that the imagination and reality are not for Stevens mere logical counters, notional opposites, such as the existence and nonexistence scrupulously examined by others, critiqued by both Nagarjuna and Jnaneshwar; nor are they in the dialectical relationship of thesis and antithesis, leading to a higher synthesis, the whole process leading to some desired end; nor do they contribute to some abstract, sustained argument, whether exemplified, for example, by the extended metaphors and analogies of Donne, or by the often intricately logical structure of Shakespeare's sonnets. Rather, the polar forces of reality and the imagination are complementary, each necessarily entailing the other, and are in a constantly changing, dynamic relationship to each other, including a potentially limitless number of provisional adjustments between the two.

In Taoism it is said that "the Tao that can be named is not the true Tao." The Tao, literally *the way*, can be seen as referring to the true path followed by the sage, a path that is in practice ever-changing, the path no doubt followed by Basho on his journeys to the northern interior. Likewise it akin to *anupaya*, the practice-less practice, the pathless path, ever spontaneously manifesting itself, which is always being blazed, not followed, by the Shaivite seer.

At the same time, the Tao refers to a principle, itself nowhere manifest, that generates the complementary poles of the yin and the yang, the one active and masculine, the other passive and feminine. These complementary forces, each entailing the other, are constantly at play, manifesting the ever-changing lineaments of the natural world. Like Stevens, Taoism deals more with *natura naturans* than *natura naturata*. Nothing is frozen, fixed, categorical. The *Tao Te Ching*, a seminal text of Taoism, though it addresses the interplay between stillness and movement, profoundly reflects an awareness that all things change, are in flux. One is reminded of the Heraclitan opening of Charles Olson's masterpiece, "The Kingfishers": "What does not change / is the will to change." The last line of Rilke's "Sonnets to Orpheus" has a distinctly Taoist feel: "Say to that earth of silence: I flow. / Say to the rushing waters: I am." For Lao Tzu as for Heraclitus no supervenient, transcendent will is involved in the Tao's unfolding of things as they are. The Taoist sage is ever aware, at every given moment, of the unique adjustment, of the always provisional balance between the yin and yang. Stevens' poems, as I have suggested, are exquisitely attuned to just such accommodations and adjustments. In his recognition that the poles of experience, which he calls reality and imagination, are aspects of a continuum that is cyclical not linear, complementary not agonistic, Stevens resembles not only a Shaivite seer but also a Taoist sage.

The second chapter of the *Tao Te Ching*, with a typical simplicity and beauty, addresses the complementarity of which I have just been speaking.

> When people see some things as beautiful
> Other things become ugly.
> When people see something's as good,
> Other things become bad.
>
> Being and non-being create each other.
> Difficult and easy support each other.
> Long and short define each other.
> High and low depend upon each other.
> Before and after follow each other.

In Shaivism, the ultimate principle, though referred to, like the Tao, by name, is unnameable and undefinable, nowhere to be found and yet manifest everywhere. Ever arising within *Paramashiva* are the inalienable powers of both Shiva and Shakti, complementary not agonistic, the co-creators and co-destroyers at every moment of all that is. Crucially, in both Shaivism and Taoism, as in Stevens' poems of summer, the complementarity of polar forces, whether of Shiva and Shakti, of the yin and the yang, or of reality and the imagination, are at play in engendering the ever-changing appearances of the phenomenal world. The adjustment between these forces is likewise ever-changing, always provisional, always, at every moment, unique. No one pole ever apocalyptically usurps the other—at least not without disastrous results. The famous graphic symbol of the Tao makes clear that even when one pole seems ascendant, the seed of the other, present within it, is waiting to germinate

Of course there are also significant differences between Taoism and Shaivism. The Tao, though it can nowhere be isolated and found in the world, is not, like Shiva, a transcendent principle. In the dominant Pratyabhijna school of Shaivism, furthermore, Consciousness is always connected to Shiva as agent. Shiva possesses the fully expanded powers or shaktis of *iccha*, *jnana*, and *kriya*, of will, knowledge, and action, of which iccha or will, as most associated with Shiva's *svatantrya*, or unfettered freedom, is *primus inter pares*. Thus in Shaivism, unlike in Taoism, there is a supervenient will behind the ever-changing flashing forth of the phenomenal world.

Taoism, like Shaivism, speaks of action in inaction, inaction in action. Sometimes, in accordance with the Tao, inaction, getting out of the way, letting the yin and the yang unfold as they will, without intervention, is what is called for, and is the truest form of action. At other times, overt action is called for. But again, action when taken in accord with the Tao is really inaction, and likewise allows the yin and the yang to unfold in proper relation to each other. Similarly, with respect to the Shaivite seer who is one with Shiva, and who cannot help but act in accordance with His will, it is specifically said that his action is inaction, his inaction action, and that that he constantly delights in the play of Shiva and Shakti, letting that play unfold as it will.

Once again Lao Tzu, in discussing the nature of the sage in chapter two, expresses this insight with an eloquence far greater than any I can muster,

> Therefore the master
> Acts without doing anything
> And teaches without saying anything.
> Things arise and she lets them come;
> Things disappear and she lets them go.
> She has but doesn't possess,
> Acts but doesn't expect.
> When her work is done, she forgets it.
> That is why it lasts forever.

I have mentioned that a peculiar feature of Stevens' poetry is its renunciation of the lyric *I*. One senses that Stevens is always observing, with minimal interference, the play of the imagination and reality both as it manifests or enacts itself in the almost autonomous play of the language of his poetry, and in the fine, ever-changing adjustments of reality to the imagination, of imagination to reality, as they manifest in the phenomenal world. One of the canonical texts of Taoism is the *I Ching, The Book of*

Changes. Stevens' poems of summer constitute his book of changes, reflecting his delight in "the metaphysical changes that occur /merely in living as and where we live."

The *Tao Te Ching*, like the *Amritanubhav*, is in some sense both a poem and a work of philosophy. It has some of the freshness, the earliness, the suggestive simplicity, of the Greek pre-Socratics, of the pithy sayings of Heraclitus or of Parmenides, though one feels it has progressed considerably further along the road on which they were traveling.

I first read the *Tao Te Ching* years ago, in Witter Bynner's translation, and I have read it in a number of translations since. But, of course, it cannot really be translated. Lao Tzu's Chinese is even more polysemous than Abhinavagupta's Sanskrit. Even in the original it evades any univocal interpretation. It has something of the resistance to paraphrase, the undecidability, the openness to multiple interpretations, that I have suggested is characteristic of many of Stevens' poems. Likewise, the *Tao Te Ching* is replete with dhvani, is inexhaustibly suggestive. Each time one reads it, it is as though one were reading it for the first time. Like Basho, Li Po, Stevens, and Jnaneshwar, Lao Tzu, too, evades the by-now tired categories of the contemplative and the ecstatic. Reading the *Tao Te Ching* with any real attention puts one in a meditative state while at the same time inspiring the profound, almost metaphysical emotion that Abhinavagupta calls shanta rasa, and that, as we have seen, certain of Stevens' poems also evince.

2.
New Thresholds, New Affinities

1.

I would like to indulge myself, and beg your indulgence, as I speak, not *ex-cathedra*, but *in propria persona*, of some of my own experiences, some quite distant in time, one recent, that bear upon the preceding discussion in ways that hopefully will soon become clear.

I spent one glorious, wild summer, the summer of 1976, at the Naropa Institute in Boulder, Colorado, just prior to the fall in which I met my spiritual teacher. The institute was the creation of an extraordinary figure, Chogyam Trungpa Rinpoche, a reincarnated master of a lineage of Tibetan Buddhism. The institute offered an eclectic array of courses on transpersonal psychology; on various New Age practices, including forms of body work; as well as, most interestingly to me, on the interface between Eastern mysticism and contemporary physics and biology.

The institute also gave shelter to the strangely named *Jack Kerouac School of Disembodied Poetics*, of which Allen Ginsberg, a particularly devoted disciple of Trungpa, was not only the founder, the impresario/master of ceremonies, but also among other poets of lesser stature—including Anne Walden, who was his co-professor in residence, and visiting dignitaries like William Burroughs, the redoubtable Gregory Corso, and Michael McClure—the primary teacher, the first among not-quite-equals.

I attended several of the classes in which, with an aspect that was more that of a kindly, avuncular, learned rabbi than that of his public persona as a charismatic New Age superstar and sexual wild man, Ginsberg expatiated on his poetics, which centered around the Buddhist aesthetic mantra "first thought, best thought."

Ginsberg believed in training oneself as a poet to catch one's consciousness, as it were, on the fly, and to transcribe the contents of that consciousness, however, exalted, however apparently mundane, however, at times, frankly and graphically sexual, in the form of poems. Keats, whom I shall be discussing later at some length in the final section of this book, wrote that the mind should be the "thoroughfare for all ideas," that it should be essentially open and nonjudgmental, that it should not preemptively seize upon any one idea or cluster of ideas through which to view and inevitably to distort the world. Ginsberg's poetry is a record or testament of the mind not only as the thoroughfare of all ideas but also as the thoroughfare of all of the non-ideational flotsam and jetsam—including abortive, half-formed scraps of fantasy, of sensory impressions, and of the inchoate, raw stuff of undirected mentation, largely habitually unconscious—that the mind is continuously generating, and that constantly flits across its screen. Ginsberg was the enemy of mental censorship of any kind, including revision of his poetic transcriptions, which resulted, it seemed to me, in several extraordinary poems as well as a number of rambling, desultory rhetorical performances.

I was a fledgling poet at the time, which meant that I was at once highly impressionable and highly resistant to any prescriptive form of poetics, and of claims of poetic authority in general. This resistance was crucial and usually won out over my impressionability; it created a zone in which I could let my own work take its own characteristic shape. And so, while at Naropa, I was resistant to Ginsberg's poetic nostrums, including particularly, "first thought, best thought," which I saw as an invitation to mere self-indulgence. I was generally unimpressed as well by the poetry Ginsberg had produced since the charmed epoch in which he had been the midwife to *Howl* and to his masterpiece *Kaddish*, as well as to a number of charming and disarming briefer lyrics.

Later, I learned to appreciate much about Ginsberg, including his quite extraordinary generosity of spirit as manifested by his endemic kindliness, his unflagging devotion to and work on behalf of his Guru, Trungpa, and his life-long engagement and political activism on behalf of the politically marginal and disenfranchised not only in the United States but around the world.

More germane to my concerns here, I began to understand and appreciate what I came to see as central to his aesthetics (though it would never be akin to my own), which was to treat all of the sometimes subliminal mind stuff that arises and subsides within the vast expanse of pure, conscious awareness on equal terms. This involved shining the light of consciousness on the scarcely conscious contents of the mind, which are often a kind of insult to our egos, our privileged but narrow sense of ourselves, and which most of us usually unconsciously but sometimes half-knowingly suppress and would never think of sharing with others. Thus Ginsberg's aesthetics seemed to involve, as in his overt embrace of an unequivocal gay identity, which far more than now exposed him to contempt and humiliation, a kind of courage, a refusal to find embarrassing or outré what might seem so to others. Thus his poetry at its best extends a kind of permission to its readers to be fearlessly open to and conscious of whatever in them is repelled and habitually repressed, rendered unconscious, by the fortress of the ego as buttressed by societal norms. His aesthetics, I later realized, were aligned with the spiritual practices and perspectives enjoined by Tibetan Buddhism, which counsels, in line with its essentially Tantric character, viewing all mental phenomena, though possessing only an equivocal reality, with a kind of equally unconditional positive regard, thereby inducing a state of balance and joyful equanimity that no nominally external force or attitude can disrupt.

But for me, the summer in question was not primarily concerned with matters poetical. Rather, it revolved around my first forays into meditative practice. For some time my first bout of poetic inspiration, which lasted about five years, had seemed, despite my attempts to fuel it with alcohol, to be on the wane. I gave up drinking and somehow sensed that meditative practice might grant me access to the source of inspiration or something close to it.

And so it was that I found myself meditating for four hours every morning as part of a group practice supervised by one of Trungpa's devotees. I eventually came to look forward to these sessions, which had at first seemed arduous. Moreover, I began to feel a kind of subtle shift in my awareness. My mind seemed to be becoming clearer, more spacious, more open.

I loved Boulder and particularly the omnipresence of a radiant, brilliant, clear sky against which the foothills of Rockies were set in a kind of high relief, a sky whose prominence was the result of my sojourning for the first time at a relatively high altitude. While my feet were planted firmly on the ground, I felt myself somehow to be immersed in the depths of this vast, sovereign, unmirroring sky. I began to indulge in extracurricular hours of meditation in a beautiful meditation hall on the second floor of a commercial building in downtown Boulder, which at that time retained something of the feel of a small Western town. I often emerged from these sessions, usually in the late afternoon, to a golden light that seemed to bathe all things with a kind of equanimity and joy.

Curiously, I never connected these experiences to Trungpa, nor was I attracted to him as a spiritual teacher. Later, however, it seemed to me that Trungpa was for me a kind of John the Baptist preparing the way for my meeting with the figure who was to become my spiritual preceptor, or Guru. Although I do not know much about Tibetan Buddhism, I know enough to know that its essentially Tantric nature aligns it as much or more with various forms of Tantric Hinduism than with other schools of Buddhism. I recall that during one of my stays in India a devotee of my Guru left him in order study with the Dalai Llama. Remarkably, he was somehow granted an audience with this venerable personage, who told my friend that whatever he could learn from the Dalai Lama, he could learn equally well from the Guru whom he had just misguidedly left. The Dalai Llama referred to my Guru as a *mahasiddha*, a term for an enlightened master, common, again, to both certain strains of Tantric Hinduism and Tibetan Buddhism, and to a lineage of masters of yoga that are likewise revered by both.

All of the above is intended as a kind of prelude providing some context for an event that has occurred quite recently. One of my friends, who had been for a long time a disciple of my spiritual preceptor, is currently studying with a Tibetan Buddhist teacher, Anam Thubten, who is the legatee of a lineage of Tibetan Buddhist masters. Parenthetically, in response to a question about my Guru by a former devotee, Anam Thubten also referred to him as a mahasiddha. Like the Dalai Llama, he was somehow cognizant, as though via a kind of underground network, or by subtle tendrils of affinity, of a figure from a different but related Tantric tradition.

As I have been suffering of late from the twin challenges of mental and physical distress, my friend asked her teacher if there was anything he could do help me. He recommended that I read a much revered Tibetan Buddhist text called *The Special Treasury of the Basic Space of Phenomena*. The text, if one excludes the facing pages in Tibetan, is relatively brief, running to about seventy pages in a fairly large typeface. This recommendation of a sacred text marked the second time a spiritual text had been specifically introduced to me by a spiritual teacher. The first had been my introduction to the *Amritanubhav* by my spiritual teacher over forty decades ago.

The *Special Treasury* is one of seven treasuries written by the great Tibetan Master Longchen Rabjam, commonly known as Longchenpa (1308–1364), who was a major teacher in the Nyingma school of Tibetan Buddhism. His major work is the aforementioned *Seven Treasuries,* which is said to epitomize the previous six hundred years of Tibetan Buddhist thought.

Upon reading this book I felt immediately and powerfully drawn to it. Like the *Amritanubhav* and the *Tao Te Ching*, it is a sublimely beautiful work in stanzaic form. These texts, which I now regard as a kind of trinity, have an extraordinary way of insinuating themselves into one's awareness, one's consciousness, in much the way that the greatest poems do. The beauty and sometimes enigmatic rightness of their expression induces in one something of a trance-like state. They transmit meaning as a kind of ineffable feeling, a feeling that is deeper and more subtle than—and that subtends, underlies—all grosser more definitive feelings. Paradoxically, their words seem imbued with the power to summon, call forth, suggest, insinuate an experience that is too subtle to be conveyed by words.

How different is reading such texts from reading the logical pyrotechnics of Nagarjuna's *Mulamadhyamakakarika*. My forced march through that text had felt to me like a form of almost tortuous mental asceticism, twisting my consciousness uncomfortably into mental Möbius strips that seemed always on the verge of breaking or tearing. I can well understand how for those of a certain temperament who spend much time with this text, their minds might eventually, through a kind of bolt of insight, crack wide open. The *Amritanubhav*, the *Tao Te Ching*, and the *Special Treasury*, however, persuade and enlighten us—if only, for most of us, partially, if only through momentary gleamings and gleanings—by gentler and more gracious means.

I am still in the process, one which I expect will be endlessly open-ended, of assimilating *The Special Treasury of the Basic Space of Phenomena*. As a way into the text, I have strung together a series of excerpts from some of the stanzas that comprise its first two sections:

> Naturally occurring timeless awareness—utterly lucid awakened mind—
> is something marvelous and superb, primordially and spontaneously present.
>
> . . . .
>
> Supreme, naturally occurring awareness is timelessly and spontaneously present.
>
> . . . .
>
> There is only self-knowing awareness, the blissful place of rest, extending infinitely as the supremely spacious state of spontaneous equality.
>
> . . . .
>
> Mind itself is an unchanging, vast expanse, the realm of space.
> Its indeterminate display is the expanse of the magical expression of its responsiveness.
> Everything is the adornment of basic space and nothing else.
> Outwardly and inwardly, things proliferating and resolving are the dynamic energy of awakened mind.
> Because this is nothing whatsoever yet arises as anything at all,
> it is a marvelous and magical expression, amazing and superb.
>
> . . . .
>
> Without underlying support, vividly apparent and yet timelessly empty, supremely spacious, and naturally clear, just as it is,
> the universe arises as the adornment of the basic space of phenomena.

What immediately struck me about these stanzas is how consonant they are with certain tenets and practices of Kashmir Shaivism. The vast unchanging spaciousness of unchanging awareness in which equivocal phenomena arise and subside reminds me of what Shaivism calls *kechari mudra*, which is a meditative experience, granted only to the most advanced of spiritual adepts, of roaming at will in the infinite sky of Consciousness. According to Shaivism, the Absolute is of the nature of *prakasha/vimarsha*, two key terms that I should perhaps have introduced earlier. Shiva is associated with prakasha, which is the vast, unbounded, ever unchanging, and above all radiant space of pure Consciousness itself. Shakti is associated with vimarsha, which is the reflexive power of Consciousness to be aware of itself as Consciousness. The vast unbounded space of pure awareness of which Longchenpa speaks seems in particular to be consonant with what Shaivism and what Abhinavagupta, again, call prakasha, the infinite, radiant Consciousness of Shiva. That this pure awareness is at the same time self-aware, known to itself, is consonant with what Abhinavagupta calls vimarsha.

A second key point is implicit in what I have just stated. The basic space of phenomena is of the nature not only of awareness but of self-knowing awareness, which Longchenpa also refers to as awakened mind. Supreme Consciousness, according to Shaivism, is precisely this timeless, infinite expanse of self-knowing awareness. As for the appearances that arise and subside in the phenomenal world, Longchenpa describes all phenomena as resting within pure self-knowing awareness even as they seem to arise and subside within it. From within the vast expanse of the awakened mind, phenomena appear, as though by magic, as products of its dynamic energy. This dynamic energy is consonant with the energy that Shaivism calls Shakti, she who creates and resorbs all phenomenal appearances, which are called by Longchenpa the adornments of awakened mind, its amazing and superb display. Thus, as in Shaivism, the appearances of the phenomenal world are not to be spurned or rejected. Just as in Shaivism all that arises within Consciousness is not different from Consciousness and is projected by Consciousness, as it were, upon the screen of Consciousness, so, according to Longchenpa,

> Everything is subsumed within all-inclusive awakened mind.
> Since there is no phenomenon that is not included in awakened mind,
> the true nature of all phenomena is that of consciousness.
> . . . .
> Given that the sphere of being, without any "hard edges," is inclusive,
> everything, just as it is, is encompassed within the expanse in which
>   there is no differentiation.

Longchenpa proceeds to examine the true nature of phenomena when perceived by the awakened mind:

> The true nature of phenomena—suchness—has no beginning,
>   middle, or end.
> This state of infinite evenness, equal to space and pure by nature, has
>   no beginning or end.
> It is beyond any time frame.
> It is unborn, unceasing, and has no substance or characteristics.
> It neither comes nor goes and cannot be characterized as some "thing."

In a previous stanza Longchenpa has said:

> Within the expanse of spontaneous presence is the ground for all that
>   arises.
> Empty in essence, continuous by nature,
>   it has never existed as anything whatsoever, yet arises as anything at all.

The phenomena that arise and subside within the self-knowing awareness of awakened mind have only a kind of equivocal status. Never existing as anything whatever, they nonetheless arise as anything at all. All phenomena arise within the spaciousness of awakened mind or self-knowing awareness as non-different from that mind and from each other. They have no independent status or existence apart from the awakened mind in which they rest. This non-difference manifests as a kind of evenness, a term that occurs frequently in *The Treasury* as a synonym, along with awakened mind, for the vast spaciousness of phenomena. These phenomena cannot be said to possess any substance or characteristics. Their true nature, rather, is that of suchness, of a kind ineffable, impossible-to-define qualitative essence, a kind of form devoid of substantive attributes suggested by the *Heart Sutra's* invocation of the form which is emptiness and the emptiness which is form, not a thing with quantity, substance, or number.

In the introduction to this book I mentioned that if not for my fear of seeming presumptuous, and for considerations of rhythm, the subtitle of this book would have read: *On Poetry, Mysticism, the Imagination, and Consciousness*. Any extended inquiry into the nature of the imagination naturally leads to speculations about the nature of consciousness. I have mentioned that questions regarding the elusive nature of consciousness, and specifically regarding how we experience the subjective quality of things as we do, remains for various disciplines—scientific, philosophical, psychological, and, to a lesser degree, literary—an unavoidable, conspicuously unsolved, hard problem. From Longchenpa's point of view, the mysterious qualitative apprehension of the world by Consciousness or by awakened mind is perhaps not so much a problem to be solved as an irreducible reality, "marvelous and magical," "amazing and superb," to be joyfully acknowledged.

As a corollary of the essential evenness of Consciousness or awakened mind, Longchenpa stresses over and over again that all phenomena are positive. I have elsewhere suggested that the category of the negative, which is in no way found in nature, is one of the most ingenious inventions of the human mind, or more specifically of the logical mind. It is a kind of virtual machine that is particularly adept at generating pairs of logical opposites, such as existence and nonexistence, presence and absence, ignorance and knowledge, delusion and enlightenment, samsara and nirvana, which appear to have an independent reality but do not. They are mere chimera of the unawakened mind, a mind that is also adept at conceptually labelling essentially dynamic phenomena, at reifying and categorizing. Such a mind is consumed with the task of fixing, delineating, and delimiting phenomena whose nature is to have no substance, no fixed attributes, and to constantly, dynamically arise and subside within awakened mind as non-different with that mind. The nature of such phenomena, again, is entirely positive, is characterized by a pervasive evenness that we can experience as a kind of equanimity.

Thus the awakened mind has much in common with my conception of the imagination as being essentially dynamic, as being a verb not a noun, a force not a faculty, and a force moreover that is essentially inimical to the fixed and the categorical, to the reified conceptual niches of which the mind, and in particular the rational mind, is so enamored. The awakened mind dissolves all such constructs—which Blake refers to as the mind-forged manacles that imprison consciousness within the confines of the ego, which is itself likewise a mental construct—into the vast, spacious, infinite, timeless expanse of pure self-knowing awareness.

I have thus far given only the most meager foretaste of *The Special Treasury of the Basic Space of Phenomena*, whose mysteries I am not competent to unlock and which, if I were, would require a compendious commentary, far longer than I have scope for here. Instead I will skip to a passage toward the end of the *Special Treasury* that refers to the state of the enlightened being whose consciousness has merged with that of the awakened mind:

> It is of no concern whether or not the nature of being is spontaneous presence.
> It is of no concern whether or not you are bound by dualistic perceptions of affirmation and denial.
> It is of no concern whether or not you have arrived at the enlightened intent of the true nature of phenomena.
> It is of no concern whether or not you follow in the footsteps of masters of the past.
>
> No matter what arises, even if heaven and earth change places,
> there is a bare state of relaxed openness, without any underlying basis.
> Without any reference point—nebulous, ephemeral, and evanescent—
> this is the mode of a lunatic, free of the duality of hope and fear.
> With unbiased view and meditation, ordinary consciousness that is caught up in reification collapses.
> Without the entanglements of wishful thinking, there is no "thing" to strive for or achieve.
>
> Let whatever happens happen and whatever manifests manifest.
> Let whatever occurs occur and whatever is be.
> Let whatever is anything at all be nothing at all.
> With your conduct unpredictable, you make the final leap into awareness
> without the slightest basis for determining what is spiritual or not,
> and so this bare state with no reference point is beyond the cage of philosophy.
> Whether eating, moving around, lying down, or sitting, day and night you rest in infinite evenness,
> so that you experience the true nature of phenomena as their equalness.
> There are no gods to worship, no demons to exorcise,
> nothing to cultivate in meditation—this is the completely "ordinary" state.

With this single state of evenness—the uncontrived ruler that has no
    pride—there is oneness, a relaxed and unstructured openness.

How delightful—things are timelessly ensured without having to be done,
and being free of effort and achievement, you are content.

What is described in this extraordinary passage is what Kashmir Shaivism calls anupaya, the pathless path of the enlightened being whose every thought, word, and deed is a spontaneous, effortless spiritual practice, or rather a practice that is beyond any practice. This is the state of the Taoist sage who by doing nothing accomplishes everything. It is the unconstrained, untrammeled, unpredictable, utterly free state, unbound by any conventional notion of propriety, of one who from the point of view of the unawakened mind can appear to be a lunatic. It is astonishingly similar to the depiction of the state of the realized master, of the mahasiddha, in "The Secret of Natural Devotion," the penultimate chapter of Jnaneshwar's *Amritanubhav*, which I do not have the space to quote at any length here, but which can be found on the web for free in a fine translation by Swami Abhayananda.

I have mentioned that there is an affinity between certain kinds of Tantric Hinduism and Tibetan Buddhism, and so perhaps it should be unsurprising that there should be such close parallels between the content, and also the form or the manner of expression, of *The Special Treasury of the Basic Space of Phenomena* and Jnaneshwar's *Amritanubhav*. Both are philosophical works that escape the "cage of philosophy" not only by renouncing any notion that there is any external point of reference from which Consciousness can be objectively apprehended, but by being couched in poetic form, a form that is suffused by dhvani, or the power of suggestion, and that deploys metaphor as a means of insinuating, conveying to the reader that which is essentially ineffable, impossible to definitively pin down in words.

Longchenpa, like Jnaneshwar, is fully aware of the rhetorical and performative character of his text—of a text that, unlike denotative works of philosophy, somehow enacts that to which it refers—and of its radically metaphorical nature:

Space is a metaphor for awakened mind.
Since that mind has no cause and is not an object that comes into being,
it does not abide in any finite way, is inexpressible, and transcends the
    realm of the imagination.
The phrase "the realm of space" is simply a way of illustrating it
    metaphorically.
If even the metaphor itself cannot be described as some "thing,"
how could the underlying meaning that it illustrates be imagined or
    described?
It should be understood as a metaphor for what is naturally pure.

Though the awakened mind transcends the realm of the imagination, that realm is not one of mere fantasy. Wallace Stevens sought, by the production of increasingly apt metaphors or of analogies that he called resemblances, to approach the vanishing point of identity in which metaphor, resemblance, and indeed language itself are ultimately lost and subsumed in bare, unadorned reality, in the vast expanse of awakened mind, and in the suchness of things as they are. Though the imagination can never grasp the realm of identity, which is the pure undifferentiated realm of the awakened mind, it is at least more equipped than reason to draw ever closer to that realm, to provide an approach to it, and ultimately to suggest what can never be grasped or defined.

2.

When, as a young man newly exposed to meditation at Naropa, I returned to Providence, where I was attending graduate school, I decided to look for a spiritual teacher and for teachings that would somehow resonate with me, feel right to me. Early in this process I visited a Zen monastery. The teacher, or Roshi, was giving a kind of brief homily. At some point he said, "Zen is like perfectly clear water. If you prefer orange soda, you should look elsewhere." As it happened, I had at that time an almost addictive love affair with orange soda. I immediately realized that I should look elsewhere. Before long I attended a weekend retreat in a Hindu monastery. The resident Guru swept like a small meteor into the hall, clad in orange robes that rustled with his stride. He gave a talk in which he seemed the quintessence of effervescence, laughing frequently, his gestures both broad and elegantly refined. I felt that I had found a kind of carbonated spirituality that did, in fact, somehow resonate with me.

As a part of my plea on behalf of the ecstatic, I have intended to argue for the experience of divine love with all of its rasas and flavors as a vital part of spirituality. Of course, divine love is a part of all or almost all spiritual paths, but traditions that give equal scope to the head and the heart, that establish a strong connection between them, are those that I find most resonant with my own predilections.

If I had to choose one over the other, however, I suppose I would give pride of place to the heart. Which returns me to the exemplary figure of Jnaneshwar. The second of four siblings, he was born a Brahmin. His father, however, impulsively broke all societal norms and left his mother to take up life as an ascetic; then, thinking better of his rash action, he committed suicide in remorse. Not long afterward, Jnaneshwar's mother, heartbroken, also died. Disgraced by his parents' sins, Jnaneshwar was stripped of his status as a Brahmin. While still a boy he appeared before a kind of Brahminical court of appeals in order, all assumed, to be reinstated as a Brahmin. He recited by heart long, sometimes particularly obscure passages from the Vedas. The judges, stunned and abashed, marveling at his superior powers, which far surpassed theirs, agreed to reinstate him as a Brahmin. Jnaneshwar refused their offer, whereupon, to ridicule the rote orthodoxy of his judges, he inspired a herd of water buffaloes in the vicinity to spout verses from the Vedas.

In Jnaneshwar, several of the strands of mysticism I have been discussing converge. He, like the great Sufi poets, was highly learned. He was, from an early age, a master of Sanskrit, thoroughly conversant with the Brahmanical strand of Hinduism, of which Vedanta was the flower. Though himself a Brahmin, he renounced that status, and identified himself with those of a lower caste. Like the great Sufi poets and like all Tantrikas, he had a profound devotion for the figure of the Guru, who in his case, remarkably, was his brother, Nivrittinath.

Jnaneshwar was a legatee of the lineage of what are called Nath Siddhas, yogis who strove, and succeeded, through intense yogic practices, to unite the microcosm—the purified and transformed human body—by means of a kind of spiritual alchemy, with the macrocosm, and who were said to possess *siddhis* or magical powers. Like all enlightened masters, however, Jnaneshwar considered these powers to be at best of no account, and at worst a dangerous distraction from the true path of yoga. Upon encountering Changdev, an arrogant yogi who vaunted various siddhis but lacked the wisdom of enlightenment, Jnaneshwar wrote a brief treatise to convince him of the error of his ways.

Jnaneshwar is most famous for his *Jnaneshwari*, a profound and voluminous commentary on the *Bhagavad Gita*, a quintessentially Vedic text, written from the point of view of the esoteric Tantric yoga of the Nath lineage. Although fluent in Sanskrit, Jnaneshwar, as previously noted, like Dante, chose to write his *Jnaneshwari* in the vernacular, in Marathi. Indeed, it is considered not only the foundational text of Marathi literature but of the Marathi language itself and is still considered its chief glory. As a Nath Siddha, Jnaneshwar, as we have seen, was predisposed to embrace the Tantric world view of Kashmir Shaivism, which he so brilliantly both explicated and redefined in the *Amritanubhav*, the second of his great poems.

Finally, though a great master of the yoga of knowledge, Jnaneshwar came to embrace the more humble path of Bhakti Yoga, the yoga of divine love. Like Ramakrishna, Jnaneshwar, in effect, pursued and consummated many different *sadhanas*, or forms of spiritual practice, including both the path of knowledge and the path of love, in one lifetime. At the age of twenty-five, he decided that the pilgrimage of his life was drawing to a close. He took what is called live samadhi. Surrounded by his dearest devotees at the local Shiva temple, at sunset he assumed a meditative posture. He passed into a state of deep meditation from which he would never emerge. He was buried in the Shiva temple, which is now itself a site of pilgrimage.

Many years ago, in 1977, when I was twenty-five and living in the ashram of my spiritual preceptor, I was myself both a poet and a would-be spiritual adept. I undertook an actual journey, a solitary pilgrimage to Jnaneshwar's samadhi shrine in that small Shiva temple in the town of Alandi. Time, like glass, became oddly transparent. I felt somehow as though I were in the twelfth century, not the twentieth. I sat and meditated under an Ajna tree at the center of the temple's small courtyard. Legend has it that if a single leaf falls on one meditating there, he is destined to be liberated either during his lifetime or at the time of death.

As I was sitting, not a single leaf fell. I had not expected it to. Still, it was good, or more than good, a real boon, although of an inexplicable kind, simply to be sitting there, basking in the still almost palpable energy of a poet/saint who had died almost a millennium ago.

As for you, my prospective reader, whoever you are, you could do worse than wind up in the company of such a poet, of such a saint.

A translation of the first chapter of Amritanubhav:

Homage to Shiva and Shakti

I bow to the God and the Goddess,
The limitless primal parents of the universe.

The lover, out of boundless love,
Has become the Beloved.
Both are made of one substance
And share the same food.

Out of intense desire each consumes the other—
Then emits the other for the joy of being two.

Though one they appear as two;
They are neither entirely the same nor entirely different;
We cannot really say what they are.

How intense is their desire to enjoy each other!
Becoming one, they never allow
Their union to be disturbed—
Not even in jest.

They are so averse to separation,
That not even their child, the universe,
Can disturb their union.

The whole universe and all that it contains,
Both animate and inanimate, emanates from them,
And yet they acknowledge no third.

New Thresholds, New Affinities

Seated on the same ground,
Wearing the same garment of light,
They dwell together in eternal bliss.

Duality, intent on enjoying itself,
Sought to find itself in them.
Instead, it found only their union—
Into which it vanished without a trace.

How sweet and mysterious is their union!
Though the whole universe is too small to contain them
They dwell happily together in the tiniest atom.

Each regards their spouse as their very life,
And neither creates so much as a blade of grass
Without the help of the other.

These two alone dwell together
In the house of the universe.
When the master falls asleep,
The mistress remains awake
And performs the functions of both.

When either awakens to the Self,
The whole house and everything in it is consumed,
And nothing but ashes remains.

To enjoy the play of diversity they seem to part,
Then long to melt back into unity.

With respect to each other
Each is both subject and object.
Thus they revel in each other's company.

Shiva alone abides
in the forms of Shiva and Shakti.
The whole universes arises from the coupling
Of these two—who are really one.

As two cymbals, when struck, sound one note,
As two roses exhale one fragrance,
As two lamps emit one light,

Some Segments of a River

As two lips form one word,
And two eyes behold one vision—
So Shiva and Shakti together
Create one universe.

And so, appearing to be two,
Each savors a dish of the same flavor.

The chaste and devoted Shakti
Cannot live without her Lord.
Without her, he becomes powerless.

His appearance is due to her,
And her existence is due to him.
How, then, can these two be distinguished?

Can one separate sugar from its sweetness,
Camphor from its fragrance?

Trying to catch hold of the radiance of a light,
We catch only the flames that emit it.
Thus it is while contemplating her nature
That we discover him.

The sun appears because of its radiance
But that very radiance depends upon the sun.
Thus all false distinctions dissolve
And nothing but light itself remains.

Through its reflection one infers
The existence of an object;
Yet without the object its reflection vanishes.

Shakti bestows upon Shiva his sovereignty;
He bestows upon her his vast creative power.

The formless Shiva himself creates Shakti,
The mirror on which he appears
As the primal Lord of all.

She glorifies him
By giving birth to the universe

From her own womb.
Yet without him she could create nothing,

Abashed at the nakedness
Of her formless husband
She weaves from her own being
The universe of names and forms,
The resplendent garment with which he is clothed.

Where there was austerity in unity
She produces abundance in diversity.

When she dissolves the universe, the body,
The Lord returns to his formless state.
When he conceals that state
Her glorious form is revealed far and wide.

Out of his desire to see her, he becomes the seer.
When he sees her no longer,
Both the seer and the seen disappear.

Though He assumes the form of the universe
Through her grace,
He is so subtle that he remains invisible
Even while manifest.

After rousing her husband from sleep,
She gives birth to the entire universe.
When she falls asleep
Her husband himself disappears.

Shiva enjoys his own bliss by embracing her;
Without her he relishes nothing at all.

Shakti is the radiant body of Shiva;
Shiva is the inner beauty that makes her glow.
Only when these two ingredients are blended
Can the feast of Love be enjoyed.

Wind and its swiftness,
Gold and its luster are inseparable.
Just so, Shiva and Shakti are inextricably one.

Just as both the Ganges and the ocean
Merge into the waters of the cosmic flood
In which the entire universe is dissolved,
So all the levels of speech, from *vaikhari* to *para*,
Merge into absolute silence
When their true nature is realized.

As wind dissolves into the stillness of space,
And as both the sun and its light disappear
Upon the cessation of the universe
Into the greater light of the Absolute,

So, in the process of beholding that light
Both the seer and the seen vanish.

Again and again I offer homage to Shiva and Shakti,
The stream in which the knower drowns,
Thereby perishing, as he attempts to drink
The waters of the known.

And yet, alas, to offer
Words in praise of Shiva and Shakti
Is to indulge that very illusion of separation,
Born of verbal distinctions, that they annihilate.

Just as fragrance inheres in perfume
And heat in fire, so Shiva inheres in Shakti.

My salutation is like an ornament
That is not different from the gold it worships.

When the word "tongue" is uttered by the tongue
Is there any difference between the word
And the object denoted by it?

When the Ganges and the ocean intermingle
There names can still be distinguished,
But is there really any difference between the two?

Though the sun is both the subject and the object
Of its own illumination,
Its unity is not thereby disrupted.

New Thresholds, New Affinities

When moonlight brightens the moon,
Or when a lamp is illumined by its own light,
Is anything thereby lost?

When the luster of a pearl
Plays upon itself,
Its beauty and purity are only enhanced.

Is the unity of the sacred syllable AUM
Destroyed because it is written with three letters?
Is the unity of the letter N abolished
Because three strokes are required to produce it?

As long as its unity is not disrupted
And an added grace is attained,
Is there any reason why the surface of the sea
Should not exult in itself
When it flowers into radiant ripples?

It is with the same delight that,
Finding no difference between them,
I bow once again to Shiva and Shakti.

When a mirror is withdrawn,
The image it contained merges with its object.
Ripples vanish when the wind grows still.

A man comes to himself
When he awakens from sleep.
Just so, I have found the God and Goddess
By laying my ego at their feet.

Surrendering its separate form,
Salt merges with the ocean.
By sacrificing my individuality,
I have merged with Shiva and Shakti.

Thus I have paid homage to Shiva and Shakti
By uniting with them—just as the inner space
Of a plantain tree merges with the outer
When its husk has been stripped away.

3.
Abhinavagupta and the Four Levels of Speech

1.

After having indulged in the above detours and divagations, I would like to focus again on Kashmir Shaivism, specifically on one aspect of Abhinavagupta's metaphysics, his theory of language, and then to examine its relevance to several Western theories of the imagination.

Abhinavagupta postulates two distinct but related views of language, and particularly of how the manifest world, or worlds, unfolds from it. Both, though they borrow elements from previous speculative traditions, assume, particularly as discussed by Abhinavagupta, an original and distinctive spin. One of these views is based upon numerous previous *agamas* or Tantric scriptures and involves a discussion of the creative power, the Shakti, instinct in all of the phonemes that comprise the Sanskrit alphabet.

In one of her aspects, according to Shaivism, Shakti assumes the form of Matrika Shakti, the creative mother or womb from which the subtle array of Sanskrit phonemes, each instinct with its own power, arises. Only later do they combine into the words and sentences through which not only language itself but the world or worlds which it denotes come into being. Matrika Shakti thus precedes what Derrida calls *la langue*, precedes any given language and its words as an inexhaustible network of mutually imbricated and endlessly ramifying meanings.

Sound in the unarticulated form of subtle unarticulated phonic energy is integral to the unfolding of the universe and its thirty-six *tattvas*, stages of creative emanation, each of which is connected to a particular phoneme, starting with syllables that comprise *Aham*, or "I Am." In general, though the phonemes involved in world manifestation have no discursive meaning, each does have a specific power or energetic charge. In this way, they are akin to mantras, many of which likewise often have no referent, either external or internal, but are powerful repositories of spiritual energy.

The phonic emanation of the cosmos is a topic far too complex and arcane for me to attempt to deal with here. So I will not discuss it further, except for stating the obvious: Sanskrit words, like all words, are comprised of phonemes that, even when not engaged in the process of cosmogenesis, retain at least a residual charge, the "unalterable vibration" to which Wallace Stevens has referred. They are particular energetic resonances in the form of sounds. Thus, as I keep insisting, for Abhinavagupta as well as for the Indian tradition in general, words are never inert, lifeless counters. They are instinct with energy, and when used by inspired poets, that latent energy manifests and shimmers with an uncanny suggestiveness.

It is the second view of language, Kashmir Shaivism's doctrine of the four levels of speech, which I will discuss here in greater detail. I will then examine its relevance, or resonance, with respect to several Western theories of the imagination. The ground traversed here and the tentative notions with which I end this chapter prepare the way for the subsequent sections of this book and for the essays on particular poets of which they are comprised.

The doctrine in question was in part borrowed from the great Indian grammarian and poet Bhartrihari (fifth century CE), a remarkably original thinker. For Bhartrihari, all levels of creation, from the most subtle to the most gross, are structured by language and by the matrix of energies associated with it. The Sanskrit language is considered by Bhartrihari not only as ancient but as without beginning, eternal. Thus it provides the blueprint through which the world is recreated after every period of *pralaya*, or cosmic dissolution.

From the time of the earliest Vedas, the notion of the world as created and sustained by the Word has been a central theme, elaborated in slightly different ways by different Vedic texts. The Upanishads further refined this essential idea. The *pranava*, or *Aum,* came to be regarded as the primal vibration or Word through which all of the worlds of creation come into being. In this context, Bhartrihari's insistence on language and the matrix of energies associated with it, itself creating and constituting all levels of manifest reality, differs not in kind but in degree from previous speculations. For Bhartrihari it is language primarily that has this creative and constitutive power.

Bhartrihari sees the process of creation as involving three stages. The first is pre-linguistic, the Word as ineffable, one with the Absolute, a kind of stirring or vibration prior to any articulated speech. The next two stages involve, respectively, the word as sounded by the mind, and as externally vocalized.

Kashmir Shaivism and Abhinavagupta adopted Bhartrihari's three levels of speech but added a fourth. The four levels of speech are most commonly discussed in descending order, from the highest to the lowest, the order that corresponds to the creation and manifestation of countless worlds. But, as usual with Shaivism, they can with equal justice be discussed in the reverse, in ascending order, from the most gross to the most subtle, corresponding to the de-creative movement through which all phenomena are resorbed back into Shiva. I will discuss the four levels first in the descending order, then in ascending order.

According to Abhinavagupta, the fourth and highest level of speech, not found in Bhartrihari's scheme, is *para-vak*, or simply *vak*, speech as the utterly transcendent, unsounded Word. But a word of caution is in order here. Andre Padoux, the great

French scholar whose book *Vak* is the definitive work on the Tantric theories of language that I am discussing here and that attain their fullest articulation in the work of Abhinavagupta, is at pains to point out that vak is a virtually untranslatable term, and that its typical translation as the Word is the best among unsatisfactory alternatives. Vak is not the Neoplatonic or Christian *logos,* the Word as the transcendent analog to the word as deployed in language. It is of an altogether different, ineffable order.

Shiva is the possessor of Shakti, whether in her quiescent form as pure potential, fully resorbed into Shiva, or in her dynamic mode as the creator, while still one with Shiva, of countless phenomenal worlds. The union of Shiva and Shakti, when Shakti is in a quiescent, dormant state, entirely subsumed by Shiva, is the very highest level, unsounded and unsoundable, of the Word. It is the highly charged silence from which the word arises. Shiva's absolute, transcendent nature, one with para-vak, is the precondition for the further unfolding by Shakti of the worlds of manifestation. He remains the transcendent, pure, unchanging, immaculate light of Consciousness that both constitutes the being of, and illumines, makes knowable, all of the subsequent worlds of manifestation.

The first of the three remaining levels of speech is *pashyanti*, which was for Bhartrihari the highest level. According to Abhinavagupta, pashyanti, though still associated with one of the levels or *tattvas* of pure creation, beyond the limits of time and space, differs from para-vak only in that it entails a very slight inclination to manifest what becomes the phenomenal world. At the level of pashyanti, word and object are still one, are as yet inarticulate, indistinguishable from each other. Pashyanti is the subtle stirring of Consciousness just prior to the emergence of articulate sounds, of words and their corresponding objects, in the mind. The root meaning of pashyanti is "to see," and pashyanti is a foreseeing, an envisioning of what is to come, the mental differentiation of word and object. It is a precognitive, synthetic awareness or intuition of what is about to be unfolded.

Pashyanti and pratibha, the flash of creative intuition, like several other sets of terms in Kashmir Shaivism, are closely interrelated, though not quite synonymous. Pashyanti is with respect to Abhinavagupta's theory of language analogous to what pratibha is to his metaphysics and aesthetics. They are both phenomena that are free of the limitations of time and space, and the differences between them are as subtle as the differences between the realms or levels of Consciousness, technically called tattvas by Shaivism, that are likewise beyond time and space. Both ultimately stem from the primordial stirring or vibration of Consciousness that is spanda itself.

In the case of great creative artists and scientists, the foreseeing and envisioning implicit in pashyanti can become visionary. It is well known, for example, that the whole structure and many of the details of Mozart's symphonic works arose in his consciousness as a powerful synthetic intuition, which he would then unfold in the written notes comprising his score. Paul Valery wrote about poems first arising in his consciousness as a kind of inchoate stirring, followed by a sense of a unique rhythmic signature that would finally unfold itself into the articulate words and the corresponding images of his poems. Einstein likewise wrote about a similar kind of stirring of consciousness, often involving intense experiences of synesthesia, which preceded all of his breakthrough intuitions, and which thereafter had to be translated, unfolded, into the symbolic language of physics. If one reads the biographies of great scientists and of their struggles to solve seemingly intractable problems, the solution often arrives in a sudden flash of intuition, which again must be expressed, sometimes in a laborious process, in symbolic language. And must often await experimental verification.

I do not mean to suggest by invoking great artists and great scientists that the experience of pashyanti is available only to a few. Indeed, there is a stirring of preconscious awareness and energy, a kind of envisioning, that precedes every word we utter, every thought that arises in our minds, every action which we perform. As we train ourselves to be aware of this preconscious stirring, according to Shaivism, we will come more and more to experience the power of pashyanti, and will be increasingly enabled to mobilize its energy,

Pashyanti unfolds into the third level of speech, called *madhyama*. At the level of madhyama, words and the images associated with them become articulate, distinct, in the mysterious spaceless space of the mind. Madhyama involves words spoken silently in the mind. The space between words so spoken and the images they invoke is indeterminate, or rather, perhaps, there is no space, or only a kind of virtual space, between them. Madhyama is restricted entirely to the sphere of the mental. It does not refer to any objective world outside of the mind. For us, empirically, madhyama corresponds to states in which we are so thoroughly absorbed in mental processes that we are scarcely aware of the outer world, states such as dreaming or daydreaming, and the kind of freely associative process we call the stream of consciousness. It is also, as we shall see, the province of the higher order functions of the intellect.

The fourth level of speech, called *vaikhari,* is associated with spoken words and with the objects out there in the real world to which they point and refer. Here a real space opens up between the word and the object to which it points, and it is at this stage that we develop the conviction that there is, indeed, a world out there with objects existing in an extended, external space. The dream-like world of madhyama, in which the mind ranges relatively freely within its own circumscribed domain, here becomes more fixed, less fluid. More than in dreams, we have the sense of ourselves as individuals, wide awake, living within the fixed parameters of given world. At the level of vaikhari, our sense of dualism becomes most extreme.

It is, however, also at the level of vaikhari that we speak with each other, that we communicate, that an interpersonal space opens up between us. Words uttered to us out loud become words that we silently speak in our minds, that are translated into madhyama, and so the ascending order of consciousness to higher levels of speech begins. It is at the level of vaikhari, too, that we hear the notes of a symphony or the words of a play, through which, if we are same-hearted listeners, we can experience pratibha, the creative intuition from which great works of art arise, and which they have the power to ignite in us. As for written texts or musical scores, they are a kind of subset of vaikhari. In perusing written texts, we translate marks on a page into words spoken in our minds, into the level of madhyama. If we are reading a great poem, once again we can ascend even higher, can experience the powerful synthetic intuition from which it has arisen.

Continuing now to examine the four levels in *ascending* order, vaikhari, just discussed above, need not be further belabored here. Madhyama, as we have seen, is experienced whenever the waking mind is absorbed in itself. I have cited as examples daydreaming, free association, the stream of consciousness. But what of the higher order functions of the mind, states in which the mind is even more absorbed in itself? What of reason and understanding, often couched in abstract language that does not call up images of any kind?

I briefly mentioned previously that these higher functions of the mind are also subsumed within madhyama. In Shaivism, as in Patanjali's yoga, to which Shaivism is in part indebted, the mind is tripartite, consisting of *ahamkara*, which is one's sense of oneself as an ego, as a limited individual; of *manas*, or that restless aspect of the mind that not only moves, at the level of vaikhari, among the objects of sense but which ranges, as it were, restlessly, rapt within itself, and which as previously mentioned is associated with dream-like states or with the undirected irrational stream of consciousness. But at its highest level the mind transcends both manas and ahamkara and assumes the form of the purified, reflective intellect called *buddhi,* the higher, more intentionally directed, intellectual factory of reason, which is a kind of spotless mirror in which still higher forms of consciousness are reflected.

Reason, of course, involves the use of concepts couched in words that do not conjure up corresponding mental images. Though I have noted at various places in this text the tendency of concepts to become fixed, categorical, and rigid, this is, of course, not always the case. Through conceptual thinking the mind can move, open up, expand from the experience of the particular to the universal, and in so doing can transcend the experience of itself as a limited ego. One thinks, for example, of what are called *pure* mathematicians, whose minds move in a kind of rarified ether in which the concerns of the ego are transcended and have no place. Just as in Shaivism, metaphysics and aesthetics are closely aligned, so higher mathematics and aesthetics are also closely aligned. Mathematicians often speak of *elegance* and *beauty* as being hallmarks of the most satisfactory proofs of solutions to long vexing problems. Thus mathematical truth and elegance or beauty are in close alignment, a point which I will discuss in greater detail in the coda to my essay on Keats that appears later in this volume.

In many Buddhist traditions, as we have seen, meditative trance and intense intellectual activity are both seen as means that can flower into states of intense insight.

Buddhism developed highly refined and complex systems of logic, which forced various Hindu traditions, Kashmir Shaivism included, to develop their own logical apologetics. In medieval Kashmir, in which a number of religio-philosophical systems concurrently thrived—much as Christianity, Islam, and Judaism happily coexisted for a time in medieval Seville—great debates, attracting large audiences, between the proponents of various schools were held, and had a powerful, practical effect, leading to the ascendancy of some schools and the virtual disappearance of others. In this context, intellectual activity served a polemical purpose.

But it also, again, served a spiritual purpose. In Tibetan Buddhism, for example, fierce, prolonged logical debate is employed as a means of exhausting all possible logical positions and of awakening a profound insight into one's true nature. In Shankara's Vedanta, continuous, disciplined self-inquiry and a refined analysis of key scriptural statements replaces outward ritual as a means to draw closer to Brahman. In Christianity, in the case of Catholicism in particular, deep theological/philosophical study and reflection has been a vital part of the spiritual path, and in the case of Catholic priests a required part. Sufism, too, draws upon a proud philosophical heritage.

What Blake calls "intellectual warfare" is also a function of *buddhi*. The constant process of combatting intellectual or philosophical error is in large part the process that Blake's long prophetic poems "Milton" and "Jerusalem" enact. Blake famously wrote, "I must create my own system or be enslaved by another man's." He wrote that his poems were allegories addressed to the reader's intellectual powers. Northrop Frye's great book *Fearful Symmetry* emphasizes the subtlety, power, and coherence of Blake's critique of Newton, Locke, and other paragons of Enlightenment rationalism. But this does not mean that Blake spurns reason. To the contrary. Much like Nagarjuna, he uses reason to highlight the limits of reason. Finally, Blake is equally opposed to what he sees as the irrationalism of a figure like Rousseau, with his nostalgic romanticizing of man in some prelapsarian state of nature. The notion that Blake is a kind of madly inspired crank is profoundly misguided.

In sum, in every mystically oriented spiritual tradition the path of the intellect is respected, but never as an end in itself. The mind is used to exhaust the intellect, to pierce beyond the intellect to some higher insight or attainment.

Continuing on our ascending course, pashyanti, as a stirring of consciousness that is just on the threshold between one state of awareness and another, is the ultimate junction point, the ultimate state of the liminal. Considered from the point of view of world manifestation, pashyanti is the precognitive moment of synthetic intuition that leads eventually to madhyama and vaikhari, to the appearance of the manifest world. But considered in the ascending order, pashyanti, as well as being creative, can also be apprehended as reflexive, as a dense throb of energy, as a wave that can be surfed, as it were, backwards, that can lead to the awareness of oneness with Shiva. Again, pashyanti is the ultimate juncture point, the interstitial space of the liminal. I have continually emphasized that liminal states are portals, openings, through which one can glimpse the nature of the unconditioned, of Shiva himself. And as the ultimate liminal state, pashyanti potentially opens out into the most powerful and direct intuitive apprehension of Shiva, an intuition that can blossom into complete union with him.

Having come full circle back to the ultimate union of the self with para-vak, with Shiva, all that remains is to look at how the liberated master experiences the other three states. The master maintains the supreme awareness of Shiva in all these states and in the transitions between them. With respect to pashyanti, which is a precognitive state, the liberated being has a full awareness that he is in a thought-free state. With respect to madhyama, to the realm of mental activity or thought constructs, he maintains the awareness that he is the witness of thought, that his pure awareness is no more tainted by thoughts than a summer sky is by clouds, and that moreover thoughts are nothing but forms of his pure, unconditioned awareness. Finally, with respect to the waking state, he does not experience himself as a limited individual in the midst of an extended, external space filled with autonomous objects. Rather, he maintains the awareness that all that he perceives not only emanates from his own consciousness but that he is one with that consciousness.

One of the hallmarks of Tantrism is that great masters can experience liberation, an identification with Shiva that entails possession of his fully expanded powers, while still alive. The liberated being experiences no difference between the state of full meditative absorption in Shiva and the extroverted state in which he is absorbed in the beauty of objects of the physical world, or observes the ever-changing scenes of human activity and interaction as though he is both the bemused author and spectator of an unscripted play.

Finally, I will now stress what I should perhaps have stressed earlier: all spatial metaphors, such as high, low, inner, and outer, with respect not only to transcendent but to immanent levels of Consciousness, are just that—metaphors. My discussion of the four levels of speech might seem, at first blush, to suggest the kind of static categorical hierarchy I have claimed is inimical to the imagination. To the contrary, as Supreme Consciousness continually engages in the process of creation and recreation, or unfolding and enfolding itself, these four levels, as well as the multiple levels of creation postulated by Shaivism, are not airtight categories but dynamically interpenetrate each other.

Moreover, they are nested within each other like Chinese boxes. Every level of Consciousness, with the exception of Supreme Consciousness itself, is contained by "higher" levels and contains "lower" levels and all are homologous, are related non-hierarchically in being both container and contained.

Finally, again, the realized master experiences Supreme Consciousness as equally pervading all levels, experiences that "there is nothing that is not Consciousness," and that all phenomena, from the most apparently exalted and spiritual to the most apparently gross and material, equally participate in a kind of divine continuum in which all boundaries dissolve.

2.

This concludes my rather hasty discussion of the four levels of speech. What, then, is of pertinence in this theory? Why should it be of interest to me, let alone to you?

When I read about the doctrine of the four levels of speech, I was initially quite captivated by pashyanti in particular. It jibed with my experience as a poet and gave me a new way to think about that experience. I should perhaps be embarrassed to say that I have never adhered to a strict routine as a poet, have never reserved particular hours every day for writing. Instead, I go to my desk when I experience what feels like a stirring within, the sense that a poem is arising, waiting to cross a threshold into articulated form. Accompanying this stirring, this original or originating impulse, is a kind of global but non-specific sense of the poem that is about to appear, sometimes the sense of a rhythm and of the landscape that the poem will evoke and inhabit.

Often the poem will pass the preconscious threshold that is pashyanti as though it had just passed through narrow straits, a kind of Scylla and Charybdis, and emerged somewhat the worse for wear. Or worse still, it will appear, as it were, abortively, with whatever potential form or forms that were instinct with its original impulse, along with that impulse itself, already somehow fully eclipsed, fatally cancelled, stillborn. Rarely and blessedly, however, a poem is smuggled—who knows how, or by what angelic bandit—relatively unscathed by its border crossing, straight to the page. Miraculous interludes, much to be cherished.

In writing poems I try to ignore these chance buffetings and miraculous passages and remain in touch with the poem's first stirring, its originating impulse, and to let the poem unfold from it, thus eventually revealing itself to me and any prospective future reader. Even or especially when writing quite long poems, I try to stay in contact with that initial stirring or vibration and sometimes strangely come to feel as though I am living within it, have become happily domesticated by it, am both building and dwelling in a kind of virtual sonic and rhythmic domicile that I am loath to leave when the poem draws to its often deferred close.

But in thus discussing my own experience as a poet I have been perhaps too glib about the translation of the synthetic insight that is pashyanti into madhyama, and from thence into the verbally articulated lineaments of the achieved object that is the poem. Shelley, in a justly famous passage in "The Defense of Poetry," speaks of the mind in the act of creation as being like a "fading coal" awakened to a "transitory brightness" by a "force, an invisible influence, a power that arises from within" but which "eludes not only the will but the conscious portions of our nature," an inspiration whose original purity somehow carries within it "the presentiment of profound, original conceptions." I hope I cannot be faulted for seeing here a discussion of something very much akin to the preconscious stirring, instinct with a powerful, synthetic sense of the form of the work that is to be unfolded, that corresponds to the level of speech that Abhinavagupta calls pashyanti.

But Shelley had an almost tragic view of what is lost in translation as one moves, as one must as a poet, from the inspired level of pashyanti to the poem as articulated in actual words. According to Shelley, inspiration and creative intuition are already on the wane even as the act of composition begins, such that "the most glorious poetry that has ever been written is but a feeble copy of the poet's original conceptions."

The discussion of originals and copies here is a clue that Shelley is in full Platonic, or rather Neoplatonic mode, a mode most fully exemplified in Shelley's poetry by "Adonais," his great elegy on the premature death of Keats. Neoplatonism bears some resemblance to Kashmir Shaivism in regarding creation as emanating in a series of stages from a sole transcendent Absolute. It is more akin to Vedanta, however, in its attitude to the world of phenomenal appearances, which are seen as degraded copies of intellectual forms that are themselves distant from the One, the unitary Absolute, which the seeker strives, through intense contemplation, to intuit.

There is a sense of painful impatience in Shelley, a near despair about living with the faded simulacra, the broken images that comprise our world, a longing to strike beyond faded copies to a purity and radiance of the ideal not available during our mortal sojourn here, an impatience and a longing that led to his own premature death. I shall explore these and other matters in more detail in my essay on Shelley in the third section of this book.

I found that Shaivism's discussion of the four levels of speech, and again, particularly of pashyanti, opened up for me a new perception and understanding of the great Romantic poets in particular. At the same time, again, it gave me an insight into aspects of my own—far from exemplary—experience as a poet. When I first read about the four levels of speech and about pashyanti in particular, I had a strong, pleasant shock of recognition. It was as if I was given a new vocabulary with which to consider some of my own most intense experiences as a poet. At the same time it affirmed those experiences as in some way real and led me to value them, to be alert to the stirrings of pashyanti, and thereby to augment and strengthen them.

More broadly, the four levels of speech represent four realms of experience; the first, a transcendent realm that when experienced bathes all other realms with a radiant light of awareness; the second, a realm of insight, intuition, wonder, joy; the third, the purely mental realm in which we are alone with our thoughts, whether we are daydreaming or engaging with the rigors of logic and reason; the fourth, the apparently outer world that, at its worst, can become a nightmare in which the isolated self confronts a world of objects frozen in an alien, external space.

The fourfold structure of the levels of speech is related in Kashmir Shaivism to other fourfold structures, most importantly and pertinently to the quaternity of the waking state, the dream state, the deep sleep state, and the state of *turiya*, or transcendent awareness; a schema that is not special to Shaivism but is widespread, common to both Tantric and Vedic traditions. Once again, the fully enlightened yogi, established in turiya, is fully awake, aware in the three other states. This wakefulness, however, is not like ordinary wakefulness. It is the pure, direct, immediate awareness of consciousness in all states, in all things. Modern science, of course, has ratified three of these states, with turiya remaining a *terra incognita* that is just beginning to be explored.

Likewise, the four levels of speech correspond to the four sets of spiritual practices or *upayas*, from the most subtle to the most gross, enjoined specifically by Kashmir Shaivism.

This fourfold scheme of the levels of speech also corresponds quite remarkably to the fourfold schema of hell, earthly life, the terrestrial paradise, and heaven that was prevalent in Western literature, particularly in epic poetry, from Dante to Blake, who rechristened these realms Ulro, Generation, Beulah, and Jerusalem. Ulro is the realm of vaikhari at its worst; of single vision; of a terrifying, frozen isolation of the self from the reified, unresponsive world and from God; of hell itself. One thinks of Satan frozen solid in a vast lake of ice at the absolute nadir of Dante's inferno.

Generation is the level of experience in which most of us, the not-yet regenerate, live our daily lives. It is the mental realm of madhyama, of the strife of contraries, including the strife of joyless or exploitative sexual congress, the strife between the individual and society, the strife between a people and the government that pretends to act in their interest, but too often does not. More productively, generation includes the higher realms of intellect and understanding; it is a state that can lend itself to what Blake calls mental warfare, the dialectical clash of contraries that can lead to spiritual and societal progress. It is the soil in which revolutions, whether ultimately benign or destructive, grow.

Beulah, the realm of the earthly paradise, of pashyanti, corresponds to the precognitive, prelapsarian state of Eden, prior to the knowledge of good and evil. The earthly paradise is sometimes called the married land, analogous to the blissful prelapsarian sexual congress of Adam and Eve. It is often represented—in Spenser, for example—as a kind of seedbed of Platonic forms that, while remaining in their ideal state in the mind of God, germinate in the earthly paradise and eventually manifest as the faded copies, the far less-than ideal things of this world. This same fourfold structure is, of course, also found in Milton's "Paradise Lost," whose depiction of the hellish state of the fallen angels, but particularly for our purpose here of the blissful state of Adam and Eve in the prelapsarian garden of Eden, have such extraordinary imaginative force that Blake famously stated that Milton was of the devil's party without knowing it. Finally, pashyanti is sometimes related to the restorative realm of deep sleep just before transitioning to the dream state. For Blake, the earthly paradise of Beulah is a realm of repose, of rest, of nights blessed by the caressing beams of the moon, of an innocent sexuality, of a blissful unity of the self with its female energies, its emanations, and with the world. However, if indulged in too long, Beulah leads to passivity and a fall back into Generation. If correctly understood as a pause, as a liminal moment, a necessary respite, it can be a stage on the way to the ultimate goal, leading to the highest realm of spiritual attainment.

For Dante, the earthly paradise is, less ambiguously, a way station, a blissful foretaste of the highest state of beatitude attained at the end of the Paradiso, at the close of which Dante beholds the ultimate vision of a radiant, thousand-petaled white rose, pulsating with love, with Christ at its center. In a remarkable homology, in yoga the highest spiritual center at the crown of the head, representing the ultimate attainment, assumes the form of a thousand-petalled white lotus, a vision radiant with bliss and love that is seen by liberated beings in meditation.

The Christian soul in the ultimate state of beatitude is wedded to Christ as the logos, the Word through which the universe is created. The Shaivite soul in the ultimate state of beatitude is wedded to para-vak, the similarly generative highest level of speech.

All of these realms, again, correspond to different states of human experience, and it is language in particular that, by assuming different forms, including the subtly undifferentiated state prior to language as we usually conceive of it, keeps translating itself, and thereby translating us, from one level or realm of consciousness to another. We are constantly crossing psychic thresholds, sometimes upward toward the Absolute, sometimes downward toward the external world. Shiva constantly revels in both the ascending and descending movements of his own Consciousness. From his perspective, beyond the limitations of time and space, a perspective shared by liberated masters of yoga, these two movements, again, alike generated by spanda, are essentially, inextricably one.

For most of us this endless translation is a process that is both habitual and necessary. For example, we must translate whatever flashes of insight we have, if we wish to communicate them, first into the unsounded words in our minds, and from thence to spoken or written words that are internalized by others; similarly but obversely, we must translate words spoken or written by others to the unsounded words in our minds, and from thence, if they are instinct with insight, to our own intuitive awareness through which their power can be recognized and experienced. In the case of an enlightened being, all states and the thresholds between them are experienced as throughly suffused, saturated with the undifferentiated light of Consciousness. For him or her alone, this endless process of translation is no longer experienced as translation. Every level of speech and the realms to which they correspond have been fully resorbed into the pure awareness of Shiva, which both contains and transcends them.

As I have been writing the above, I have felt, from the beginning, the presence of a somewhat disheveled yet titanic figure looming, glancing over my shoulder. I am referring to Samuel Taylor Coleridge. I cannot help but feel there are resonances in my discussion of the four levels of speech to Coleridge's once much-revered, now no longer derided but simply ignored, theory of the imagination. Here, then, are his unusually succinct words on the imagination in the thirteenth chapter of the *Biographia Literaria*:

> The Imagination then I consider either as primary, or secondary. The primary Imagination I hold to be the living power and prime agent of all human perception, and as a repetition in the finite mind of the eternal act of creation in the infinite I AM. The secondary Imagination I consider as an echo of the former, co-existing with the conscious will, yet still as identical with the primary in the kind of its agency, and differing only in degree, and in the mode of its operation. It dissolves, diffuses, dissipates, in order to recreate:….it struggles to idealize and unify. It is essentially vital, even as all objects (as objects) are essentially fixed and dead.
>
> Fancy, on the contrary, has no other counters to play with, but fixities and definites…equally with the ordinary memory the Fancy must receive all its materials ready made from the law of association.

A preliminary note: wherever in the ensuing passages I refer to Shiva, Coleridge, a committed Christian, would have referred to God, whom he only obliquely references here as the infinite "I Am." The fact that the two are virtually interchangeable is remarkably telling.

The primary imagination is related to the eternal act of creation in the infinite "I Am." This is a phrase to delight any Shaivite. As touched on earlier, creation as phonetic emanation begins with Aham, which quite literally means "I Am." In the infinite "I Am" there is an eternal act of creation. Creation in Shaivism is not something that happened once but that rather continually happens, as Shiva, through Shakti, constantly both emits and resorbs all worlds. The infinite "I Am" is Shiva himself, and his eternal creation is effectuated by Shakti in the form of para-vak, the highest level of speech.

The infinite "I Am" is the living power and prime agent of all human perception. Shiva, unlike the Brahman of Vedanta, who is without attributes of any kind, is always both the prime agent and his power of action. This living power, the power not only of action but of knowledge and perception as well, is Shakti, with whom Shiva is inextricably one. We remain here on the very highest plane of Consciousness, in the realm of para-vak.

Though he adverts only glancingly to this subject in the above passage, Coleridge would have referred, in the place of para-vak, to Christ as the transcendent Word, the logos, through whom all things come into being. The infinite "I Am," engaged in an eternal act of creation by means of a living power, is an implicit reference to the creative Word or logos. The logos is a living power that eternally creates just as Shakti in the form of para-vak is a living power that eternally creates.

The primary imagination is the reflection of this highest level of consciousness in the finite human mind. The primary imagination, as a faculty of the human mind, is not entirely one with this highest level of Consciousness but faithfully reflects it.

The secondary imagination echoes Aham, the unsounded sound of para-vak. The word *echo* nicely suggests the kind of not yet articulate resonance or vibration that is pashyanti. But poems need to translate that vibration into articulate words. Creation here requires conscious will on the part of a figure who is clearly now an artist, a poet, one who is still, like Shiva, an active agent, a creator, or more properly, a re-creator.

Coleridge coined one of his many neologisms to convey the nature of the imagination. He calls it the "esemplastic power," a term borrowed from the Greek and meaning "to shape into one." The poet's creation is suffused and unified by this shaping power, reflecting the essential unity of all things as one in Consciousness. His work clearly flows from the vital, synthetic intuition that is pashyanti, which is akin to pratibha, the creative intuition from which all great works of art unfold. Coleridge makes much of the true work of art as being vital, full of life, fluid, responsive, as though supersaturated with the enlivening, shaping power of Shakti. The poem both embodies that power and conveys it. It is in no way static, inert, fixed.

Poems of the fancy are of a different sort altogether and are a clear step down from the synthesizing intuition of pashyanti to the level of madhyama. The first great philosophical influence on Coleridge was David Hartley, who felt that poems were unified by the mind's associative power, a power that was the crux of his philosophical system. In our own era Freud, though a far more complex figure, often relies upon association or free association—as in his *Interpretation of Dreams*—as an interpretive tool to reveal hidden, unconscious meanings. We have seen that the purely mental level of madhyama is one in which dreaming and daydreaming predominate. But madhyama also includes the perception of an almost mechanical cause and effect, in which a more rigid form of associationism reigns. Coleridge, as is clear from the above passage, came to thoroughly repudiate associationism. Rather than aligning itself with an active, vital shaping power, working with malleable materials, association deals with inert, lifeless counters, with the merely contingent, with fixities borrowed from memories, faded copies of a physical reality. Blake in particular felt that the imagination is inimical to "the rags of memory." This was one of his chief objections to Wordsworth's great autobiographical poem "The Prelude" and to one of his greatest lyrical poems, "Tintern Abbey," which rely respectively on memory and on the return to a remembered scene. To the extent to which fancy and the associative power deal not only with memories but with other lifeless counters, frozen shadows, fixed, definite, obdurate, links in an associative chain, they lead to a further step downward to the level of vaikhari, of objects fixed and frozen in an external space.

To briefly retrace our steps, critical confusion has reigned regarding the difference between the primary and secondary imagination. The problem lies with the fact that the primary imagination, as described by Coleridge, mirrors the imagination of God, of

Shiva, of the great "I Am" constantly creating a living universe. The primary imagination is said to reflect this power. But reflection is passive in nature. It cannot itself be a shaping power. It cannot actually produce poetry.

The secondary imagination, however, is the imagination of the poet as maker, not that of God or Shiva. It is allied with Shiva's active power, impelled by a creative intuition that manifests itself as poems. The activity of the secondary imagination is aligned with and analogous to the creative activity of the divine. It is, however, neither one with it nor, as is the case with the primary imagination, a perfect, passive, Platonic reflection of it. It is telling that Coleridge, with respect to the role of the poet, uses the word *recreate* rather than *create*. The secondary imagination is indeed secondary. Nonetheless the poet creates, in his poems, virtual worlds, analogues of the work of the prime agent and his creative action. As remarked upon by both Sir Phillip Sidney and Shelley in their respective exquisitely eloquent defenses of poetry, in the world of the poem, unlike that of mundane so-called outer reality, the laws of time and space are temporarily suspended, and the poet experiences an exhilarating increase of freedom, in Coleridge's case the freedom to dissolve and dissipate the frozen fixities of the mundane world, almost as by some alchemical process, and through his esemplastic power to recreate a vibrant, coherent world in which all things are unified, just as all things are unified in Consciousness. What is Coleridge's esemplastic power if not an analogue of the creative, shaping power of Shakti herself, through which he attempts to bring some kind of vital order out of the mundane chaos of the merely incidental and contingent?

Sidney defended the poet as the creator of idealized, golden worlds that are truer than the mundane world, that are not mimetic of its trivial actuality but patterned after a quasi-Platonic realm of ideal forms. Abhinavagupta writes that great poetic and dramatic works are both real and unreal. Great poems are, as analogues, recreations of God's primary act of creation, resulting in virtual worlds that are more real than the relatively unreal mundane world. To imaginatively participate in them grants the viewer or spectator access to a realm of enhanced freedom, a realm in which a multitude of possibilities replaces the fixed, frozen counters of the outer world. As the products of pratibha, creative intuition, and pashyanti, the visionary force whose stirring precedes the manifestation of the duality of the word and its referents, the poem is close to, aligned with, the primordial vibration of spanda within Shiva himself, a vibration that, from the point of view of Abhinavagupta's theory of language, is the first stirring within the transcendent Shiva, or para-vak.

It is reflective of the genius of Abhinavagupta and of Shaivism that they developed this notion of the four levels of speech, some of whose resonances I have clumsily been trying to suggest. It is reflective of the genius of Coleridge that in the very succinct discussion of the eternally creative, infinite "I Am," and of the primary imagination, the secondary imagination, and of fancy, he has touched upon all four levels of speech—para-vak, pashyanti, madhyama, and vaikhari. At his greatest, as the author of the "Rime of the Ancient Mariner" and "Kubla Khan," Coleridge, like Shelley, was a truly visionary poet, a term I am using with pashyanti, and its root meaning of seeing or foreseeing, in mind.

Finally, I want to point out that in the vast realm of Western semiotics and theories of language, in this epoch of the linguistic turn that keeps on turning, I know of no theory even remotely like this one. Somehow, it has always fascinated me, has felt right to me, as true to experience. For me, as potentially for others, it has provided a new, illuminating perspective, and has shed new light on a few old problems. I will now proceed to cite several of them.

From the very beginning of my life as a writer I have felt oddly hostile to the Freudian notion that great works of art somehow emerge from the murky wellspring of the unconscious. Perhaps surrealist works do, but I have never been attracted to surrealism. From whence, then, do poems arise? The doctrine of the four levels of speech greatly clarified this question for me. It now seems clear to me that complex works of art arise from the preconscious, from the powerful, energized moment of precognitive synthetic intuition that is pashyanti, not from the unconscious. It is as though densely gathering, powerfully poised waves of not-yet articulate conscious energy, both similar to and different from other such waves, foresee the actualization of the potential within them, and urge the artist to unfold, articulate, and thereby accomplish this actualization. The artist must translate, in work requiring both great skill and practice, this higher order of synthetic insight into a pattern of words on a page, or notes of a score, that will most effectively realize it. If this sounds slightly grandiose, I would point out that waves appear in an infinite variety of sizes.

During the course of my always somewhat random reading, I discovered that George Oppen, an intellectually scrupulous, rigorous twentieth-century American poet, an elegantly austere thinker-in-poems, whose work is very unlike mine but whom I greatly admire, had come to this same position—that poems arise a from precognitive intuitive flash of insight. Quite specifically, they do not, Oppen declares, arise from the Freudian moil of the unconscious; nor from the chaotic transformations of dreams, which are preeminently in the realm of free association; nor from the rational, logical operations of the mind, both of which, as previously mentioned, pertain to the realm of madhyama, to the mind sealed off from the outside world.

Poets have traditionally called upon some higher power, whether the muses, God, or in the case of Marlowe's and Goethe's "Faust," Mephistopheles, for the gift of inspiration. Rilke, in typically histrionic fashion, reports that he cried out upon the battlements of Duino, hoping to be heard by angelic orders of a somewhat indeterminate and dubious provenance. Stevens and Valery, too, show an odd disinclination to let go of angels, which keep cropping up in their work. The impulse of the poet is to call upon a phenomenon of a higher order to aid in a lower order task and then to account for the lower with a grateful reference to the higher. Pashyanti, or precognitive, synthetic intuition, if it is a real phenomenon—and I both believe and feel, based on my own experience, that it is—is a demystified version of such a higher order phenomenon.

To imagine that poems that spring from the unconscious or from dreams can enact —without the aid of either the intellect striving to pierce beyond itself or of creative intuition itself—a perilous and incongruous leap from a lower order phenomenon to a higher one, seems at best unconvincing, at worst deluded. It is to account for the higher with an appeal to the lower, which, though appropriate with respect to emergent biological phenomena, has always seemed to me to be reductive when applied to artistic creations, conducive to weak interpretations of works of art. How many dreary Jungian interpretations of Blake, for example, have sprung up like brightly colored mushrooms. Their authors' time would have been far better spent by using a reading of Blake to enrich and complicate some of the more simple-minded notions of Jung, the collective unconscious among them.

In pursuance of my interest in Oppen, I learned that he had in part been inspired to return to poetry in the early '60s by an encounter with a book by the Catholic scholastic philosopher Jaques Maritain, with whom Oppen, though a Jewish socialist, had felt an unlikely but profound affinity. The book, *Creative Intuition*, argues that genuine works of art arise from a space of luminous interiority, from the stirring of a preconscious intuition, essentially spiritual in nature, which is not, he explicitly argues, to be equated with the Freudian unconscious—the automatic, autonomous, instinctual realm of biological drives that Freud calls the id or primary process, which is distinct from higher order functions of the mind. With respect to precognitive creative intuition, Maritain stresses that it is associated with an experience of inner illumination or luminosity correlative with an immediate, direct, simple act of seeing, unfiltered by any conceptual screens. It bears within it a powerful, synthetic intuition of a form, which unfolds as the particular form of the poem or of whatever work of art emerges from it. Finally, according to Maritain, creative intuition, upon being translated into poems and other works of art, to some extent loses itself, objectifies itself.

What Maritain is evoking with his idea of creative intuition is almost eerily identical with the characteristics of pashyanti or pratibha as stressed by Abhinavagupta. Creative intuition is characterized by luminosity, just as Shiva himself and the higher realms of consciousness, of which pashyanti is one, shine with a preternatural radiance. It is precognitive. It is involves a direct, immediate seeing or foreseeing. Inherent within it is a kind of synthetic intuition of form that becomes the form of the articulated poem or work of art. Finally, in the very process of being articulated, translated into words on a page or notes on a score, creative intuition becomes to some degree objectified.

Maritain does not simply deal with the rarified realm of pashyanti. He goes on to discuss the realm of vaikhari and the relationship between the now fully differentiated, embodied self and the things of this world. Initially, according to Maritain, we awaken to ourselves and to things of the world "simultaneously." Both are grasped by an experience or knowledge that has "no intellectual framework." They are grasped immediately by an intuition that is prior to both—prior to the differentiation between subject and object. Not only works of art but the self and the things of this world arise from this precognitive intuition. Subject and object are not set against each other but integrally entail each other, emerging from a state in which they are one—or perhaps more precisely from a state in which they do no yet even exist. Indeed, Maritain writes, "things are grasped in the self and the self is grasped in things, and subjectivity becomes a means of grasping obscurely the inner side of things." Our awareness of ourselves grants us access to things, even to glimpses of the inner side of things, of the otherwise unknowable Kantian thing in itself, and our awareness of things grants us access to ourselves.

I would now like to turn to a famous passage in Wordsworth's "Tintern Abbey" that beautifully exemplifies Maritain's notion of things being grasped in the self, and of the self being grasped in things. The passage reminds me that Wordsworth at his finest was a true visionary poet, again a word that I use with the root meaning of pashyanti as to see or to foresee in mind. In this excerpt the word *them* in the first line alludes to prior instances of attending to natural phenomena.

> To them I may have owed another gift,
> Of aspect more sublime; that blessed mood,
> In which the burthen of the mystery,
> In which the heavy and the weary weight
> Of all this unintelligible world,
> Is lightened:—that serene and blessed mood,
> In which the affections gently lead us on,—
> Until, the breath of this corporeal frame
> And even the motion of our human blood
> Almost suspended, we are laid asleep
> In body, and become a living soul:
> While with an eye made quiet by the power
> Of harmony, and the deep power of joy,
> We see into the life of things.

This excerpt from "Tintern Abbey," like a number of Wordsworth's more sublime passages, seems lit from within, suffused by a visionary gleam, a peculiar and powerful radiance. In such passages he describes a profound reciprocity between the self and the things or forms of nature. In the excerpt quoted, Wordsworth begins by praising these forms, which he has previously been contemplating, because he owes to them "another gift / of aspect more sublime," a blessed mood. As Wordsworth explores the deepening of this mood, he exquisitely describes the physiological stages of entering into a deep state of meditation. Finally, he becomes a living soul and sees into the life of things. The moment of becoming, inwardly, a living soul and seeing, outwardly, into the life of things is one moment. Seeing things in the self, turning inwardly, reflexively, toward the wellsprings of one's being simultaneously involves the outward, expansive movement of seeing the self in things, which thereby appear more and more alive, more and more to be lit from within. This is an inextricably reciprocal process. Whether one starts from the vantage point of meditative introspection—of quieting one's mind and breath and drawing closer to the interior of the self—or from the vantage point of ecstatic absorption in the things of nature makes no difference. The practice of seeing the self in things, things in the self, continually deepens until self and world are constantly, immediately, recognized as one in the radiance of a higher awareness, not merely that of the subjective ego, that suffuses and constitutes both. To cite another passage from "Tintern Abbey,"

>   —And I have felt
> A presence that disturbs me with the joy
> Of elevated thoughts; a sense sublime
> Of something far more deeply interfused,
> Whose dwelling is the light of setting suns,
> And the round ocean and the living air,
> And the blue sky, and in the mind of man:
> A motion and a spirit, that impels
> All thinking things, all objects of all thought,
> And rolls through all things.

When one rereads this passage, it is readily apparent why Coleridge originally felt such a deep kinship with Wordsworth.

In discussing pashyanti as the origin of great poems, or as a level, beyond time and space, in the evolution of the universe, I do not wish to obscure the fact that pashyanti is fundamentally and simply a mode of human experience, the experience of an intuition, devoid of any intellectual framework, in which we are on the verge of awakening and then awaken to our connection with things. It becomes the state of direct, unfiltered, immediate seeing through which we ourselves and the world are grasped together as one.

We have all, I believe, had experiences in which our minds, for whatever reason, briefly cease to churn out thoughts, and in which we are able to feel and see, in a heightened, intuitive way, our immediate connection with things. Think, in thinking of pashyanti, of the many who have these kinds of experiences in relationship to nature. Think, for example, of how during long walks along forest trails a sense of a deepened connection with things can flower and grow; or think of rock climbers as they intuitively move, always on the brink, from position to position, on the living, ever-changing contours of the rock face, with which they must maintain a more than merely literal—an almost spiritual—contact, must remain alert, awake, from moment to moment, knowing that one moment of unconsciousness can be fatal; or think, in an entirely different realm, of a young mother raptly, intently observing the changes of expression on a newborn's face; or of Emily Dickinson's lines,

> There's a certain Slant of light,
> Winter afternoons—
> ...
> When it comes, the Landscape listens—
> Shadows—hold their breath—

or of the same kind of hush that can equally fall over a landscape on late afternoons toward the end of summer; or of that radiant energy that bursts forth unexpectedly in any setting while one is mindfully performing the simplest of tasks. Think, finally, of the experience of being in love, an experience in which one's own consciousness, the beloved, and the world around one seem surcharged with a special radiance. I could multiply examples almost endlessly, examples of when we awaken, through a simple act of undistracted awareness, to a more than usually heightened sense of our connections with others and with the things of this world.

I suspect that almost every day we have fleeting moments in which we awaken to this kind of heightened awareness and connection. The more we remain alert, on the lookout for them, the more they will seem to occur. More proactively, according to Shaivism, we can try to pause during moments of our days and open ourselves to the possibility of experiencing such moments. We can train ourselves to attend to both the first, inchoate stirrings of awakening, then to the awakening itself, of the pure, immediate, intuitive awareness in and through which we apprehend the integral connection between ourselves and the things of this world. We can, to paraphrase Blake, seek to kiss the moment not, in this case, as it flies but the moment just before it flies and as it flies.

Again, there is nothing occult, no mystification, no mystagogy involved in the apprehension of such moments, nor are they strictly the property of initiates, seers, shamans, artists, or great scientists. On the contrary, their essence is a luminous clarity and they are available at all times to all.

And yet, as pashyanti unfolds, via madhyama, to vaikhari, to the realm "out there," extended in space, in which all of us as embodied beings dwell, most of us come to lose, to a greater or lesser degree, a sense of the unalienable interconnection and reciprocity between ourselves and the things of this world. This is Wordsworth's great sorrowful theme. We become estranged both from ourselves as subjects and from things of this world as objects. As mentioned before, vaikhari is the realm of spoken speech, of the individuated self confronting objects situated in an external space. At its worst, it becomes a realm in which frozen, reified, isolated subjects confront an obdurate world of equally frozen objects. It becomes the nightmarish realm that Blake called the limit of contraction, and that Coleridge calls "death in life" or "life in death," a realm like a cave in which we cower, shrinking inwardly, solipsistically, in mute terror, in danger of entirely losing both our sense of ourselves and our sense of the world outside of the cave. Or it becomes like the world of the Ancient Mariner who aimlessly drifts "alone, alone, all all alone" on a vast sea, the sole survivor of its depredations, a soul who is no longer an agent, who has become a passive object to whom things happen but who initiates nothing. Having forfeited the capacity to act, he can merely endlessly, aimlessly suffer.

How do we overcome our own, likely far less dramatic, sense of estrangement? Maritain felt that the function of artists is to reawaken in us the essential connection between self and world. Artists, and poets in particular, possess the gift of bypassing the discursive intellect and, through creative intuition, of grasping the self and world together in their integral unity. The poems produced by genuine poets are stamped by the intuition from which they have arisen, an intuition that they can awaken in the reader.

I would like to cite here, with minimal commentary, one such poem, a brief and compelling meditation by the American poet James Wright that seems almost as though it could have been written by Basho, the great Zen poet of the maximally minimal. It suggests how deeply attending to the life of the things of this world can grant a transformative insight that powerfully affects one's perspective on and experience of one's own life.

Lying in a Hammock at William Duffy's Farm in Pine Island, Minnesota

> Over my head, I see the bronze butterfly,
> Asleep on the black trunk,
> Blowing like a leaf in green shadow.
> Down the ravine behind the empty house,
> The cowbells follow one another
> Into the distances of the afternoon.
> To my right,
> In a field of sunlight between two pines,
> The droppings of last year's horses
> Blaze up into golden stones.
> I lean back, as the evening darkens and comes on.
> A chicken hawk floats over, looking for home.
> I have wasted my life.

Beginning with the invocation of a very specific place in the title of the poem itself, Wright meticulously stations himself within the world, precisely mapping his position with respect to the twin coordinates of time and space, in large measure by attending to and registering the sensory phenomena of the things of this world. It is by so thoroughly placing himself, experiencing himself, as in and of the world, and by attending to that world with such care, that he experiences the transformed sense of self attested to by the poem's final line.

In "Tintern Abbey," Wordsworth becomes a living soul and sees into the life of things. Here Wright sees into the life of things and becomes a living soul. Both thereby are restored to a condition of vital reciprocity with the things of this world.

Wright's language until the last line—including even the alchemical reference implied by horse droppings blazing up into golden stones—completely attends to the sensual, the concrete. Wordsworth's language is notably more abstract, states rather than infers. Indeed, the language of one of the greatest English poetic extollers of nature is often to a surprising degree abstract, usually only briefly, and judiciously, referring to concrete sensuous detail. That language is unusually sparing in its use of metaphor as well. This tendency toward abstraction is one of the often overlooked strengths of Wordsworth poetry. The lineaments of his discourse are laid bare in clear, direct, declarative strokes, in a flexible free verse sensitive to the modulations of the human voice. Again, no mystagogy, no mystification obtain here. Wordsworth does not simply address his bond with nature but straightforwardly addresses his readers as a man speaking to men. And presumably to women (not simply to his sister Dorothy, often invoked and addressed in "Tintern Abbey") as well.

And yet Wordsworth strongly associates, as we have seen, the precognitive intuition of which I have been speaking, particularly in his "Ode: Intimations of Immortality," with childhood. This precognitive intuition is inevitably dispelled by language acquisition, with the acquisition of reason, and its prevalent use of abstraction, dealing intuition a fatal blow. It is with the advent of madhyama, with the awareness of self, of the airtight mental realm of unsounded words and images unrelated to external space, that the visionary gleam of childhood fades. For Wordsworth, we can gain glimpses of this state of interconnectedness in adulthood, but its immediacy is inevitably more and more replaced by the compensatory mediations of the philosophic mind.

For Maritain, to the contrary, we perhaps initially awaken to ourselves and to the things of the world at some point during childhood. But crucially, we can't truly awaken to things until we awaken to the self. Moreover, preconscious, precognitive creative intuition is in no way fundamentally a childish or primitive state. It is an order of experience higher even than that of rational thought. It is a state that can be cultivated, and can lead us closer to the experience of the divine.

In what follows, rather than continue to read Maritain closely, I will freely, or somewhat freely, riff on his concept of interiority, a virtual space in which we draw close to the preternatural clarity of the divine within us, to the preconscious, precognitive realm of pashyanti in which the subject and the object, ourselves and the things of this world, are as yet undifferentiated. From the outset, I want to make clear that Martian's use of a term translated as *inferiority* seems, misleadingly, to suggest the primacy of an inner, subjective self. Rather, as Maritain uses the term, and as I will use it here, interiority, I wish to stress strongly, suggests a medial or middle way between, beyond, and inclusive of both subject and object, a way suggested by the Sanskrit word *madhya*, for which there is no equivalent in English. This way includes both introspection and paying loving attention to the things of this world. If our subjectivity becomes a means of grasping obscurely the inner side of things, profound attention to or absorption in the things of this world can lead us to grasp—at first obscurely, then hopefully with increasing clarity—the inner side of ourselves, to discover depths we may not have known we possess. Again, whether we begin with inner or outer absorption makes no difference. A process of increasing reciprocity, a kind of virtuous cycle occurs, in which each movement is seen inextricably to involve the other. The inner side of ourselves and the inner side of things draw closer and closer together, eventually becoming one as inner and outer, subject and object merge in the immediate intuition from which they have emerged, in the luminous space of pure awareness. Though it has not been my focus here, a similar reciprocal process can, of course, also occur in our relations with others leading, in cherished instances, to a shared place of pure love.

Our embodied individuality and the existence of things do not, of course, dissolve in intuitions of the state of ineffable unity of all things in Consciousness, but our lives are immeasurably enhanced by them. Never again can either the self or the things of this world be accorded special privilege, nor can they be considered as opposing counters between which one must choose, thus leading to the dead end of either subjective idealism or of reductive materialism. Exploring one's interiority is not yet another of the ego's/subject's attempts to gain ascendancy over itself, over others, or over an exploited nature seen as mere matter. It is an attempt to draw closer to the divine luminous awareness whose light, at the higher levels of consciousness, dissolves both subject and object, the same light which, when subject and object manifest as the self and the things of this world, illuminates, permeates, constitutes both.

If we choose to embrace and explore our interiority, we will have chosen a life of vital relationship, in which—at least to some degree, as we attempt to approach more closely to the wellsprings of our own life—we will become a living soul who sees into the life of things, things which will then further quicken and enliven our own lives. We will also see ourselves in the other, whether in the form of a human being or a blade of grass, of others instinct with a life that is also our own life, or that is in no way essentially different from it, and whose otherness is therefore to be acknowledged, to be accorded full respect.

Just as we come to apprehend our own life in the things of this world, so, according to Shaivism, when awakened we behold inanimate matter as instinct with consciousness. The electrons in a slab of stone are no less alive than those in the hand that is now writing what you are reading. A rock to a geologist, or to a rock climber, is not a matter of indifference, is nonetheless vital and absorbing for being inanimate. And temples, of course, are built of stones, even of stones that a previous builder has foolishly rejected. All things participate in an unbroken, living continuum that stretches from wayside rubble to the highest non-dual awareness. Finally, through entering fully into and participating in that continuum, through embracing our interiority, we will be in a position to return to the preconscious, luminous source of both ourselves and the things of this world, to the ecstatic stirring of pashyanti itself. Perhaps from thence we will penetrate still further toward some kind of intimate contact with or absorption in the divine—regardless of whatever name we choose to give it or not to give it.

If we neglect or refuse to embrace our own interiority, if we lose touch with the wellsprings of our lives, we will lose touch with that which is alive both in ourselves and in the things of this world. We will become facades confronting facades, masks confronting masks. We will not see other human beings and the things of this world as instinct with their own lives, their own prerogatives, their otherness worthy of being acknowledged and respected, but as lifeless counters to be appraised and manipulated. We will live in the space of the external, external to ourselves and external to others and to the things of this world, a place of perpetual exile. As our hearts harden we will harden, become more obdurate, fixed, dense. Finally, we will have little sense of how to approach, let alone to reenter, the luminous source that is the origin we share with all.

Having come this far, I see now that an important problem I formulated in my wayward little book *Providence* was formulated, perhaps, in the wrong terms. In portions of that text, I was much exercised about the evacuation of the subject, of its replacement by such ugly, abstract monikers as the subject position or the author function, monikers that seemed the thinnest of veils hiding the effaced face of an essential nihilism. Now I have come to a place where notions of the subject and of subjectivity need no longer be clung to with such tenacity. In previously using the word *subject*, I was heedless of, or set aside, the awareness which that word carries with it, inevitably, connotations of subjective idealism—a position with which my not quite imperial "I" is uncomfortable—and of the logical or dialectical opposition between subject and object. To the extent that these terms are useful at all, I have tended to see them as complementary, not as antagonistic. In defending the word *subject* I was dragging its long shadow into an argument that might have better been conducted using other terms.

In speaking of interiority, I have been speaking of a mode of apprehension that avoids two traps, that of subjective idealism on the one hand, and of a reductive, skeptical materialism on the other. It is our interiority—not our subjectivity as circumscribed by the ego with its endless self-aggrandizing designs—that is now increasingly under threat from multiple forces unleashed by our current meta-evolutionary, exponentially speeded-up epoch. Current academic discourse is as suspicious of any notion of interiority as it is of subjectivity. Interiority is likened to capitalist private property with all of its attendant ills. Indulging in its seemingly private space comes to seem almost immoral. We would be better off declaring ourselves bankrupt and divesting ourselves of it. But it seems to me, on the contrary, that the numinous awareness that is our source and end, and that includes all of us, is in fact highly democratic. It is thoroughly in the public domain. All have experienced it. Many of us fail to recognize it for what it is, associate it with whatever fleeting context accompanies it. Nor are we aware of how to initiate or to remain in contact with it. Others block it from their view, fearful of its life-altering disclosures. Despite all of this, some will continue to grasp it in moments of glowing intuition, and others will press on still further toward whatever remains to be experienced, or to the blissful annihilation of experience as we know it.

4.
Concluding Unscientific Postscripts

1. The Seer, The Act of Seeing, and The Seen

1.

I have mentioned in the first chapter of the first section of this book that two revealed texts, the Shiva Sutras and the Spanda Karikas, are regarded as the foundation of Kashmir Shaivism, which came to be comprised of two shastras, or lineages of teachers and commentators. The first of these, the Pratyabhijna Shastra, whose commentators focused primarily on the Shiva Sutras, was emphasized in my initial account of Kashmir Shaivism. The second lineage of teachers and commentators, the Spanda Shastra, focuses primarily on the Spanda Karikas.

The Pratyabhijna Shastra, again, which regards Shiva as the fully expanded, transcendent "I" or subject, as at once the agent from whom all else unfolds, as the witness of that unfolding, and as he to whom all in the created world ultimately refers, can be seen as a form of subjective idealism. Indeed, one of the greatest scholars of Kashmir Shaivism regards the Pratyabhijna Shasta or school of Shaivism as anticipating, many centuries before the fact, the philosophy of Fichte and Schelling, the first of the German Romantic proponents of subjective idealism.

On the other hand, there is no mention in the various commentaries that comprise the Spanda Shastra of Shiva as the Supreme "I" or witness to whom all in creation is referred. Nor is there any suggestion that the disciple practice I-consciousness, reminding himself of his unity with Shiva as supreme ego. The Spanda Shastra focuses on Supreme Consciousness itself as the Absolute.

Kashmir Shaivism, which is often referred to as *trika* after the three-pronged trident of Shiva, frequently references metaphysical triads as forms or modes of the one Supreme Consciousness, among which are the perceptual triad of the seer, the act of seeing, and the seen, and the cognitive or conceptual triad in the form of the knower, the act of cognition, and the known. Both the perceptual and cognitive triads can be seen as subsumed under the fundamental triad of the agent of consciousness, the act of consciousness, and the object of consciousness. With respect to this triad, in the

Pratyabhijna Shastra, Shiva in his role as supreme agent is preeminent. In the Spanda Shastra, the middle term, Chit Shakti, Supreme Consciousness itself, the energy or power of pure awareness encompassing all levels of creation, unattached to any subject or object, seems first among equals.

My own sympathies, as one who is neither a theist nor a subjective idealist, and as one embarking on exploring the intimations of a middle way between subjective idealism and objective idealism, lie with the Spanda Shastra.

These somewhat arcane matters came to be an almost obsessive concern for me as a result of two years spent on translating and writing a commentary on Jnaneshwar's *Amritanubhav* which, as I have mentioned, adopts an outlook that seems entirely in consonance with Kashmir Shaivism, and in particular with the Spanda Shastra. I have mentioned that in much of the *Amritanubhav* Jnaneshwar ceases, for the most part, to use any theistic terms. His relentless focus is on what he simply calls the Ultimate Reality. Nowhere does he reference either I-consciousness, or witness-consciousness, or any notion of the ultimate reality as Absolute Ego, all of which are mainstays of the Pratyabhijna Shastra. He discusses in great detail, however, the aforementioned triad of the seer, the act of seeing, and the seen. The seer, for Jnaneshwar, clearly corresponds to Shiva, and the act of seeing and the seen to Shakti. As I delved more deeply into the *Amritanubhav,* it increasingly became clear to me that in discussing the ultimate reality, Jnaneshwar was positing yet another, higher principle both beyond and between Shiva and Shakti, beyond the seer, on one hand, and seeing and the seen on the other, beyond any notion of subject or object, inside or outside.

This intuition led me back to Abhinavagupta, whose magisterial *Tantraloka* synthesizes not only the Pratyabhijna and the Spanda Shastras but several other prominent, related strands of Tantrism—into all of which he was initiated, and with all of which he was thoroughly conversant—with the intention of seeing whether there was any warrant for, any indication in his writings, of such a notion. And indeed Abhinavagupta sometimes uses the term *annutara*, which means, essentially, that beyond which there is nothing, to indicate or suggest a principle that is beyond even Shiva Himself in his role as the seer. Even in commentators prior to Abhinavagupta the term Paramashiva is occasionally used. The suffix *para* means beyond or above, so Paramashiva, again, seems to hint at a Shiva who is paradoxically beyond or above even Shiva Himself.

I have mentioned that Shiva, when not engaged in the joint project with Shakti of emitting and absorbing innumerable words, withdraws into himself, while Shakti, entering into a dormant state, in effect dissolves into Shiva. In this phase, as there is no longer anything to see, Shiva is no longer the seer, while at the same time Shakti is purged of her status as the seen. In the *Amritanubhav* Jnaneshwar writes: "The Ultimate Reality is a kind of seeing which manifests as the seer and the seen but transcends both." In the very highest, unmanifest level of consciousness, as I have discussed, Shakti is fully resorbed into Shiva, who abides in a quiescent state. When

Shiva thus withdraws the universe into himself, nothing remains to be seen, and perception or seeing vanish as well. Jnaneshwar writes, "When he vehemently desires no longer to see, he withdraws into himself and reposes there." And again: "If he desires that seeing should cease, the state of seeing nothing is instantly attained." In this, Shiva's ultimate, unmanifest state of repose in himself, he is no longer the seer, and likewise seeing and the seen have fallen away. In this state, Jnaneshwar writes, "He is like no one seeing nothing. And yet, finally, even this not seeing is a kind of seeing."

As noted above, the triad of the seer, the act of seeing, and the seen is synonymous with the triad of the conscious agent, consciousness, and the object of consciousness. Thus the higher seeing that remains when the seer and seen have fallen away is synonymous with Supreme Consciousness itself. Jnaneshwar writes: "The Absolute, being vision itself, is neither seeing nor not seeing. He is the cause of both." Crucially then, it is Consciousness, the middle term, that precipitates both the conscious agent, the seer, and the object of consciousness, the seen.

And so, in sum, in Jnaneshwar it is indeed Supreme Consciousness, the ongoing act of pure awareness itself, lying between and beyond Shiva as the supreme perceiver and all he perceives, independent of any subject, even the supreme subject, and of any object, but the precondition of both, that is, with respect to the triads I have been discussing, preeminent, first among apparent equals.

One must always bear in mind, however, what is perhaps the central paradox of Kashmir Shaivism: that even as Shiva, having resorbed Shakti, is fully withdrawn into himself, he is at the same time always fully engaged with Shakti in flashing forth as countless phenomenal worlds. Spanda, likewise never abating, is the initial stirring of Shakti within Shiva. I have described it as a simultaneous inward and outward vibration of Consciousness within the Absolute. In its inward moving aspect, it begins to establish the pole of Shiva as supreme subject, and in its outward moving aspect it begins to establish what will later become the objective world. At the highest level of manifestation, *aham* and *idam*, the *I* and the *this*, are still one, oscillating together as spanda, as a pure, luminous, supremely conscious throb of awareness, continuously reflecting itself while at the same time, projecting itself, as it were, outward. Spanda is the living, vibrating heart of what will later become both subject and object. Focusing on neither the subject nor the object, but instead on the middle term, the act of consciousness, and by extension the act of cognition or perception, leads to an experience of the resonant heart of both subject and object that is one with Supreme Consciousness itself.

Consciousness as the middle term between the agent and the object of consciousness resonates, I hope, with my previous discussions of the liminal, the in-between, as conducive of the achievement of a more expanded state of awareness. Indeed, I have discussed at some length that an aspect of the spiritual praxis of Shaivism involves, for example, focussing on the space between thoughts, between the incoming and outgoing breaths, between waking and sleeping, and so on. In the following passage in the *Amritanubhav*—the sole passage, remarkably, in which Jnaneshwar refers to spiritual practices of any kind—he emphasizes focusing on the interval, on the "space between" of the liminal, as integrally related to the state of pure, ongoing awareness of Consciousness itself.

> Such a state is like the surface of water where one wave has subsided and another is about to arise
>
> Or like the moment when sleep has just ended but we have not yet fully awakened;
>
> If you wish to think of it, think of sight when it ceases to regard one object and, not yet resting on another, hovers in the gap between visions,
>
> Or of how at sunset, just before night has arisen, the horizon flares, then fades from our sight;
>
> Or think of a moment when you have just exhaled a breath and are about to inhale;

At the very highest levels of Consciousness, Jnaneshwar writes:

> The natural state of the Self lies in the interval between the destruction of the seer and seen and their revival.
>
> The natural state of the Self is like this. It abides between both.

The interval between the destruction of the seer and seen and their revival is the moment when the Absolute is withdrawn into its unmanifest state, the moment when a seeing that is not seeing, that is pure Consciousness itself, prevails. Jnaneshwar writes that the triad of the seer, seeing, and the seen itself constantly flashes forth and subsides, and advises us to catch hold of the moment between its flashing forth and its subsiding. At the same time, from a slightly different perspective, this interval can be seen as the moment between the unmanifest and the emergence of the manifest, when spanda, the first stirring of Consciousness, begins to oscillate.

More broadly, I would like to look at the concept of the imagination from the perspective I have just discussed, with the notion that it participates in the act of a pure Consciousness that is beyond and between seer and the seen, the conscious agent and the object of consciousness, the subject and the object, but precipitates both. I wrote in my introduction to this volume, as regards our prevailing notion of the imagination: "I, too, dislike it. It reflects, as a noun, the mind's and particularly the Western mind's tendency to hypostasize or reify not only the abstract but the dynamic into reassuringly stable, seemingly substantial categorical niches." The imagination is reduced, along with reason, to a supposed mental faculty, an attribute of the subject. At the same time, it accrues to itself something of the allure and prestige of a reassuringly stable reality that we associate with nouns that denote objects in the so-called real world. I would suggest, to the contrary, that the imagination is uncategorical. It is not a faculty, but a force. Not a noun, but a verb. Not a fixable idea, but an energy, not knowable in itself but glimpsed in its fugitive instances. Who knows—it may even be an energy that is independent of the human mind, a force that the mind draws upon but does not control.

Our default assumption is that the imagination, like Consciousness, is a faculty or attribute of the subject, and that when this attribute is, as it were, exercised as a result of the prompting of another attribute—the *will*—it will result in the work of art as a kind of definitively achieved product. According to the alternative model I am suggesting, the imagination is inspired and activated by the ongoing act of Consciousness, a pure awareness that is not simply an attribute of the subject, but is prior to both subjects and objects.

I am reminded, in this context, of my discussion of Li Po and of Basho and what I called the poem of pure percept. Seen from a slightly different perspective, such poems not only evoke but reenact a single, immediate act of perception. It is this act of perception that precipitates the poem as pure percept and the poet who, though not asserted as a subject, registers with the reader as the conveyor of the subtlest of moods and emotions.

But of course the imagination is not limited to the perceptual. As previously mentioned, the triad of the known, the act of knowing, and the object of knowledge is also subsumed under the broader triad of the agent of consciousness, the act of consciousness, and the object of consciousness. Thus in the poetry of Stevens, as we have seen, it is the act of thinking that precipitates both the poet as subject in his various guises and whatever provisional, incidental ideas toward which the poet is pointing. Indeed in Stevens' the subject as lyric "I" is barely asserted at all, and the conceptual content of his poetry is of little concern except in so far as it provides material for the poem as an ongoing act of thinking.

Poems are, of course, not limited to either perception or cognition. They are also, often, affairs of the heart, and they almost always convey at least some degree of affect. In devotional poems the affective is at least an equal partner with the conceptual or the perceptual. And so here yet another triad—that of the lover, the act of loving, and the beloved—comes into play. What I have been calling Supreme Consciousness is associated, in virtually every spiritual tradition, with love. In Christian devotional poems it is God's act of loving, the working of the Holy Spirit, itself the mediator, the active term between the father and the son, that precipitates both the poet as lover and whatever particular form of the divine beloved—whether Christ, or Mary, or God with or without form, or, indeed, the forms of his fellow man or of nature—is experienced by him.

Similarly, in the love poems of the great medieval troubadour poets and their successors, the act of loving, preeminently expressed in the act of writing poems, is of far greater concern than is the particular nature of either the poet as lover or of the beloved, who is described in pat, conventional, ideal terms, who eludes the poet's grasp, and who in fact, as in the case of Petrarch's Laura, may even have been entirely fictional.

It seems to me that Jnaneshwar's evocation of an aspect of ultimate reality that is the ongoing act of a Supreme Consciousness or pure awareness, that is neither subject nor object but the precondition of both, is analogous to my preferred conception of the imagination, referenced previously. The imagination is not itself Supreme Consciousness, but is that within us that resonates with it, which picks up its frequency and draws upon its vast reservoir of energy. And which is itself only realized as the act, say, of writing a poem, an act whose genesis is prior to, is the necessary precondition of both the emergence of the poem itself and of the identification of its author as author.

Jnaneshwar's portrayal of Supreme Consciousness as involving the ongoing act of pure creation recalls Coleridge's notion of the "eternal act of creation of the infinite I AM," but with the difference that the "I" drops out of the equation, replaced by the act of Consciousness itself. Coleridge speaks of the imagination as reflecting this eternal act. But as I have noted, mere reflections are passive and reduplicative, not creative. It seems to me that the imagination participates in or draws from, rather than merely mirrors, Consciousness as the eternally present, ever ongoing act of creation.

Finally, I would like to revisit my discussion, in the previous chapter, of the self and of the things of this world with an emphasis on the notion that both are precipitated by this ongoing creative act of Consciousness itself.

The self and the things of this world, both precipitates of the act of Consciousness, are dynamically implicated in each other. As previously mentioned, when the inner side of the self and the inner side of objects, drawn together by the Consciousness that comprehends them, are fully aligned in the state of the realized being, there is no longer any outer side, any fixed façade, to the self or to things of this world. Nor is there any occult inner side. There is nothing outside of Consciousness, the container in which all is contained, nor is there anything other than Consciousness within it. All phenomena, whether thoughts or things, are recognized as precipitated, projected by Consciousness as forms of Consciousness upon the screen of Consciousness, with no real difference between the projector and the projected. Moreover, just as the self and the things of this world are vitally, dynamically implicated in each other, so all phenomena of whatever scale, are vitally, dynamically implicated in each other. All things vibrate, pulsate, resonate with the primordial yet ever-renewed vibration, the ongoing act of Consciousness itself. And it is this act upon which the imagination draws and in which it participates when it apprehends, in an act of preconscious, synoptic intuition, an insight which it then unfolds, creating the lineaments of a work of art or the outlines of an elegant, heretofore unrealized scientific theory.

2.

I confess that in grappling with the *Amritanubhav* I had trouble wrapping my head around the notion of Supreme Consciousness as an energy of awareness ultimately independent of any subject or conscious agent. In our ordinary experience, consciousness is always associated with a conscious subject. It is almost as difficult to conceive of a Consciousness independent of any human being as it is to imagine Einstein's fourth dimension

And yet, finally, in sum, I confess that as a result both of my experiences as an unofficial, ultimately failed spiritual aspirant, and from my likewise unofficial experiences as a more-than-usually successful if unknown poet, I have come to feel that the universe is pervaded by a non-localized Consciousness with respect to which the terms subject and object, inner and outer, are meaningless, and whose essential nature can be intuitively apprehended by us in a myriad of different ways—as that which inspires awe and wonder; or as that which registers as a profound meaningfulness beyond yet pervading any particular meanings; or finally as that which assumes the nature of a supremely playful trickster who delights in concealing what he ultimately reveals, who is not only sublime but sublimely funny, even if for a time at our expense —all these and many more besides are the myriad faces of one face.

The sense that I am growing toward here I found confirmed when I read Longchenpa's *Special Treasury of the Basic Space of Phenomena*. Longchenpa, too, postulates Consciousness, or the pure self-knowing awareness that he also calls awakened mind, as that from within which all phenomena, including both subjects and the objects which they apprehend, arise and subside. Such phenomena have only a kind of equivocal, dependent reality that results from their resting within Consciousness or awakened mind even as they dynamically appear and then disappear within it. Once again, Consciousness is primary; it is Consciousness that precipitates both subjects and objects. When rightly apprehended, such phenomena are apprehended not as self-subsistent entities. They are perceived, rather, in their suchness, not as substantive but as uniquely qualitative, fleeting phenomena, each imbued with its own unique form. Just as no human subject is merely a replica of other subjects, so no object of perception is experienced as definitively like any other such object.

Here I have stumbled upon what, as mentioned in the introduction to this text, Western neuroscientists, philosophers, and psychologists regard as the greatest remaining enigma, what they call the "hard problem" of Consciousness itself, of how it is that we subjectively experience phenomena such as pain or the redness of a rose as we experience them. Shaivism, as I have pointed out, like Longchenpa, regards both subjective and objective as real insofar as they are such appearances—manifestations of the flashing forth in form—of Consciousness itself, but unreal in so far as they are considered to be self-subsistent entities. The brain, according to later proponents of this view of Consciousness, is uniquely suited to pick up on intimations of a non-local Consciousness and to translate them into local forms. In a sense the material is regarded as an epiphenomenon or emergent property of the spiritual.

Those of a more materialistic bent prefer to regard Consciousness as an emergent epiphenomenon of the brain itself, the spiritual as an emergent property of the material. Consciousness, in this account, if not infinite space, is packed into the grey matter bounded within the fragile nutshell of the human cranium.

Still others might—or rather do—regard Consciousness as simultaneously evolving from the top down and from the bottom up. This is the view of Kashmir Shaivism.

Apparently, a number of proponents of whatever position regard it as unlikely that the problem of Consciousness will ever be definitively solved. And so I must acknowledge that what I intuitively feel to be case—that there is some form of Consciousness independent of either the mind or of the body, of the subjective or of the material—may well be proved to be entirely wrong.

I would prefer, however, that the hard problem of Consciousness remain unsolved and unsolvable, that we continue to live with a sense of the mysterious, that it remain neither conquered by the imperial mind nor co-opted, comprehended by the spirit of the divine that, according to both my own spiritual teacher and Christ, dwells within all of us.

This sense of the mysterious need not involve, as Blake seemed to think, trafficking in obscurantism. Rather, it is a recognition of our limitations, the kind of limitations, for example, that arise when either poets, mystics, or scientists attempt to definitively say the unsayable, or that we feel when we gaze upward, as finite beings, at the incomprehensible vastness and plenitude of the night sky.

2. The Synchronic and the Diachronic/Kairos and Chronos

I would like to introduce here two sets of terms that are relevant to the notions I have already discussed at considerable length in this text. I have mentioned that the same-hearted reader or spectator of a work of poetry or drama becomes attuned to the state of creative intuition experienced by the poet as giving rise to a given work, and that he or she in a sense becomes the imaginative co-creator of that work. For my purposes here, I would like to stress an aspect of Abhinavagupta's notion of the same-hearted reader that I have not yet sufficiently emphasized. The same-hearted reader is also the qualified, the more than merely-competent reader. And to become a qualified reader, one who is able to grasp the intuition of the poet/artist, a deep and extensive familiarity with works of art is necessary. The more, for example, one has had experience of, say, poetry in general, the more likely it is that one will have developed the creative intuition that has given rise to any given particular work. Just as artists work long and hard at their craft as a precondition to being granted moments of creative intuition, so the same-hearted reader must devote much time and energy to extensive reading before he or she can be quickened by the impulse that has given rise to any particular work.

Here I would stress, likewise, that the more often a spectator/reader has seen/read any given play or poem, the greater will be his or her imaginative attunement to and alignment to the work in question, and the greater his or her apprehension will be of the inspiration on the part of the playwright/poet that gave rise to it, and, finally, the more effectively he or she will be its virtual co-creator. Some such attunement will occur as a same-hearted reader sees or hears the poem or play unfold sequentially for the first time, but it will come into play more fully after a given work has been seen or heard in its totality. On one level, this is simple common sense. Surely it is a typical experience that the more one reads a great play, the more one will grasp various of its inexhaustible nuances and the more complete one's picture of it will become.

But something else as well happens in the process I am describing, and here the formidable but now unfashionable literary critic Northrop Frye will be my guide. The more often one has read a given poem or play, the more it assumes a kind of spatial form, like a diorama, a kind of immediate whole that one can apprehend, as it were, all at once, immediately, as a significant totality. In such a case, that which is at first apprehended sequentially, in the linear order of time, is grasped more and more as a kind of spatial, atemporal whole. At the same time, significant details, various of the inexhaustible nuances of the work are, as it were, increasingly filled in and come to stand in a kind of high relief. The more one exposes oneself to a work of art the more detailed one's grasp of the whole picture becomes.

Here, finally, I will conjure up the first of my aforementioned paired terms, the synchronic and the diachronic, terms that are associated with structuralist poetics, but which I will here use in a different, more simple sense. The diachronic corresponds to that which one apprehends in one's first experience of a poem or play as occurring sequentially in linear time, much as one habitually experiences the events of one's life. The synchronic is a span of time that one experiences immediately, atemporally, all at once. The more one experiences a work of art the more one experiences the transformation of diachronic, sequential time, into the synchronic, into that which is grasped immediately, atemporally, as presenting itself as a kind of spatial form that transcends linear time. But the metaphor of spatial form should not be taken too literally. The synchronic includes both the temporal and the spatial, while transcending both.

Having looked at matters from the point of view of the reader/spectator, I will turn again briefly to that of the poet/playwright. What I have called his immediate, precognitive, foreseeing of the emergent poem or play as a significant whole—in which pratibha (creative intuition) and pashyanti (the initial stress or impulse, still non-verbal, that gives rise to articulated work) come into play—is not only synoptic but synchronic. The more the poet/playwright works, in real, sequential, diachronic time, on the poem or play as an emergent significant whole, the more its details are filled in, until finally it has been translated into fully articulated form.

The experience of the poet/playwright is thus the inverse of that of the same-hearted, qualified reader/spectator, or rather each is the inverse of the other. The former translates the synchronic into the diachronic, the latter the diachronic into the synchronic. They are the joint laborers, the original creator and the subsequent co-creators of the work of art as a significant whole. Both have apprehended the synoptic, synchronic intuition from which the work has arisen as an immediate totality, and both have as it were filled in its details. That creative intuition that gives rise to the work of art, however, according to Abhinavagupta, transcends both the poet/playwright and the reader/spectator. Its source is the creative impulse, the initial vibration or stress within the divine, within Shiva, in which both poet and reader equally participate, and which likewise transcends both.

One last point needs to be made about the reader/spectator as co-creator of the work of art. He or she does not merely reduplicate, in inverse order, a process realized by the author, thereby completing the circuit through which the poem is realized. He or she also finds in the work much of which the author himself was unaware. Thus the work of interpretation is also a kind of ongoing work of creation. Like the poem itself, the work of interpretation is inexhaustible, which is to say that no one interpretation is exhaustive. Through the reader, the poem is continually recreated and oriented toward the horizon of a future in which it will continue to live.

What, if anything, does the synchronic have to do with the phenomena known as synchronicity? Synchronicity involves the experience of coincidence, of moments when events come into what seems like a miraculous, almost impossible alignment. The realm of the synchronic is that in which, as we have seen, things are taken in immediately, all at once, as with a single glance. In the synchronic dimension of time, all things, as it were, happen at once, in a realm beyond time and space; all events, as it were, co-inhere in each other and in that Consciousness, which is likewise beyond time of space. This order in which synchronicity holds sway is inexhaustible, cannot be wholly apprehended by us, just as great works of art are inexhaustible, cannot be wholly apprehended by us. We can only, if we are not enlightened beings—and even, perhaps, if we are, assuming that such beings exist— catch glimpses of this order glancingly, partially, as though through a glass darkly, as though to preserve the mystery and the wonder that remain, for us, at the heart of all things.

The second set of paired terms to which I will here refer, in some sense analogous to the synchronic and the diachronic, are the originally Greek terms *kairos* and *chronos*. I will brazenly cite here a particularly apt and pithy introduction of these terms cribbed from Wikipedia: "(καιρός) is an ancient word meaning the right, critical, or opportune moment. The ancient Greeks had two words for time: *chronos* (χρόνος) and *kairos*. The former refers to chronological or sequential time, while the latter signifies a proper or opportune time for action. While chronos is quantitative, kairos has a qualitative, permanent nature."

These terms were later picked up on and deployed in Christianity, in which kairos becomes sacramental time, or any moment or span of time, ranging from Blake's pulsation of an artery to the performance of the ritual of the Eucharist, in which Christ's presence or grace is particularly imminent/immanent. Kairos is time as wedded to the eternal while chronos is time as related to the secular, linear, sequential clock time. Both the Greek and the Christian sense of kairos are at play in *Hamlet*, in which Hamlet keeps seeking the right, the opportune, the auspicious moment in which to slay Claudius, the time that, moreover, accords with God's will. As Hamlet says with respect to the ripeness of time, echoing Christ's words in the Gospels, "We defy augury. There's a special providence in the fall of a sparrow. If it be now, 'tis not to come. If it be not to come, it will be now. If it be not now, yet it will come—the readiness is all." When one experiences the sacramental nature of time—time as one with eternity—one experiences the things of this world in a different light as well. One experiences them as not merely quantitative but as qualitative. While chronos is quantitative, kairos has a qualitative nature. One experiences things, as the Buddhists say, in their suchness. Or as Jacques Maritain says, one experiences the inner, qualitative side of the things of this world, which is one with the inner qualitative side of ourselves, until inner and outer merge. Once again, the mystery of how we experience things qualitatively is at the heart of the so-called hard problem of Consciousness to which I have referred at several times throughout this volume.

Inspired poems, poems that arise from pratibha, from creative intuition, poems whose impetus is derived from the Consciousness that is their source, are instinct with that Consciousness, and participate fully in the order of kairos. The poet, so inspired, finds the right, the opportune, the auspicious, the ripe word or words, words that according to Wallace Stevens possess the acutest vibration, that participate in the divine, creative vibration that is their source. They are pregnant with the ineffable. They participate in the qualitative, not merely the quantitative. They grant access to the synchronic, the immediate totality of the things of this world, not merely the diachronic, the chainlink fence of linear time that partitions the world into meager segments. They glow with the radiance that is their source. To read them sameheartedly is to be, if only fleetingly, transformed, to be oneself instinct with their energy.

3. The Intelligence of the Head/The Intelligence of the Heart

1.

When I was nineteen, I experienced a long period of agitated depression. Its onset was sudden, and it was so severe that I was considered unsafe to myself and was hospitalized. Of course, I thought that this hellish episode would never end. After nine months, however, for no apparent reason, the cloud of depression and terror lifted as suddenly as it had descended. I was summarily released from the hospital, and before returning to school, I spent a month at my parents' apartment.

During this interregnum and for a number of months thereafter, I experienced what was for me a kind of altered state. My heart felt open, alive, attentive, susceptible to a whole range of feelings. I felt, as though for the first time, that my head and heart were connected, that there was an easy commerce between them, and that their prior disconnection, occasioned by trauma, had been the source of my depression and the years of malaise that had preceded it.

At some point during my brief stay at my parents' apartment I casually pulled a book from a bookcase. It was Sylvia Plath's *Ariel*. As neither of my parents read poetry, I have no idea how it got there. I spent perhaps an hour perusing Plath's poems, after which I sat down for a considerably longer period and wrote, as though in a trance, several poems of my own. By the end of this session I had a clear, emphatic, incontrovertible conviction that my vocation in life was to be a poet, which, for better or worse, for richer or poorer, has turned out to be the case. When I returned to college I immediately enrolled in a poetry workshop, during the sessions of which I felt strangely and happily at home.

Almost from the outset of my life as a poet, I considered poetry, among the arts, as particularly well suited to the task of forging an alliance between the head and the heart, between thought and feeling. Unlike most music, for example, poetry contains some measure of the discursive, of ideational content, of thought, while being, at the same time, fundamentally non-discursive. Because its medium is language, poetry seemed well positioned, too, to effectuate a kind of homeopathic cure of the mind, to liberate the mind from habitual thought patterns, themselves comprised of words, by means of using those same words, but raised to a higher power. Raising words to a higher power seemed to me to entail, at least in part, baptizing them in the energy of an open heart. I regarded not only my own depression, but also much of the malaise of society as a whole, as having arisen from a disconnection between head and heart, between thoughts and feelings, between the mind's executive and its empathic functions.

I thought of writing poetry as an exercise through which my head and heart might be drawn into closer proximity and of poems, when successful, as virtual crossroads of the head and the heart to which the reader, or readers, might travel, and thereby have access to feeling as thought, thought as feeling.

Even now the poems that move me involve some kind of merger or alliance of the head and heart. This alliance is yet another of aspect of the imagination, one that I have not sufficiently discussed. If, in the process of writing a poem, the head is hypertrophied, the resultant poem will likely feel aridly intellectual. If the heart is hypertrophied, the resultant poem will feel naïve and sentimental, slack. It is vital that some kind of balance be struck.

Virtually all popular books on creativity emphasize evading the strictures of an inhibiting critical mind. This advice, to be blunt, is fine for those whose intent is to write poetry recreationally or therapeutically, but is of little use to those who have committed themselves to the difficult project of writing poetry as an art form that makes its own demands on the poet. Allen Ginsburg's oft repeated valorization of the aphorism "first thought, best thought," which entails a principled but misguided refusal to revisit or revise poems, is fine advice perhaps, if one is writing poems of the pure percept, or is a master calligrapher, both of which require years of rigorous discipline and practice of their own kind to master. But with respect to the composition of poems of any length, with respect to most Western poetry, which I chiefly have in mind here, "first thought, best thought" usually results in poems that feel slack, entropic, self-indulgent.

On the other hand, if the inner critic is too strong, if one cedes the field to him in advance, if he becomes one's master rather than one's servant, then the poems that emerge, if they emerge at all, will feel dry, inert, and attenuated. Writing poems that successfully integrate the head and the heart requires heeding both the abjurations of the inner critic and the promptings of a heart that remains open, alert, alive, in the course of writing, to almost infinite linguistic possibilities, as well giving rise to unique nuances and resonances of feeling. The poem that successfully marries head and heart is a soundscape not only of meaning but of the resonances of an affect, of a feeling which, as we shall see, ideally transcends the sentimental release of what Eliot, whom I rarely cite as an authority, called undisciplined squads of emotion.

Any discussion of the role of the inner critic opens up to a broader discussion of the role of analytical intelligence, and of reason in general, in fashioning works art. The analytical intelligence is too often considered as inimical to, or the opposite of whatever is said to be the source of creativity, the wellspring of the imagination. The imagination is regarded as synthetic, intuitive, creative, whereas the intellect is too often considered the enemy of the intuitive. Analytic intelligence can be seen, accurately, as reducing wholes to their constituent parts, but as I have tried to indicate throughout this text, reduction and de-creation are, or can be, in a complementary relation to the intuitive, the creative, the synthetic. The imagination is the exclusive domain of neither of these poles. It involves a kind of higher synthesis in which both work together.

Reason, moreover, when it takes on an abstract, speculative cast, moves away from the particular toward the general and the universal. As Stevens recognized, the abstract can, or to use his more emphatic word, must be enlisted as an ally of poetry. Perhaps the most sublime instance of sustained abstraction in the service of poetry is provided by Dante's "Paradiso," with its evocation of a world that resolves itself into ever more abstract, yet numinous, formal patterns that in their elegant simplicity and spareness are antithetical to the clogged and teeming realm of the Inferno.

Finally, even formal logic can be an ally of poetry and of the imagination. In Mahayana Buddhism, as we have seen, it is not only meditative practice that leads to progress on the spiritual path. An intense and exhaustive training in logic also leads, in particular, to prajna, to a sudden, transformative, non-discursive flash of spiritual insight.

Great scientists and mathematicians think long and hard about seemingly intractable problems before the flash of insight or a series of insights reveals previously unseen fields of possibility from which the long sought solution arises. One thinks in this connection of Zen students whose minds are engaged, sometimes for years, in pondering a knotty koan before a sudden insight that leads to an experience of no-mind irrupts. Great poets not only assiduously practice writing poetry, but also are constantly engaged in thinking, if sometimes subliminally, about poetry, and I assume this is equally true of great musicians and of great painters.

Again with rare exceptions, it is only those who have been intensely engaged in some discipline—who have not only thought deeply but have refined their skills relevant to that discipline over many years—who are granted the kinds of insight that result in truly original work. Such insights are vouchsafed to those who have developed the capacity to translate them into complex, resonant form. Alas, however, they are granted only to a small subset of those who have spent their lives diligently laboring in their chosen discipline. The poet/critic Randal Jarrell has likened the discipline of writing poetry to spending a lifetime venturing outside during thunderstorms with the hope of being struck, whether once or several times, by lightening. Sadly, most of such determined but quixotic adventurers are never rewarded with the strange privilege of being struck by lightning at all.

When I was a young poet, and even now, only a blessed few of my poems have felt successfully realized to me. I somehow recognized early on that writing poetry was an art that would require both sustained self-discipline and much trial and error, and I knew that even after a lifetime of such discipline, poems that accomplish the poet's purposes are rare, and are often experienced as a kind of gift.

The process of writing poems, for me, typically involves a shuttling between my sense of an evolving whole and a concentration on the parts, at the most basic level the words, which are charged with articulating and communicating that whole. In the process of the poem's emergence, a continual readjustment of the parts to the still-evolving whole takes place. All of this happens on the fly, is a kind of guided improvisation. Ultimately, after having become practiced at writing in this way, one begins to feel that the part and the whole, the analytic and the synthetic, are almost homologous. Once I have written the first draft of a poem, a still further process of adjusting the parts to whole takes place. The poem, when it finally somehow seems, perhaps arbitrarily, finished, is not static, but is a kind of allegory of its own emergence, and moreover only becomes authenticated as it is received and is interpreted further by the hearts of its same-hearted readers.

My mode of writing poems seemed simply natural and right for me, but was also influenced, no doubt, by the remaining traces of the New Critical notion of the poem as an autonomous, self-organizing artifact, each word of which must contribute to the whole, and which progresses, as though through an inner telos, to an inevitably strong and definitive closure, a kind of boundary or *temenos* that sets the poem apart from all that is not within the sacred precincts of the poem itself. My conception of the poem, too, was influenced by my having been exposed, during my revelatory summer spent at the Naropa Institute, to a number of New Age preoccupations, including holography, in which the whole of a projected image is contained in each part, just as each part inheres in the whole.

I was drawn, too, to the Romantic notion of organic form that sees the unfolding of a poem as analogous the growth of a plant, as emerging, again, through a kind of inner telos, a self-organizing principle, passing through a number of preordained phases until realizing, as though inevitably, its final form—although I recognized the points at which this analogy, like all analogies, breaks down. Poems evolve both more intentionally and more randomly than does any individual biological organism. A poem that accomplishes a poet's purpose can have about it an aura of inevitability, of finality. But at any given point while writing the poem, the poet could have made an almost infinite number of other choices; the words that comprise the poem have been plucked, always to some degree arbitrarily, from the inexhaustible matrix of language.

Were it not, however, for some kind of concentrated, guiding intent, or, to a lesser degree, of formal constraint, a poem would succumb to the merely random, the excessively entropic. The various iterations of the avant-garde, from surrealism to futurism, to Dada and beyond, many of whose avatars have adopted a programmatic, messianic tone, have intended to involve a kind of automatism, an experimentation with different means of censoring the intellect in the hope of discovering in the unchecked, random flow of mentation not only the new but the radically, apocalyptically new. Instead, reading the resultant poems is too often of little more interest than reading the transcript of someone else's chaotic and grandiose dream.

Much of the work of the by now wearisome and tame American poetic avant-garde over the past several decades has involved the devising of rules, designed to suppress any intent save that enshrined in the rules themselves and to ensure the generation of outcomes that are so relentlessly random that they lack even the slightest element of surprise. These procedures are almost entirely aridly intellectual and completely bypass the intelligence of the heart. The result is work that suffers, paradoxically, from both from an excessive, too rigid intent and from too much randomness. Some kind of balance, too, some kind of ongoing adjustment or calibration not only between part and whole, head and heart, but also between order and entropy, the intentional and random, seems optimal for the writing of healthy, viable poems.

Finally, of course, my poetic process of shuttling between part and whole was also validated by Kashmir Shaivism, particularly by its notion that every level of creation—as both contained by higher levels and containing lower ones—is homologous with all others, and that Consciousness is fully present in all things just as all things fully participate in Consciousness

I am not speaking about my own mode of writing prescriptively. Indeed, over the years I have cultivated an increasing respect for the fragmentary, the disjunct, the discontinuous, the terminally open-ended in poetry, and in poetry as an ongoing process whose products, discrete poems, need not be fetishized or reified as self-enclosed, definitive, finished objects.

Every poem has its own implicit poetics, as does every poet. Of course, not all poets feel the need to make the implicit explicit, to develop and communicate their own aesthetic, which is, of course, itself liable to change over time. My own implicit, informal aesthetic, my impulse as a poet, though expressed in varying ways, has been to seek a synergy of analytic intelligence and synthetic intuition, of the intelligence of the head with the intelligence of the heart.

2.
What do I mean by the intelligence of the heart?
In attempting to answer this question I will turn from consideration of the necessary if vexed role of the intellect, the intelligence of the mind, in facilitating creative endeavors, and will emphasize the perhaps more than coequal role of the intelligence of the heart not only with respect to such endeavors, but in cultivating a self, and more broadly a culture, a society, that is not blighted by a hypertrophied intellect, by a severance of the head and heart, and by extension of the head and body, the disastrous consequence that is the result of such a severance.

What then, again, do I mean by the intelligence of the heart, which seems a pleasant enough locution, although perhaps suspiciously wooly?

Surely by now many know that the heart is densely packed with neural cells, that it is in fact, not merely metaphorically, intimately connected to the head. But the head has, of course, many more such cells than does the heart. Does this mean, as it might to a reductive materialist, that the head is more intelligent than the heart, which is, after all, merely a kind of glorified pump? Surely this is not what I intend to suggest.

One thing I do intend to suggest is that the intelligence of the heart is akin to the preconscious, synoptic vision of a soon-to-be emergent whole, the creative intuition which Abhinavagupta calls pratibha or, in a slightly different context, pashyanti. It is the intelligence of the open heart through which we are capable of entertaining countless possibilities, through which the future flows into the present, through which alone we are capable of creating or of manifesting anything genuinely new. The open heart is synthetic or, to use Coleridge's term, esemplastic. It has the capacity to forge new connections, just as the brain has the capacity to form new neural pathways between previously disparate realms of experience, thus disclosing hitherto unseen realities.

But again, isn't it a bit sentimental or weakly metaphorical to speak of an open heart? Here a thought experiment occurs to me. Surely one can think of a hypothetical person as having an open heart and an open mind. We can equally plausibly think of a person of having a closed heart and a closed mind. But does it make sense to think of a person as having a closed mind and an open heart, or as having a closed heart and an open mind? Perhaps, but only if we strain credulity or ignore common sense. If we are considering an actual rather than a hypothetical person, the answer is likely to be no. Which leaves only two possibilities. One can either have an open heart and an open mind, or a closed heart and a closed mind. In the first case, the mind and the heart work together, work synergistically. In the second case they fail to properly work apart. Which is to say that the disjunction between the head and the heart leads, sometimes tragically, to a radical dysfunction. Typically when the mind and heart are severed, it is the mind which retains its peculiar brilliance and power and lords it over the cowering, closed heart. It has free rein to wreak untold havoc in the name of reason. Its extreme of logic becomes illogical. It becomes blind to its own blindness, and its brilliance blinds others. Thus blindness begets blindness.

When the heart and the mind work together, however, the brilliance and power of the mind serves the intelligence of the heart. When the intuitive, synthetic, esemplastic intelligence of the heart is wedded to the keen, analytic, extraordinarily powerful intelligence of the mind, intuitive insights are translated, rendered into often-complex, articulated forms.

The task of the poet is twofold: to keep his heart open to its intuitive stirrings, and through the skillful means honed by a disciplined mind to manifest, to actualize, to render intimations of a wholeness that would otherwise remain latent. This twofold task, which resolves itself into one task, is preeminently the work of the imagination, through which the rift between the head and the heart is healed, and through which a pernicious dualism gives way to the apprehension of a richly differentiated whole

What, if anything, does our erstwhile paragon and guide Abhinavagupta have to tell us about the intelligence of the heart?

At the literal level the heart is, of course, neither opened nor closed but is constantly opening and closing, is the pulsating source of our lives. At a slightly more subtle, but as we now know, literal, actual level, the heart is subject to the vicissitudes of positive or negative emotions.

At the same time, Abhinavagupta deploys the Heart as a technical term synonymous with *annutara*, with that beyond which there is nothing, and with Paramashiva. It is the highly charged silence that is in some sense prior to para-vak itself. Thus it is the Heart from which the boundless energy of Shakti, one with para-vak, the word beyond any word, prior to any generative language, constantly arises, and to which it constantly returns. It is a fountain that keeps overflowing, that we all, even without knowing it, share.

What Abhinavagupta calls the cave of the Heart is also suggestively designated as the "womb" of matrika Shakti, a kind of cosmic incubator subsuming a vast reservoir of potential energy from which the phonemes, the as-yet-inarticulate sounds that eventually combine to comprise words, arise. At this level, however, all remains ineffable, unconditioned by time and space, in a realm beyond not only any particular meanings but beyond meaning itself.

From articulate words, in turn, language, and the world or worlds denoted or connoted by it, is unfolded. The words of which language is comprised, endlessly imbricated, endlessly ramifying, are like the pearls of like Indra's fabled necklace, each of which both reflects and is reflected by every other pearl. Any given language is itself a matrix of inexhaustible potential, comprising an infinite number of possible combinations and permutations of words, only an infinitesimal number of which are *actualized,* unfolded in either works of art or in the speech acts of individuals. When one considers not the subset of any particular language, but the set of all possible language, the mind boggles at what it cannot even begin to comprehend.

Yet even the words that are *actually* unfolded, whether written or spoken, from this inexhaustible source, remain charged with its power

Through the intelligence of the heart we are attuned to the resonance of the sacred, to the vibration of the primordial wordless word, as a result of which we become not only synchronous with, attuned to, ourselves, but also attuned to others, to the earth that we share, and to whatever realms lie beyond the earth. With time, this experience of attunement gives rise to an awareness, even if at first only temporary, of the essential, blissful unity of all things.

Abhinavagupta uses another technical term, *kechari*, which refers to an experience of the advanced yogi in deep meditation soaring through the infinite, indescribably luminous sky of the Heart. At the higher levels of Consciousness, the resonance and luminosity of which I have just spoken, and indeed sound and light themselves, the root of what will later become the word and its referent, are experienced as one. Each constantly, in a kind of divine reciprocity, gives rise to the other.

My preceptor's preceptor, unlike his prized disciple, was a man of few words. When he did speak it was often to reiterate one fundamental injunction: "The heart is the hub of all sacred places. Go there and roam." This injunction hints at what Abhinavagupta explicitly emphasizes, the centrality of the heart. It is from this pulsating center that all things, even our most apparently negative, frightening thoughts or experiences flow. If we are able to concentrate on the intensity and power of these experiences, of their essential nature as spanda, as the primordial vibration from which all things arise and into which they subside, they become not our masters but our servants, propelling us back to their ecstatic center and source.

Myriad and wondrous are the attributes of the intelligence of the heart!

It is the intelligence of the heart that sponsors freedom, *svatantrya*, that most cherished of Shaivite values, and that encourages in us a free play, unrestricted by habitual patterns of thought, that is one with the play of Consciousness itself. It sponsors, too, a kind of metaphysical humor, the trait so prominent in Jnaneshwar. Reading him, it is as though we are playing a game of hide and seek with both Shiva and Jnaneshwar himself who, ever concealing and revealing themselves, are constantly playing with us.

It is through the intelligence of the heart that we become as children again, that we experience the world, with awe and wonder, as though it were being created anew at every moment. Indeed, the word *chamatkara*, or wonder, is a key term in Abhinavagupta's aesthetics, which denotes not only the response of an open heart to the miraculous, ever-changing things of this world, to the whole spectacular sound and light show of Consciousness itself, but also more specifically the response of the same-hearted spectator or auditor to great works of art.

I have spoken of my youthful experience of being moved by poetry. And yet the poems that most moved me did not seem to generate in me any particular, identifiable emotion. They had a kind of refinement and power that seemed to connect me to a transpersonal, or supra-personal, feeling that at the same time seemed to underly all merely personal emotions. At the time I had no vocabulary with which to describe to myself this kind of feeling.

I now know that I was experiencing what Abhinavagupta called shanta rasa, the rasa which underlies all other rasas, all of the other feelings that a work of art may induce in us. Its nature is that of a kind of surpassing peace and bliss that Abhinavagupta explicitly identifies with the state of Lord Shiva himself. To awaken, as a same-hearted reader or spectator, to such a state, is to awaken to what I have been calling the intelligence of the heart. Same-hearted, of course, is another of Abhinavagupta's often repeated, technical—but more than merely technical—terms.

During my time at the ashram, my experience of meditation remained remarkably constant over the years. After about a half an hour my mind would become calm, whereupon I would feel a subtle stirring in my heart and in my throat. Technically, I was experiencing my heart chakra, which is yet another resonance of the word *heart*, here referring to one of the seven main nodes or centers of the subtle body that the Kundalini Shakti, awakened by the spiritual preceptor, purifies. The heart chakra is the center and seat of love. The throat chakra, I discovered, is the seat of the imagination, the wellspring of art and music, but especially of poetry.

For much of my time in the ashram my heart was open. I experienced a kind of quietly joyful love without an object. I also, in my scant spare time, was able to remain faithful to my vocation as a poet. In retrospect I can recognize how remarkably valuable these experiences were, surely as valuable as the flashier experiences of many of my fellow devotees which, for a time, I so ardently longed for.

Above all, the intelligence of the heart is the awareness of love, the love that Dante describes as moving all things, the source of the compassion that binds us together in a world experienced as a whole, as one with us, not as the shards of some explosion detonated by the disenfranchised head, the disenfranchised heart—a world of tragic delusion that is all too real, that is perpetuated by a specious casuistry that encourages us to embrace a pernicious, Manichaean dualism. A world that, perhaps now as much as ever, still cries out to be healed.

I have mentioned, or perhaps hinted, that throughout my life I have experienced profound, abrupt, and sometimes unaccountable shifts in my consciousness, the sudden onset of long periods of despair and agitation, and the equally sudden and unaccountable emergence from such states, which invariably felt like miraculous awakenings, experiences of rebirth, like lightening bolts of prajna radically resetting, rebooting my consciousness, my hellishly constricted frame of mind, inaugurating what would reliably manifest as periods of enhanced creativity and joy—before the darkness would yet again roll in, a darkness that is even now, as I write this, subsuming me.

How fondly, and sadly, I look upon the youth whom I once was, with his self-appointed task of merging, through poetry, the head and heart, and thereby doing something to heal the rifts of a torn and broken world.

That project still seems to me an entirely valid one.

Years later, when my voice was seized—and yes, inspired—as though by some daemonic other, I wrote a long narrative poem in the voice of Orpheus called "Talking Head." Ah, yes, Orpheus, the *ur* musician and *ur* poet, a kind of Greek Saint Francis, his lyre taming and pacifying not only nature but whatever ferocious beasts came his way. Few recall or know the end of his story. After he is dismembered by a band of oddly stately matrons, Orpheus' severed head, still alive, still conscious, and terribly destined to remain conscious, was tossed into the river Hebron, launched into a kind of posthumous existence like the death in life and life in death undergone by Coleridge's mariner, and likely experienced all too frequently by Coleridge himself.

In my youth I had written poems in which I had attempted to marry the head and the heart. Now I was writing a poem about their disastrous severing.

The poem now reads to me like a prefiguration of my present state, a kind of warning to myself. Written not long after 9/11, a prodigious, quasi-apocalyptic tearing and rending that took place less than a mile from my apartment, on the roof of which bits of what seemed like ticker tape smoldered and burned for hours, the poem is also, I think, an indictment of a world continually and sometimes abruptly, spasmodically, losing its collective mind.

But it is far from my intention to leave you with such an indictment, but rather to extol, one last time, the intelligence of the heart. Words that arise from that intelligence are, and will continue to be, available to us, and will retain the capacity to transform us even when the world, and the things of this world appear to us in the guise of a nightmare from which we cannot awaken.

Some Segments of a River

III. INESCAPABLE ROMANCE

1.
Keats' Middle Way and the Intelligence of the Heart

1.

In the following remarks, I wish to suggest that Keats is perhaps the truest exemplar among the English Romantic poets of one who instinctively, intuitively grasps both the inside of the self and the inside of the things of this world, and who then unfolds these intuitions—with the aid of his powerful, always questioning intellect—into always provisional but never less than powerful speculations about the nature of poetry and of the imagination. These speculations are given voice both in his letters and more obliquely in his poems. I will be concentrating on the former here, though I briefly address the latter as well.

In the second chapter of the second section of this book, I cited a passage by Wordsworth that exemplifies a kind of third or middle way threading itself between subjective idealism on the one hand and objective materialism on the other. Keats, however, in his famous letter discussing "negative capability," regards Wordsworth as more typically an avatar of the egotistical sublime, a mode of discourse in which everything is referred back to and attaches itself to the self or the ego of the author, which is thus prone to a kind of sublime dilation. The ego, the "I," thus dilated, can become overweening, overbearing. Wordsworth's poetry of the egotistical sublime is prone, too, to waxing didactic and often has, as Keats says, too obvious designs upon the reader, designs that too insistently dictate to him or her the requisite responses. Though "The Prelude" contains surpassingly beautiful moments in which self and other interpenetrate each other on equal terms, it contains more passages—many still beautiful, still formidable—that justify Keats' respectful indictment. During the writing of "The Prelude," Wordsworth was dependent upon Coleridge's subjective idealism, largely pilfered from German Romantic metaphysicians and from Schelling in particular, to furnish its philosophical framework.

Keats' notion of negative capability is an antidote to the egotistical sublime, to the shortcomings of subjective idealism. Negative capability, famously, involves tolerating being in "uncertainties, mysteries, doubts without any irritable reaching after fact or reason." Its greatest exemplar was Shakespeare, whom Keats steadfastly wished to emulate. It is the characteristic of the imagination to receive intimations, glimpses of, and much more rarely full-fledged insights into both the nature of the self and of the things of this world. "Consequitive [sic] reasoning," on the other hand, whether deployed to buttress objective materialism or subjective idealism, does not rest until it arrives at what it imagines to be certainty.

Keats regarded Coleridge's philosophical obsessions as inimical to the imagination, and thus as responsible for Coleridge's abandonment of poetry—or of poetry's abandonment of him. Keats writes of Coleridge that he would "let go by a fine, isolated verisimilitude caught from the Penetralium of mystery, from being incapable of remaining content with half-knowledge." We recall here Stevens' depiction of the imagination as dealing with the half color of quarter things. Writing about his friend Dilke, Keats complains that Dilke's sense of identity is bound up with making up his mind, with coming to a definitive decision about even trivial matters. On the contrary, according to Keats, the only means of strengthening one's intellect is to make up one's mind about nothing—to let the mind be "a thoroughfare for all thoughts."

Consecutive, rule-bound, syllogistic reasoning, on the other hand, is a mere subset of reason, let alone of the intellect. It arrives at a limited kind of certainty by establishing whether discrete propositions are true or false. Such reasoning has its place, but it should be clear that when Keats uses the term *truth* he is not referring to binary propositional truths. The intellect more broadly addresses itself to the experiential truths which consecutive reasoning cannot grasp, and upon which it can make no definitive pronouncements. When syllogistic reasoning attempts to poach upon this broader arena, the results are inevitably, all too predictably, falsifying and reductive. Keats states that he does not perceive (a word which he characteristically uses where one might expect conceive) how consecutive reasoning, with its binary propositional truths marching in lockstep in a sequence determined in advance by arbitrarily privileged axioms, postulates, or first principles, and with its categorical, conceptual constructs that reify, pigeonhole and freeze the objects of an always external world, can get at the broader truths of human experience.

As an undergraduate, I studied with the great Keats scholar Walter Jackson Bate, who remains a cogent and reliable exegete of the tensions in Keats between consecutive reason and the imagination. In *Negative Capability: The Intuitive Approach in Keats,* he writes:

> "Consequitive reasoning" is the power of categorizing and representing objects as externally related to each other. It is almost *quantitative*, so to speak, embracing what is measurable. It is mediate, in contrast with the Imagination which is intuitive and immediate; it analyzes rather than synthesizes... It is essentially an outward view of phenomena... The Imagination is the direct opposite; it looks inward, grasping by an effort of sympathy and intuition the hidden intention and reality of life.

To Bate's account, which culminates by postulating the kind of creative intuition that I have been examining in this volume, I would like to add one caveat. Once again I must confess that the word *interiority* is problematic. It implies an inward motion of consciousness that fastens upon the subjective pole of experience, on the ego, and particularly on the ego that, as in Wordsworth and Coleridge, is inflated into the egotistical sublime, which philosophically aligns itself with subjective idealism. Rather, I am envisaging arriving at a state bypassing the ego and its fixed identity, a state that is characterized by a highly-charged awareness that includes and transcends, while wending its way between both the subjective and the objective. This state of awareness —as previously discussed—can be arrived at either by turning inward in meditation or contemplation, or by turning outward in ecstatic identification with the things of this world. And so I do not agree with Bate that the outward view is the opposite of the inward one, but regard each as implicated in the other.

Indeed, though he subjected himself to an enforced isolation and contemplation in writing "Endymion," and though he turned to a more contemplative mode in his most mature work, Keats seemed almost constitutionally inclined to revel in the things of this world. In one of his earliest letters Keats exclaimed, "O, for a Life of Sensations rather than of Thoughts!"

Much has been written of the extraordinary sensuousness of Keats' language and of his depictions of the world. And indeed virtually every page of his poetry or prose reflects the intense aliveness of his senses, not just the senses of sight and hearing, but of touch and taste as well. Keats' senses were exquisitely, passively open to experience, but they were also unusually active and intentional, keenly deployed, moving out into the world to touch their objects.

It is the default position of many to view the senses as simply passive, impinged upon by the things of this world. It is Keats' contention, to the contrary, that the structure of perception is intentional, that the mind carves out of the sensory manifold that which it perceives, which usually involves carving out and perceiving that which it has perceived before. Our perceptions tend to become a closed loop, so fixed, repetitive, and habitual, and finally unconscious that we fail to realize that they are intentional at all.

Keats stresses the intentionality of perception not only in man but in animals. In a particularly vivid passage, he writes:

> The greater part of Men make their way with the same [intuitive, intentional] instinctiveness, the same unwandering eye from their purposes, the same animal eagerness as the Hawk...I go among the Fields and catch a glimpse of a Stoat or a fieldmouse peeping out of the withered grass—the creature hath a purpose, and its eyes are bright with it.

Bate, a student of Bergson, stresses the homology between instinct and intuition, but I think it is more important to stress their differences. It is Keats, and those few men and women like him, not "the greater part of men," who have the capacity, the negative capability, to observe a stoat or a field mouse with an extraordinary intuitive sympathy bordering on identification, with an ecstatic going out of the self. Perceiving the world instinctively and perceiving it intuitively both involve immediacy and directness, but only in man, and only in those men and women who have been fortunate enough—and who have been willing to work hard enough—to develop beyond what is merely instinctual, habitual, and unconscious in their nature, does such perception become fully conscious. Such consciousness is not instinctive; it arises only after one has stripped away the habitual concepts, emotional presuppositions, and oppressive quotidian routines that reify the sensory manifold, obscuring a world that is essentially vital, dynamic. This stripping away involves becoming more and more conscious as one's identity becomes less and less fixed and defined.

The immediacy of the world perceived through the senses, rather than the world perceived as mediated, often unconsciously, by concepts, accords with the immediacy and clarity of the world perceived imaginatively through creative intuition. Negative capability has much in common with the Taoist notion of *wu wei*, in which the ego is content to get out of the way, to allow thing to unfold in accordance with the Tao. Rather than interfering with the perception of things as they are, wu wei grants an unmediated access to them. Negative capability accords too, with what in previous discussions of Chinese and Japanese poetry I have called "the poem as pure percept." The writing of such poems required a highly refined and disciplined mind, and many of these poems were embedded, as we have seen, in larger structures. But for Keats as a Western poet, the intellect, too, the intellect that is a "thoroughfare of all ideas," including abstract ideas, must be as open and alive as the senses, and all of its resources are required in translating creative intuition into finely articulate poems, which are themselves charged with a unique identity.

Such an intellect, when not only "schooled by the heart" but wedded to it, operates close to the quick of the energy of the imagination, an energy that lovingly draws together subject and object, the inner side of the self and the inner side of the things of this world. It is to this schooling, after a brief interlude, that I shall turn.

2.

Before proceeding further with matters theoretical, I would first like to look at the unusually large role that the objectively material played in Keats' life—unusual, that is, in comparison with most great English poets, who have tended to be safely ensconced in the upper middle class, like Shelley, or more rarely, like Byron, in the upper class. Keats' father, the owner of a stable, died when Keats was young. His inheritance was put in the hands of a trustee who was excessively cautious and chary in doling out funds. It was clear that Keats would have to earn a trade, make a living. After a particularly happy time at what we would call secondary or high school, during which he received a solid education and his imagination became deeply stirred by literature, Keats apprenticed himself to a surgeon, which required both intensive, objective study of human anatomy and practical experience in the form of dressing patients' wounds and the tortuously painful process of resetting bones. These experiences put him in direct contact with the intractability of human pain and suffering, sometimes as its necessary cause, a contact later cruelly augmented by the experience of taking care of his brother Tom as he was dying of tuberculosis.

It is impossible to gauge how harrowing this responsibility must have been for him, considering Keats' propensity for an empathic identification with others and his deep bond with all of his brothers.

The objectively real, for Keats, also involved his small physical stature (he was only five feet tall) and more importantly, the social class into which he was born. The response of Byron and the Tory establishment to Keats and to his poetic confreres, the circle that formed around the politically progressive Leigh Hunt, whom they contemptuously dubbed "Cockney poets," was one of outrage not only at their political ideas but at their pretentious dabbling in an avocation that was clearly above their station. More fundamentally, their antipathy took the form of an almost physical revulsion toward such poets, who were considered, by virtue of their class, vulgar voluptuaries, incapable of linguistic, intellectual, or imaginative refinement. This revulsion was reflected, for example, in Byron's references to Keats as a "tadpole" and a "mankin," and as an onanistic, masturbatory "frigger of the imagination." Much worse flowed from the pens of lesser Tory reviewers of Keats' first book, which was published after his risky decision to abandon his apprenticeship.

Byron, of course, as Lord Byron, had far more scope for the consummation of his libidinous impulses than did Keats, and he was an arch-seducer. Both men and women, and even his half sister, were prey to his capricious advances, though his unpredictable psychopathic rages were primarily reserved for women. His contempt for Keats was in part that of a man of carnal knowledge who recognized that Keats had none, and that therefore his poetic epiphanies of sensual gratification were in fact onanistic fantasies without basis in experience. But something darker was operating as well. Byron, though physically beautiful, was also painfully deformed by a clubbed foot, and was ever aware of and ever embittered by this deformity, which he came to regard as something like the mark of Cain. Thus Byron fastened on Keats' own physical vulnerability, his diminutive stature, as a point open to attack. Byron himself, though strikingly lacking in empathy for individual others, was an odd hybrid of idealism, championing the cause of the downtrodden, and dissolute hedonism. He had something about him of the allure of a daemonic fallen angel. Though he, like Keats and Shelley, died relatively young, his death was more pathetic than tragic.

Just as Byron pronounced judgement on Keats, Keats pronounced judgement on Byron. Keats wrote that Byron merely depicted and transcribed that which he saw and experienced, whereas he, Keats, depicted what he freshly imagined. In Coleridge's terms, Keats thought of himself as a poet of the imagination and of Byron as a poet of mere fancy.

Keats' ambivalent relationship with Shelley is also instructive. Shelley, very much the scion of a wealthy upper-class, though not a noble, family, still clung, even in his impetuous renunciation of that family, to a sense of his aristocratic prerogatives. As a young man he had the coddled aristocrat's arrogant certainty of his own moral impregnability. In the name of lofty and abstract political and social ideals he inflicted appalling cruelties on others, particular women, whom he was first attracted to, then banished from his circle. Much of his poetry had a powerful, idealizing, Neoplatonic strain, engendering exquisite if airy productions like "Episychidion." These unworldly and willful idealisms reflected Shelley's contemptuous impatience with mundane human affairs. Shelley, tempered by suffering, grew greatly as a man and a poet, but Keats, despite the kindness and respect that Shelley extended to him, was never really able to admire or appreciate him or his poems, and experienced him as inadvertently condescending. Ironically, "Adonais," Shelley's great elegy on Keats, was perhaps the most fully realized of Shelley's platonizing lyrics. Keats, from whatever perch in heaven, must have felt nonplussed by being so summarily snatched up into the "white radiance of eternity."

Keats, unlike Shelley or Byron, was thoroughly baptized in all of the ways described above, in the objectively real and its conditions. He was therefore immunized against the untethered flights of idealism. At the same time, he was too much a poet to see the world as merely objectively material—a position that even more than subjective idealism tends to reify reality, to fix the essentially dynamic, and moreover to render it stonily impervious to human values. Keats, then, was predisposed to seek a new way—tentative, provisional, constantly probing—between subjective idealism and objective realism, a kind of third or middle way that now passes under the general rubric of "negative capability" but includes much else besides.

3.

In what, then—beyond the ability to remain in mysteries and doubts, free of the falsifying and reductive incursions of fact and reason—does what I am calling Keats' middle way consist? It consists, in large part, in recognizing the imagination as the way of love, and as entailing the recognition of the kinds of truth that such a way pursues. Such truths can never be ugly; they always entail, for Keats, an apprehension of the beautiful.

At the outset of this discussion I would like to refer back to my prior discussion of poetry among other art forms as being particularly well situated to effectuate the marriage of the head and the heart, to serve as a model of the generative nature of consciousness when neither heart nor mind are hypertrophied, when both work together. In Western culture, again, it is the head that tends to be hypertrophied, leading to some of the disastrous consequences outlined earlier.

Keats's poetic project, more than that of any other poet in this volume, is fundamentally and consciously concerned with the effectuation of a marriage between the intelligence of the heart and that of the mind. It is through the imagination that the medium of poetry, language itself, raised to a higher power, realizes its potential as preeminently well situated to engender such a union.

In Keats' earliest reference in his letters to such matters, he writes,

> I am certain of nothing but the holiness of the heart's affections and the truth of the Imagination—what the Imagination seizes as on beauty must be truth—whether it existed before or not…The imagination may be compared to Adam's dream—he awoke and found it truth.

Here we have in embryo the Keatsian association of the imagination with love, beauty, and truth—with love, the holiness of the heart's affections, as a crucial term. I will return to this key passage later, but Keats' view of love, of the schooling of the intellect by the heart, receives perhaps its finest, most mature treatment in his famous letter to his brother George, including a well-known passage on the "Vale of Soul-Making."

This letter is extraordinarily dense, and I cannot do it justice here but must emphasize those aspects of it that are most relevant to the context of the current discussion. There is quite a long preamble in the letter, often overlooked, to the passage on the vale of soul-making itself. The thrust of this whole passage is to acknowledge the exigencies of what I have been calling objective reality as they inevitably impinge upon man. Keats, quoting Shakespeare in *King Lear*, says that initially man in relation to nature is a "bare, forked animal." Man, as embodied in himself, is both a part of objective reality and subject to its vicissitudes. As he improves his position, adjusts to reality, attains something like happiness, fresh annoyances and hindrances present themselves. And still there remains one final, unavoidable objective reality to be confronted. Keats writes, "I can imagine such happiness carried to an extreme—what must it end in? —Death—and who could in such a case bear with death?" Death, as we shall see, eventually becomes for Keats the final term, affecting all the others, in the series of terms that Keats associated with the imagination.

As an embodied being dwelling in a material world and subject to its vicissitudes, man can never achieve perfect felicity. "In truth I do not at all believe in this kind of perfectibility—the nature of the world will not admit of it—the inhabitants of the world will correspond to itself."

Conceding that such a viewpoint corresponds to the conventional notion of life as a vale of tears, Keats launches into more life-affirming speculations about the education of the intellect and of the soul. Keats begins by admitting, as a heuristic principle useful to his speculations, not as a belief, the notion of God, and in speaking now in the "highest terms for human nature," he similarly provisionally admits nature to be immortal. We enter the world as "intelligences," as "sparks of divinity," as sparks that are God but that are as yet inchoate, unformed, atoms of the barest sentience, lacking in any identity. Through their experience in the vale of soul-making what were mere inchoate intelligences become unique, realized identities, become souls.

How is this accomplished? Through the interaction of "the Intelligence—the human heart (as distinct from the mind or intelligence)—and the World or Elemental space as suited for the proper action of the Mind and Heart on each other." The interaction of these three elements is ideally suited to the "purpose of forming Soul or Intelligence destined to possess the sense of identity." It is the heart which is "the Mind's Bible, it is the Mind's experience, it is the teat from which the Mind or Intelligence sucks its identity." The elemental world provides the circumstances, the experiences, that enable this interaction between heart and mind.

> and what are circumstances?—but touchstones of his heart?—and what are touch stones?—but provings of his heart?—and what are provings of his heart but fortifiers or alterers of his nature? and what is his altered nature but his soul?

Through its experiences in the vale of soul-making, both painful and joyous, what was originally a mere spark of intelligence becomes a fully realized, unique identity that is capable of experiencing the love that is proper to it, and that ultimately returns to God as a fully distinctive soul. Finally, out of the experience of being concretely embodied, out of the experience of the elemental world and its vicissitudes, of which experiences of sorrow, loss, and pain are unavoidable, the soul or spirit as a realized identity, no longer restricted only to the objective and material, emerges, comes into being. I have been at pains throughout to stress that, due to his life experiences and social position and no doubt his temperament as well, Keats is never cavalier about the objective world. It is only by being forged in the crucible of that world that the spirit realizes itself.

I have just noted that the achievement of a realized identity is the goal of man's sojourn in the vale of soul-making. And yet, speaking of himself and of his vocation as a poet, Keats writes in his letter on negative capability,

> As to the poetical Character itself (I mean that sort of which, if I am anything, I am a Member, that sort distinguished from the Wordsworthian or egotistical sublime; which is a thing per se...) it is not itself—it has no self—it is every thing and nothing ...A Poet is the most unpoetical of any thing in existence; because he has no Identity...

We are confronted with an apparent paradox. It appears that the identity of the poet is to have no identity. But Keats is not guilty of sophistry here. He is not suggesting that a poet is a mere cypher or blank. The poet, rather, is analogous to the Buddhist or Hindu or Taoist sage whose realization, far from theoretical, is that they have no fixed identity. They perceive the world and the things of this world clearly, uncategorically, directly, immediately, intuitively, and consciously, unclouded by unconscious habitual concepts or presuppositions. Keats writes that when free from the speculations of his own brain, when in a thought-free, meditative state, which was apparently quite often the case, he was "continually in for and filling some other body." In such states, he writes, "not myself goes home to myself: but the identity of everyone in the room begins so to press upon me that I am in a very little time annihilated." In the act pure perception, unclouded by thought, the sense of oneself as separate, isolated ego vanishes, is temporarily annihilated.

How does one who has no fixed identity experience the world? Precisely because he has no fixed identity, the poet or saint is able, like the Taoist sage, to recognize the identity of the things of this world. Each man or woman's realization of his or her identity is, as we have seen, the ultimate achievement in an individual's sojourn in the vale of soul making. A thing's or a person's identity, that which it uniquely, qualitatively is, whether a rose in full bloom or a particular human being's uniquely characteristic mode of being, is of paramount value for Keats. Seeing a thing's or person's identity, which Buddhists call *suchness*, is to see it qualitatively, is to experience it as uniquely and intrinsically valuable.

Crucially, again, it is the poet's lack of a fixed identity that allows him to venture out of himself, to gently grasp, to apprehend his identity with the things of this world. The soul's intentional, avid moving out of itself, its glorying in, its intuitive, direct, immediate embrace of the other as other, its acknowledgement of the other as uniquely itself, is the soul's and the imagination's movement of love, its greeting of the spirit through which mysteriously the things of this world come into their own, and through which human others are encouraged to become, if only for a time, unique, essential versions of themselves.

Shelley writes, in a passage from "The Defense of Poetry" with which Keats would have concurred:

> The great secret of morals is love, or a going out of our nature, and an identification of ourselves with the beautiful which exists in thought, action, or person, not our own...The great instrument of moral good is the imagination.

In the early letter cited above, Keats says that "the imagination is like Adam's dream; he awoke to find it truth." Such truths are deemed valid, "whether or not they existed before." The imagination is thus potentially productive of new truths, new realizations. It is not difficult to conceive of the imagination of the inventor, for example, as productive of new actualities. The imagination of the greatest of scientists is likewise productive of insights that alter our conception of what is true of reality, and proposes, as it were, new truths that are then objectively verified. But in what sense are the imaginative productions of the artist, which seem mere airy fabrications, true, and why are these truths, for Keats, always connected with beauty?

The imagination is characterized by Keats as instinct not only with a heightened awareness but with love and joy. What the imagination seizes upon or identifies with, it apprehends lovingly, and when apprehended lovingly the essential truth, the inner side of a thing, is revealed, often as though for the first time. What is thus apprehended lovingly, and with the full force of the imagination, cannot be apprehended otherwise than as beautiful, and the consummate artistic expressions of such truths likewise cannot be other than beautiful even when, as we shall see, they involve the tragic.

Keats statement near the end of the "Ode to a Grecian Urn," "Beauty is Truth, Truth Beauty," seemed to the New Critics, and would likely still seem to anyone of a positivist bent, a kind of scandal. Clearly, from their perspective, the sentence as it stands is mere nonsense. Ingenious New Critical attempts were made to rehabilitate it, such as stressing the putative proposition's dramatic propriety in the context of the poem as a whole. But Keats' assertion, of course, is not a logical proposition but a strange species of metaphor. To equate beauty with truth is to equate a felt quality with the mother of all abstractions. Some perspicuous critic has noted that Stevens felt his thoughts, that for him thinking was a mode of feeling. This is perhaps true of all genuine poets, the more so if poetry is recognized as a discourse ideally suited to effectuate a marriage of the head and the heart. It is quintessentially true of Keats. And it was both quintessentially and broadly, extensively, from the most unreachable heights to the fathomless depths, true of Shakespeare, Keats' "great presider." Perhaps because I *do* view poetry as a discourse ideally situated as a marriage of the head and the heart, I have always instinctively accepted Keats proposition/metaphor at face value. I have no problem with it. Indeed, I concur with it, if one can concur with a metaphor. Or perhaps I assent to it as the expression of an existential truth that has at different times been proved "upon my own pulses." That poets think differently, sometimes subtly differently, from philosophers does not, of course, mean that they do not think or that their thinking is invalid.

Keats, falsely accused by some as indulging, all too often, in a kind of escapism, seems on the contrary never to have lost an awareness of suffering as an inescapable aspect of being embodied in the flesh and being embedded in the natural world. He never, as I have been at pains to suggest, gives objective reality short shrift. Like Nagarjuna, he does not attempt to logically reconcile subjective idealism and objective realism. He realizes that the real and the ideal can never, at least in this world, be fully reconciled, just as man can never fully attain perfectibility. Granting primacy neither to subjective idealism nor to objective realism and giving neither, as at least in part abstractions, the status of reality, Keats, like Nagarjuna, situates himself between them. Nagarjuna arrives philosophically at a place characterized by a radical not knowing, the absence of any epistemological or ontological certainty, the very certainty that Keats, in his discussion of negative capability, disavows from the outset. From this place of uncertainty, love is hazarded. Love has nothing to do with the overweening ego of subjective idealism. It has the rare capacity to transcend the self-interestedness, however sublime, of the ego, and to largely dissolve it, while at the same time recognizing the so-called material world as well as human beings as alive and instinct with spirit, as genuinely other, and as having the prerogatives of the genuinely other. Love's path, the path between subjective idealism and a reductive materialism, is contingent, subject to vicissitudes of this world and leads to no state of ultimate felicity. It is a path to be followed moment by moment for its own sake, not from some misguided ulterior motive. Keats, again, never expected his consummate moments of imaginative fulfillment, with their accompanying strengthening and liberation of the soul, to be ultimately and definitively reconciled with the sometimes brutal exigencies of the objective world, including the exigency of being embodied and subject to the thousand natural shocks that flesh is heir to.

Keats' recognition that the spirit can never be truly reconciled to the very world that has schooled it is shared by Shelley (although Shelley lacks Keats' respect for the material) and to a lesser degree by Wordsworth. It differentiates Keats both from Blake and more significantly from Coleridge and from his German mentors. The burden of the first phase of German Romanticism, primarily the work of philosophers (including the work of Schelling, from whom Coleridge drew, or plagiarized, many of his philosophical ideas), was an attempt to reconcile these apparent opposites, to reveal natural philosophy and subjective idealism as inextricably related to each other, and to systematically delineate, by means of consecutive reasoning, a rapprochement that such reasoning is by its very nature woefully ill suited to achieve.

Of course, the final gift or curse of the real to which we cannot fully reconcile ourselves is, again, death. Death, for Keats, was quite possibly simply annihilation—though at the same time its true nature remained ultimately, radically unknowable, at least to the living.

In one of his earliest poems, Keats implored the muses, somewhat strangely, for a mere ten years in which he could devote himself to poetry. In fact he was vouchsafed far fewer. One senses that Keats somehow sensed, even before contracting tuberculosis, that his life, like his brother Tom's, would not be a long one. It is as though the pressure of impending death was felt throughout his poetic career, contributing to its intense urgency. Death, for Keats, became, as previously mentioned, the final term in his imaginative triad of love, beauty, and truth, contributing to the extraordinary poignancy of his work, a poignancy that became even more prominent when Keats finally experienced, with the first signs of tuberculosis, the summons of an imminent death. Such a disease, a final, terrible objective reality, could not, again, be reconciled with Keats' imagination, with its contemplative or ecstatic experiences, the expressions of a love that was about to be snuffed out, that would never be consummated on the earthly plane.

4.

The scope of this essay does nor permit me to address, except in the most broadly generalizing terms, Keats' poems, but it would be, if not a crime, at least a misdemeanor, not to refer to them, if only briefly.

Of course, given the near fusion in Keats of the imagination and love, he was more attracted to romance as a genre (from his important testing of his fledgling poetic wings in "Endymion," an uneven venture that nonetheless occasionally soars; to the consummate, ecstatic expression of romance as a genre that is the "Eve of St. Agnes"; to the mysterious evocation of a darker side of romance that is hinted at in "Isabella" and more fully realized in "La Belle Dame Sans Merci"; and finally to the suave, bitter perversion of romance that is "Lamia") than was any other major Romantic poet. His first teacher was Edmund Spencer, and Keats' poetry never entirely abandoned his affiliation with romance.

Keats, though an eminently sociable poet, also recognized the vital role that solitude played in poetic creation. It had always been a part of his temperament as a poet. "Endymion," Keats' first full-fledged effort as a poet, though in general maintaining the light, fanciful, wayward tone of romance, was in fact undertaken as an exercise with high stakes. Keats demanded of himself that he write a long narrative poem consisting of four books. The poem was to be written in complete solitude, calling for an unbroken contemplative absorption, during a month's sojourn on the Isle of Wight—a circumstance chosen entirely consciously to enact a kind of testing or proving of Keats' heart insofar as it pertained to his vocation as a poet.

As the circumstances of his life darkened Keats produced, as I have just indicated, increasingly troubled and troubling versions of romance, like his compelling lyric "La Belle Dame Sans Merci," which is a kind of wasteland in miniature, in which the beloved female figure of romance becomes, if not a figure of death itself, at least deathly, an agent of sterility, paralyzing the once-heroic figure of the knight who now merely loiters, turning pale, as he declines toward death. Perhaps too, "La Belle Dame Sans Merci" suggests the ravages of a love—that of Keats for Fanny Brawn—that was destined to remain unconsummated.

We are here at a far, antithetical remove, it would seem, from Keats' consummate realization of romance as a genre in "The Eve of Saint Agnes," in whose penultimate stanza Porphyro, after surmounting myriad challenges, enters Madeleine' chamber, a scene that is a feast of synesthesia, in which all the senses are evoked, engaged, and satisfied, not cruelly mortified. In my memory of the poem, it ended here. Rereading it, I was reminded that in the poem's concluding stanza Poryphyro and Madeleine, without explanation, exit the safe confines of her chamber and brave the howling winter storm that rages outside, reminiscent of the storm on the heath in King Lear. It is not given to us to know where they are headed. A foreshadowing, perhaps, of things to come.

Keats' odes, arguably the greatest lyric poems in the English language, are, like his romances, increasingly shadowed, though less bitterly, by intimations of mortality that are expressions, as well, of an increasingly tragic view of life. But they are also ever deeper expressions of interiority. They are reflective of the meditative, contemplative movement of Keats' consciousness, are quintessential expressions of the inner side of the subject drawing close to the inner side of things—whether to a Grecian urn, to a nightingale, or to the experiential and sensory essence of autumn, its vitality poignantly flaring even while fading. The contemplative movement of consciousness can have an essential quietness to it, as in Keats' contemplation of the Grecian urn, through which, almost rapt out of time, he achieves, if only for a time, a kind of silent communion with the timeless. Sometimes it can be signaled by a kind of drowsiness or drowsing off, a state that Keats calls "indolence," as in the case not only in his "Ode on Indolence" but more powerfully in the "Ode to a Nightingale," in which the poet's consciousness, half dreaming, turns outward and identifies with the source of song.

Increasingly, as mentioned above, the shadow of mortality darkens and deepens Keats' poetry. In the "Ode to a Nightingale," the drowsiness, the state between dream and waking that I have described, is associated with "easeful death," a death to which the speaker of the poem seems subliminally attracted. This constantly increasing awareness of death is, again, the final term in the imaginative complex of love /truth / beauty in Keats' work. It intensifies all of the other terms which, in their evanescence, attain an almost unbearable poignancy. With Keats' own awareness that an early and painful death was in store for him, his shift toward concern with the tragic naturally intensified.

This concern, which began to work itself out in the odes, more fully preoccupies Keats in his abortive attempts to write epic poems that depart from the spirit of romance. Keats, it seems, had a strong sense of the proper unfolding of the career of a great poet. After having written his romances and his odes, Keats was keenly aware that two very difficult stages, two genres of poetry, both characterized by a high seriousness, the epic and the tragic, remained to be assayed. In turning to epic, he naturally turned to Milton, who progressed in his poetic career from lyric poems, culminating in "Lycidas," to his great epic, "Paradise Lost," and finally, in "Sampson Agonistes," to tragedy. In "Hyperion," Keats' model is Milton. He adopts some of Milton's mannerisms, not only his twisting of syntax, his famous Miltonic inversions, but also Milton's exquisite stationing and vivid framing of his characters. The opening scene of "Hyperion," depicting the fall of Saturn, is marmoreal in its finality and its stasis. It is Satan's tragic fall that is Keats' true subject. As soon as the poem turns to a triumphant Apollo it loses energy and is soon abandoned.

Keats also realized that he needed to free himself from Milton's sound and syntax, to discover a voice more distinctively his own. In "The Fall of Hyperion," his second attempt at an epic poem on the same theme, Keats turned for inspiration from Milton to Dante, and to the dream vision that had always been a feature of Christian poetry, disclosing worlds more real than the quotidian world of the waking state, visions in which vital transformative insights or glimpses of a future, eternal felicity are typically vouchsafed to the dreamer.

After drinking, ingesting a potion, the speaker of "The Fall of Hyperion" drowses off, then awakens to a dream realm that seems more intensely real than the experience of waking consciousness. This drinking/ drowsing, as mentioned, is a typically Keatsian trope. Crucially, however, in this instance Keats awakens into a dream that is initially a scene of desolation, of strewn refuse testifying to the recent rout of the old order of gods, rather than of felicity. As his dream vision unfolds, Keats eventually encounters the mysterious, hieratic figure of Moneta, a spectral, almost deathly moon goddess who is at once a dispenser of commandments, a keen judger of souls, and an oracular sibyl.

Unfortunately, I must quote selectively from a long passage whose beauty and power constitutes perhaps Keats most sublime achievement in narrative poetry, a narrative that is instinct with the intensity of lyric. It is Keats' most concentrated treatment of a question that had long troubled him: what was the essential nature of the role of the poet?

After surveying the scene of majestic desolation just described, Keats is eventually led to the steps of the temple of the Goddess. Through the curtains that veil her already spectral face, Keats hears, as though twice removed, her stern words—injunctions, commands, urgent calls to action. Whether or not Keats accomplishes the task enjoined by her is a matter of life and death. And indeed in responding to it Keats endures all the stages leading up to such a death. Through a tremendous effort of will Keats manages to reach the lowest step that leads to the temple. Only by reaching a kind of nadir does ascent become possible. Only by experiencing what is tantamount to death does his rebirth as a true poet become possible.

> "If thou canst not ascend
> These steps, die on that marble where thou art.
> Thy flesh, near cousin to the common dust,
> Will parch for lack of nutriment; thy bones
> Will wither in few years, and vanish so
> That not the quickest eye could find a grain
> Of what thou now art on that pavement cold.
> The sands of thy short life are spent this hour,
> And no hand in the universe can turn
> Thy hourglass, if these gummed leaves be burnt
> Ere thou canst mount up these immortal steps."

> I heard, I look'd: two senses both at once,
> So fine, so subtle, felt the tyranny
> Of that fierce threat and the hard task proposed.
> Prodigious seem'd the toil, the leaves were yet
> Burning, when suddenly a palsied chill
> Struck from the paved level up my limbs,
> And was ascending quick to put cold grasp
> Upon those streams that pulse beside the throat.
> I shriek'd, and the sharp anguish of my shriek
> Stung my own ears. I strove hard to escape
> The numbness; strove to gain the lowest step.
> Slow, heavy, deadly was my pace: the cold
> Grew stifling, suffocating, at the heart;
> And when I clasp'd my hands I felt them not.
> One minute before death my iced foot touch'd
> The lowest stair; and as it touch'd, life seem'd
> To pour in at the toes: I mounted up
> As once fair angels on a ladder flew
> From the green turf to Heaven. ...

Having reached, through experiencing great depths, these heights, the speaker of the poem is granted an extended audience with Moneta, who assumes her role as an oracular sibyl. His immediate concern is to determine why he has been singled out to experience such an audience. The speaker, having just successfully responded to Moneta's command and as a result, having passed her test, has "felt / What 'tis to die and live again before / Thy fated hour." He thus becomes privy to the mysteries of the Goddess, of the sibyl. Keats' own sense of having experienced what it to confront one's mortality, and yet to live on, need not be belabored here.

Moneta continues to dutifully answer the speaker's questions. Prompted by Keats' continued perplexity as to why he alone is standing on the steps of her otherwise deserted temple, Moneta discriminates between three classes of men. The first are those who by a failure of love, of imaginative sympathy, "thoughtless sleep away their days," remain unconcerned with those suffering from the travails of this world. The second, to the contrary, are those "to whom the miseries of the world / are misery, and will not let them rest," and who actively, directly, pragmatically strive to better man's state. The first class are absent from the scene because were they to profane the temple's steps they would immediately "rot and perish." But why would men of the second class, the speaker wonders, not be granted the vision that the speaker is granted? Why are those "Who love their fellows even to the death; / Who feel the giant agony of the world" and who "like slaves to poor humanity / Labour for mortal good" not granted access to the steps of Moneta's temple? Moneta replies that not being dreamers or visionaries, who constitute the third class of men, but practical servants of the general good, the thought of a temple such as Moneta's does not and need not even occur to them. Hence they, although diametrical opposites of the callous minions of the first class of men, likewise do not haunt the precincts of the temple.

Keats quite naturally continues to wonder about the nature of the class of men to which he belongs, and about why he, unlike the practical benefactors of man, is granted an audience with Moneta. To which the Goddess/sibyl responds:

> ...thou art here, for thou art less than they.
> What benefit canst thou do, or all thy tribe
> To the great world? Thou art a dreaming thing,
> A fever of thyself.

The term, "a fever of thyself," as well as multiple concomitant references to chills, cannot help but resonate with the fever and chills of illness, particularly and concretely with the fever that destroyed Keats' brother Tom and was to destroy Keats himself. But it also suggests that to be a dreamer or visionary is itself to suffer from a kind of illness. Moneta anatomizes the ways in which the dreamer and visionary can never be at home in the world, can never hope to experience the bliss proper to it. Again, "the greatest poverty is not to live / in a physical world, to feel that one's desire / is too difficult to tell from despair." Moneta declares,

> Only the dreamer venoms all his days,
> Bearing more woe than all his sins deserve.
> Therefore, that happiness be somewhat shared
> Such things as thou art are admitted oft
> Into like gardens thou didst pass erewhile
> And suffer'd in these temples: for that cause
> Thou standest safe beneath this statue's knees.

Dreams, once again, are hardly associated with felicity. On the contrary. It is precisely the dreams of the visionary, his impotent longing for some other state or condition, that prevent him from reconciling with the world, from finding a home in it. As with the poet of Shelley's "Alastor," whose dreams goad him first into a wilderness of solitude, and finally to extinction, and as with Shelley himself, whose feverish imaginings of some platonic realm of beatitude led him to feel contempt for the world, the dreams of the visionary ultimately become the subtle instruments of his own torture, and are associated with illness and death, not life.

The visionary, who is at least attuned to human suffering, is superior to the first class of men, those who are callously impervious to it, but is inferior to the second, to those who, sadly reconciled to the suffering of the world, devote themselves practically to alleviating it. The third class of men, the dreamers and visionaries, those not at home in the world, are by no means malefactors and therefore are deserving, according to Moneta, of at least some measure of happiness. Appropriately, that happiness is afforded by the temporary realization of their visions, such as the very dream or vision that the speaker is experiencing, and which Moneta herself, pale and spectral, the lone survivor in a scene of devastation, hardly herself bursting with vitality, seems particularly charged with granting.

Interestingly, it is the speaker himself who envisages a fourth class of men:

> ...tell me: sure not all
> Those melodies sung into the world's ear
> Are useless: sure a poet is a sage;
> A humanist, physician to all men.

Moneta replies to this question by affirming what the speaker already knows, that he is a mere dreamer and visionary, but in doing so she affirms that the true poet, the fourth class of men, are as praiseworthy and perhaps even more exalted than the more practical philanthropists of the second group.

> Art not thou of the dreamer tribe?
> The poet and the dreamer are distinct,
> Diverse, sheer opposite, antipodes.
> The one pours out a balm upon the world,
> The other vexes it.

As is the case so often, throughout this whole passage Shakespeare is at the back, or at the front, of Keats' mind. As Theseus in act 5, scene 1 of *A Midsummer Night's Dream* famously declares, "the lunatic, the lover, and the poet /are of imagination all compact." The lunatic sees the world as a hellish nightmare; the lover sees the beloved as more beautiful than Helen of Troy; the poet gives to "airy nothing / A local habitation and a name." As all three are compact of imagination, surely the poet is susceptible both to the hyperbole of the lover and to the delusions of the madman. When Moneta accuses the poet/speaker of being a "dreaming thing, a fever of thy self," Keats is giving voice to his own almost habitual self-reproach. Throughout much of his career as a poet, Keats was vexed by the notion that poets and he in particular among them are mere, unmanly dreamers, perhaps too conversant with airy nothing, visionaries whose sometimes pathological visions are too often fever dreams that add nothing, and certainly nothing salubrious, to the available stock of reality. Finally, however, Keats arrives at the notion that the true poet is a kind of physician, a healer, whose poems pour a balm upon the world. Again, when through a loving apprehension of the things of this world, the imagination seizes upon beauty as truth, truth as beauty, and what would otherwise remain airy nothings are given, in a successfully realized poem, a local habitation and a name, then something new, something every bit as real as some new datum reported by the senses or some new world discovered by intrepid explorers, is indeed added to the available stock of reality. The poet awakens to discover that his dream is real and that it is in some sense perhaps more real than and an intensification of what we normally conceive of as reality.

With respect, again, to the little matter of the truth, there is a snatch of dialogue in *The Tempest* that has always delighted and enthralled me. Antonio and Sebastian are making sport of the love-struck Ferdinand, who is somewhere safely offstage.

> Sebastian: How lush and lusty the grass looks. How green!
> Antonio: The ground indeed is tawny.
> Sebastian: With an eye of green in it.
> Antonio: He misses not much.
> Sebastian: No, he doth but mistake the truth totally.

Head over heels in love with Miranda, Ferdinand has an eye of green that transforms the inhospitable island on which they are stranded after a shipwreck into a kind of paradise. Ferdinand, in effect, is so elated by love that everything appears lovely to him, that the island is apprehended by him as a gloriously New World. Yet Ferdinand's vision may not, in fact, be a mere delusion; it reflects the hope that the brave seafaring explorers of Shakespeare's era would stumble upon a kind of new Eden. For Shakespeare the perceived is always affected by the perceiver. There is no one correct view of reality that floats free of all partial perspectives. Therefore Ferdinand's perspective is not simply to be dismissed out of hand; there is likely to be at least a kernel of truth in it.

The last two lines quoted above are true not only of lovers. Conversely, when taken, with poetic license, out of context, as I confess I habitually do, they are also true of those who are so engrossed in anatomizing the details of a given problem or a situation, who are so obsessed, like good logical positivists, with being right on every point, who are so convinced that their perspective is definitively true, that they are curiously blind with respect to the whole picture. In their pursuit of truth, they may not miss much, and yet they risk mistaking the truth entirely. The role of the poet and of the imagination is to obscurely apprehend, synoptically, with respect to any given reality, both the details and the whole picture, and thereafter to fill out that picture by shuttling between the two—with the hope that thereby, although one can never grasp the truth entirely, it is at least possible draw closer to it. The role of the mystic, on the other hand, is not only to draw close to the truth but somehow, by a supreme and unremitting act of intuition, to fully comprehend it. Whether or not such comprehension is attainable most of us will never know. It is, of course, possible that even the most revered mystics are also always on the way, are themselves engaged in an ongoing process of drawing closer to the truth. Meanwhile, poets continue to produce imaginative models of reality that are an intensification of it, models that suggest new possibilities, new modes of apprehending the world and comporting oneself toward it, that the same-hearted reader can realize, thus transforming the possible into the actual.

What distinguishes the dreamer and visionary from the true poet who pours balm upon the world? Presumably, again, higher dignity is afforded the epic poet and higher still the tragic poet who directly confront the reality of human suffering in their work, just as do those who toil more concretely to alleviate it. The true poet, pouring balm upon the world instead of vexing it, becomes a kind of healer. It is telling that Moneta uses the word *physician*, with associations to Keats' past life of close engagement with the suffering of others, to characterize the essential nature of the true poet.

The speaker of the poem becomes determined to transform himself from a member of the dreamer tribe into such a true poet. To what extent is the speaker a figure for Keats? Perhaps toward the end of his career as a poet, Keats came to regard the romances written at the beginning of his career—including poems as fine, in long stretches, as "Endymion," and as perfect in their way as the "Eve of Saint Agnes"—as fledgling efforts. He had long since begun to write poems that accrued to themselves the aura of the tragic. Likely he felt that poems that addressed the profound burden of the mystery of human suffering were uniquely able to touch the inner side of the human heart, of the human predicament. Indeed, Shakespeare had always been his lodestar.

In sum, the speaker of "The Fall of Hyperion" should not be too closely associated with Keats. By the time he wrote "The Fall of Hyperion" surely Keats realized that he had already written poems that were not mere fever dreams, that were attuned to the still, sad music of humanity, and that showed the promise of sounding the still deeper, more exalting and troubling music of the tragic, an art form that at its best incorporates not only the extreme exigencies of objective reality but circumstances ideally constructed as provings and soundings of the human heart.

And so, after trying his hand at epic poetry, it would have been to his lodestar; to the great presider whose picture was the only possession he had brought with him years before to the Isle of Wight; the exemplar of negative capability; the man of no identity who even now has bequeathed us no biography; who was uniquely able to go out of his own nature and to touch both the inner sides of his characters and of the worlds in which they moved; who had created in *King Lear* an unsurpassed literary testament, the heart's Bible, an inexhaustible teat from which the intellect could drink; who had indeed poured out a balm upon the world—it was to Shakespeare to whom Keats would have wished, after trying his hand at epic, to turn. But both "Hyperion" and "The Fall of Hyperion" were abandoned, lay in magnificent ruin, the briefest of epics, never to be completed.

It might seem that tragedy has much in common with the Buddhist's notion that suffering is the fundamental reality of human life. But tragedy does not deal with human life in general but with some particular human life that is singled out, for reasons that remain largely mysterious, for suffering of a particularly intense kind. Tragedy, with its unrelenting focus on the human individual, is a quintessentially Western art form. It so happened that Keats, in his own life, was singled out for such suffering. As soon as he realized that he had contracted tuberculosis, his previous attempts to discover and follow a kind of middle way between apparently opposite extremes became moot, overwhelmed by his physical illness, by the exigencies of a brute, material reality that were not to be denied—the very reality that he had always acknowledged, had always afforded a measure of respect. He who had wished to be physician to all men was reduced to being a patient, to being, quite literally, a fever of himself.

The question of whether or not Keats would have become a successful tragic dramatist is moot. Wordsworth and Coleridge had both written eminently undistinguished dramas upon which they expended considerable energy trying, unsuccessfully, to convince theater owners to stage. Byron's "Cain" and Shelley's "The Cenci," not to mention "Prometheus Unbound," are considerably more interesting, but they were never intended to be produced and performed on stage. There have been very few eras and cultures that have proven conducive to the creation of compelling tragedies. The Romantic era, at least in England, was not one of them.

Less than a year after writing "The Fall of Hyperion," Keats, suffering from full-blown tuberculosis, heading for Italy, was definitively severed from all those whom he loved, most grievously from Fanny Brawne. Ultimately he would be severed from love itself, would be forced to live out the remains of an essentially posthumous existence. His days as a poet were over. An illness as brutal as that which Keats suffered causes a disintegration of the personality. How intense the experience of pain must have been for Keats; the exquisite sensitivity and power of his senses turning against him must have been experienced as a kind of protracted torture. Pain, anger, and fear, in one whose body is destined to suffer so savagely, progressively blot out every trace of love, and the imagination turns against itself, envisaging only the fresh horrors that are to come. It is almost unbearable to imagine Keats suffering such a disintegration, in which the lineaments of a finely and assiduously developed character were erased, in which all that was so bravely done was so brazenly undone. Joseph Severn, Keats' remarkably steadfast companion during his last days, was deeply distressed to witness the disintegration of Keats' ego, which modern psychiatrists now refer to, in a charming neologism, as decompensation. A fatal dose of morphine that Severn had intended to administer to Keats when his suffering became too intense was misplaced. One can only hope that this ordeal was for Keats a final, terrible, proving of the heart after which no further proofs would be required.

5.

Lionel Trilling wrote a lovely essay on Keats' letters entitled "The Poet as Hero." The poet as hero has a tendency to too easily segue into the poet as saint. Much writing on Keats, until the advent of our age of debunking, involved panegyric, almost hagiological accounts of his character. Even Bate's great book on Keats betrays something of this failing. Despite the toils of later biographers, the myth of Keats is unlikely to die, in large part because he was indeed an exemplary character. The only drawback of this myth, perhaps an important one, is that Keats becomes a kind of monumental exemplar of all that is good and true more than a merely human character, and begins to recede from our view.

In less than a year after Keats' death, Shelley, who so beautifully eulogized Keats in "Adonais," drowned when his skiff, characteristically outfitted for speed not stability, capsized in a sudden winter squall off the coast of his beloved Bay of Lerici.

I would like to turn here to a strange and strangely touching poem that eulogizes both Keats and Shelley. It was written by the Late Modernist poet George Oppen, who, you may recall, appears in an earlier chapter of this book, and provides a vital link in the argument that led me to the notion of interiority that I have been further exploring, with Keats as my exemplar, here. Oppen's poem has the considerable advantage of startlingly humanizing two young poets whose reputations and achievements have monumentalized and distanced them.

BOY'S ROOM

A friend saw the rooms
Of Keats and Shelley
At the lake, and saw 'they were just
Boys' rooms' and was moved

By that. And indeed a poet's room
Is a boy's room
And I suppose that women know it.

Perhaps the unbeautiful banker
Is exciting to a woman, a man
Not a boy gasping
For breath over a girl's body.

This poem also has the virtue of calling attention to something lacking in this essay —the almost embarrassing degree to which Keats' imagination, so centered around the apprehension of love and beauty, expressed itself not only in his poetry but in his intensely obsessive erotic attraction to the idealized figure of Fanny Brawne, an attraction which, of course, was not destined to be consummated. Oppen's deliberate and deliberately prosaic diction, so unlike that of either Keats or Shelley, is all the more poignant for that, and poignant, too, is his tacit admission that he also remains a boy writing in a boy's room. Keats, and to a lesser degree Shelley, were very unlike the worldly figure of the generic yet preferable unbeautiful banker. Keats would never have the experience of sexual consummation, of gasping above a woman's body. The reference to an unspecified lake in conjunction with gasping in the poem suggests a labored breathing that is not only sexual but that refers as well to the deaths of Keats and Shelley, to their last gasps as both drowned, their lungs filling with fluid. We as readers, like the friend who is a stand-in for Oppen, are of course more likely to be moved by the tragically premature deaths of Keats and Shelley than by the exploits of any unbeautiful banker. And Oppen's poem intends that we be so moved.

Keats' conceit in his letter about souls being unformed intelligences emitted by God, later to return to him as individual souls, was, as I have mentioned, just that—a conceit. Keats had little hope that his soul would outlast his body. He did not even experience the cold comfort of feeling that his work would survive. He famously wrote his own epitaph, inscribed on his tombstone: "Here lies one whose name was writ in water." And yet, of course, his poems, the best of them expressions, manifestations of an imagination in which love transformed, assimilated to its identity all that it reached out to touch, revealing not only the inner side of this world but also of the heart that embraced them, have yet to vanish. Revealed by his imagination as standing in their truth, the things of this world could not help but be seen by Keats as beautiful, perhaps especially in their transience.

But enough! It appears that I, too, am beginning to wax hagiographic.

6.

Finally, as a kind of coda to this piece, I will perhaps obsessively attempt to further vindicate what should require no vindication, Keats' dictum "Beauty is Truth, Truth Beauty," and thereby to rescue it from the carping of petty positivists or of New Critics of a positive bent who resort to weak arguments, such as the notion that Keats' scandalous proposition has been dramatically prepared for by the poem of which it is the conclusion, and that therefore, in context, it is (barely) excusable. As I have mentioned, Keats' proposition seems valid to me whether in or out of context. I have no problem with granting it something like my unconditional assent. Beauty is associated with the intelligence of the heart, truth with that of the mind, and it is the role of poet to effectuate their union.

I will here buttress Keats' position by taking recourse to the practitioners of an intellectual discipline that at first blush seems quite different from poetry but which in fact has some quite striking affinities with it. I am referring to mathematics. And particularly to pure, not applied mathematics. The explorations of pure mathematicians need have no relationship with the material world, with what is or is not the case. Strictly speaking, they are as much at home with being useless as with being useful. Their explorations are pursued, without ulterior motive, for their own sake. And yet, though this activity is in some cases eminently non-pragmatic, it is at the same time one of the most exalted activities of man, an activity in which the human mind exercises and experiences the freedom that is proper to it, unencumbered by external constraints. Poetry, of course, is similarly useless, and yet it, too, at its finest, is an expression of man's sovereign intellectual and imaginative freedom.

Mathematicians, moreover, regularly refer to the elegance or beauty, or the lack thereof, with respect to the proof of theorems. The beauty—or lack of it—of specific proofs is correlated with their relative significance and importance. Elegant, beautiful solutions tend to be considered more profound, more significant, in a sense more true than inelegant solutions, which tend to be considered trivial and relatively unimportant.

Great mathematicians are, of course, fully cognizant of the aesthetic dimension of their discipline. Indeed, they are at pains to make us laymen aware of it. Bertrand Russell, the great English mathematician and logician, was for a long time a collaborator with Wittgenstein, a figure who features somewhat prominently in my essay "On Mysticism and Poetry." In a remarkable passage, Russell wrote:

> Mathematics, rightly viewed, possesses not only truth, but supreme beauty—a beauty cold and austere, like that of sculpture... sublimely pure, and yet capable of a stern perfection such as only the greatest art can show. The true spirit of delight, the exaltation, the sense of being more than Man, which is the touchstone of the highest excellence, is to be found in mathematics as surely as poetry.

A clearer endorsement of Keats' equation of beauty and truth could not be hoped for. Of particular note in this passage is that mathematics, though its beauty is stern, also involves an exhilarating experience of exaltation in which man experiences himself as "more than Man." Mathematics thus is not simply stern and austere but is also conducive to what can only be seen as a kind of ecstasy. Russell would have likely concurred with Blake's notion that exuberance is beauty. Beauty is not only succinct and self-contained but also prolific and overflowing. Also notable in the above passage is that "delight" is seen as intimately connected with mathematical activity. Delight is almost always, in writers on aesthetics prior to the twentieth century, particularly germane to discussions of poetry. Poetry is often said to instruct by means of delight. But this is a utilitarian appropriation of the role of poetry. More often the association of delight with poetry is simply accepted, without ulterior motive, as one of its unalienable and cherished qualities. Quite simply, as Stevens noted, the poem must give pleasure.

Of course, this association of the mathematical with the aesthetic is not peculiar to Russell. Indeed, it seems to be shared with most great mathematicians. The great Hungarian mathematician Paul Erdos, when asked why numbers are beautiful, replied with an almost exasperated tone: "It's like asking why is Ludwig van Beethoven's Ninth Symphony beautiful? If you don't see why, I can't tell you... If they aren't beautiful, nothing is." Erdos is proclaiming, in effect, "Let those with ears hear. Let those with eyes see." The rest, the unregenerate and obtuse, are of no account and can be simply passed over. Of particular interest here is Erdos' comparison of mathematics with music, which is peculiarly free of the referential. The use of language in poetry also tends to float free of the referential, and the poetic imagination tends to construct virtual linguistic universes that obey their own laws, laws which sometimes include a kind of sovereign lawlessness.

A number of mathematicians have been quite clear that mathematics is as much an art as it is a science. For our purposes, we might say that, though it has analogies to both, mathematics is neither exactly an art nor exactly a science. It is yet another instance of what I have been calling a third way, a way that bypasses apparent antinomies, that operates in its own domain.

Mathematicians in general also stress that mathematics is an activity to be known only in and by the practice of it. I have attempted to suggest that the imagination, likewise, is an activity or the conductor of a force that realizes itself as an activity.

Finally, many great mathematicians, like the remarkable French polymath Henri Poincaré, testify to the experience of their most important discoveries as arising, almost full-blown, in moments of inspiration, an inspiration that tends to have side effects, to be concretely experienced in a variety of ways. Indeed, Einstein himself described his moments of overwhelming insight as presaged by intense kinesthetic sensations and by flashes of an unusual luminosity. I will not multiply here what is a wealth of such examples, an embarrassment of riches. I will, however, note the affinity of mathematical insight with certain kinds of mystical experiences, particularly with the flashes or bolts of insight, which Buddhism calls prajna, or with the creative intuition that Shaivism call pratibha.

I have already noted the quite commonly observed connection between higher mathematics and the experience of beauty. But it has been too little noted that the discoveries of great scientists and mathematicians are often registered as sudden, awe-inspiring irruptions of the heretofore unimagined into the precincts of the real, and that as such they involve an experience not only of beauty but of sublimity. The sublime and the beautiful are together, of course, the preeminent concerns of Western aesthetics. Encountering the sublime is, unlike the relatively detached contemplation of beauty, an experience in which the mind loses its self-possession when confronted with that which, in its awe-inspiring immensity or power, overwhelms it. Such an experience involves precisely the kind of exaltation to which Russell refers. It also involves an experience of self-transcendence, the sense, again using Russell's words, of being more than Man.

These irruptions of the new, of which Einstein's theory of relativity is perhaps the supreme example, are often felt—and have been described by many of those to whom they are disclosed—as having a kind of numinous quality. They are often experienced as having been vouchsafed, ready-made, from some source, akin to the poetic muses, outside of the self. I have been conjecturing in this text whether there is some Consciousness which, though registered by the self, exists in some way independent of it. I wish to tread lightly here, however, recognizing that what I have been putting forth as a conjecture is just that, a kind of hunch writ large, one that is unverified and perhaps unverifiable. It is, however, an empirical truth that very few of the great scientists and mathematicians of the past century have been reductive materialists. Just as the insights of great mystics ossify into religious dogmas, so the insights of truly creative scientists, who have been sensitive to and respectful of the spiritual, tend to ossify in the hands of their successors—the consolidators of the charismatic insights of their forebears, time-serving priests, potentates, or plenipotentiaries presiding over the church or state of the un-wonderful and disenchanted—into mere scientism, into the passionless embrace of the apparently reasonable but relentlessly close-minded dogma of scientific materialism, which itself becomes a kind of militant religion. Too many of its acolytes have the unassailable arrogance of those whose minds, no longer the free and lawless thoroughfare of ideas, have already been made up.

Of course I am grossly exaggerating here—both for the sheer joy of exaggerating and to make a point. Those who consolidate and extend the insights of scientific geniuses in fact play an important and even a vital role in the enterprise of science. One simply wishes that some of them would exhibit more humility and less arrogance. After all, how awe-inspiringly minuscule, how partial, how tentative, whether we are poets or scientists, is our knowledge of reality. And how essential it is, lest we succumb to an absurd grandiosity, to keep this in mind. Only idiot questioners, to borrow a sobriquet from Blake, profess to have all the answers or imagine that those with differing perspectives have none of them.

But I have digressed from my main task here, which is to briefly explore the connection between mathematics and the experience of beauty, in pursuance of which I would like, finally, to examine what it is that makes a given proof beautiful or elegant. What are the criteria that differentiate elegant or beautiful proofs from inelegant ones? Here, I will abjectly confess that, not having the time or strength to conduct deeper researches, I will rely upon Wikipedia, which lists several criteria that link elegance and beauty to what Russell calls truth, all of which can be seen to happily coexist with what I have been calling the imagination. An elegant proof, then, is:

1. A proof that has a minimum number of additional assumptions or previous results.

2. A proof that is unusually succinct.
3. A proof that arises from an apparently unrelated theorem or collection of theorems, that links together previously unassociated realms of mathematical study.
4. A proof that is based upon new and original insights. The unexpected.

Since criteria 1 and 4 are closely related, I will begin with the second criteria, that of succinctness. A succinct proof is that which requires a minimum number of steps to arrive at a conclusion. Again, succinctness is associated with elegance, with beauty. I think here of Basho's poetry of the pure immediate percept and indeed of Japanese aesthetics in general, with its economical, astonishingly skillful use of highly economical means, from Zen rock gardens to the elegant, ingenious use of space in contemporary Japanese urban apartments.

Though lyric poetry in both the West and East in general can be seen as succinct, as tending to be both condensed and concentrated, as a fine distillation of experience entailing a relative economy of means, it seems to me that Japanese aesthetics in particular tends to emphasize the beautiful as succinct, corresponding to what in mathematics Russell calls austere, as exemplifying a stern perfection. To apprehend not only works of art but also the apparently quotidian things of this world aesthetically is to recognize, immediately, their unique and irrefrangible quality; what in Buddhism, as we have seen, is called suchness.

But Russell also refers, as I have noted, to the practice of mathematics as involving a kind of exhilaration, an exaltation that makes man feel like more than man, a kind of self-transcendence. This ecstatic, expansive notion of beauty or, more properly speaking, of sublimity is perhaps more aligned with Western than Eastern aesthetics.

The third criterion, which finds mathematical beauty in mathematical theorems that draw upon theorems that are usually considered to be unrelated, or that reveal surprising links between fields of mathematics that had previously seemed relatively airtight and distinct, seems likewise to me to be profoundly imaginative. I have perhaps too little stressed in this volume the role of the imagination, akin to that of metaphor itself, in forging connections between realms of experience not normally regarded as connected. This kind of linkage can, of course, connect disparate realms of scientific inquiry, resulting in startling and fresh insights.

With respect to the literary, I think of Keats' beloved Shakespeare and of how *King Lear*, for example, ranges—by means of metaphor and other figures of speech, by means of skeins of related imagery that form inexhaustibly complex webs—from the macrocosmic, from attention to heavenly or hellish portents, often associated with the sky and manifested in a storm that feels almost like a world-ending dissolution and slide into metaphysical entropy and chaos, to the meanest manifestations of the biological—all of which are in turn associated with the many levels or expanding circles of the microcosm, of the sphere of human experience; from the sexual to the familial, to the religious, to the political; from infancy to palsied old age as a cruel second childhood, thus forming an even *more* glorious and inexhaustible complex of meanings.

The fourth criterion that separates the mathematically beautiful and elegant from the inelegant is that of originality and unexpectedness. I need not stress the prevalence, particularly in the West, of the assumption that the truly creative is also original. As for the unexpected, poetry operates, as Keats avowed, by means of a "fine surprise." All genuine poets, of course, provide us with refreshing and delightful or existentially jolting shocks of surprise. I think in this connection, for example, particularly of Emily Dickinson's reference to her "bolts of melody" with their cognitive, harmonic, and rhythmic dissonance, their contrapuntal undertow, their tendency to bring us up short; characteristics which, along with their author, are discussed in my book *Elective Affinities*, which is a kind of sequel to and extension of this one.

I seem to have taken a somewhat circuitous route in vindicating, by appeal to authority of mathematicians, not normally thought of as soft-minded, Keats' association of beauty and truth. In so doing, I have also suggested some analogies between mathematics and poetry as imaginative disciplines. Keats, with his training in the sciences, would, I suspect, have appreciated such analogies.

Ultimately, however, the simple sentence, "Beauty is Truth, Truth Beauty," should cause no problem for those who have ears capable of hearing it and should be passed over in silence, not reductively traduced, by those who do not.

2.
Blake's "London": On Inspiration and the Poetic Genius

1.

I shall now turn, with some relief, from the two poets who I have thus far discussed at some length—from Stevens, with his multiple strategies of indirection and evasion, and from Keats, with his always complex and provisional speculations—to William Blake, a poet of a different stripe, one who had his mind clearly and defiantly made up about almost everything. What Blake called "the Poetic Genius" does not entail, as some imagine, the would-be poet/prophet's acting as a passive medium or channeler taking dictation from heavenly voices, a misapprehension arising primarily from a few sardonic passages in Blake's exuberant satire "The Marriage of Heaven and Hell," in which he is making a sport of shocking what would later come to be called the bourgeoisie. That Blake probably, like many mystics, experienced sublime visions and auditory visitations—whether or not, as he reports, in naked comity with his beloved wife in the enclosed garden of their suburban cottage—is largely, with respect to the execution and our evaluation of Blake's work both as an artist and a poet, beside the point. Blake's work as an artist/engraver involved meticulous, intensive, time-consuming labor. One of his patron saints, as we shall see, is Hephaestus, the artist as artisan perpetually toiling away at his fiery forge.

Blake's notion of the Poetic Genius entailed what he called "intellectual warfare," the unremitting act and struggle of a consciousness engaged in separating truth from error, in painstakingly tracing and illuminating, through the light of the spirit, the lineaments of a redeemed world. I take what Blake calls the Poetic Genius to be analogous to the inspired notions of the various seers and poets I have consulted in this book. For Blake, too, the imagination is preeminently an act or activity of Consciousness.

In turning to what Blake calls Poetic Genius I will also be turning, or returning, although implicitly, to my discussion in this book of what Maritain called preconscious, creative intuition; of what Abhinavagupta in the context of his theory of language called pashyanti, and in the context of his metaphysics and aesthetics, pratibha; of Shaivism's notion of spanda, the prodigious stirring of the resonance of Consciousness itself, which the imagination as Poetic Genius assimilates, then translates into poetic form. It will be the burden of this essay to suggest that this stirring, this resonance, this vibration ripples both in every word of Blake's poem "London" and in the network of uncountable currents that pulsate between them—like Indra's fabled necklace, each pearl of which both reflects and is reflected by all the others. In short, I shall take Blake's notion of Poetic Genius seriously, with "London," to borrow a phrase from business, providing a kind of informal proof of concept.

It seems to me, quite simply, that without an imagination baptized in, activated by Consciousness, and thereby alive and stirring, in moments like the "pulsation of an artery," with precognitive, synoptic intuition—an activity which Blake, again, chooses to call the Poetic Genius—it is impossible to account for the fact that "London," a poem of astonishing resonance and density of implication, was apparently dashed off quickly and with the exception of only two altered words, without revision.

First, however, a few words addressing context, both the context of Blake's poetic work as a whole, and of the society which that work indicts, are a necessary prelude to the closer examination of "London" itself.

2.

Blake, of course, considered himself quite literally an heir to the prophet/poets of the Bible, prophets whose brief was, clearly, directly, and unambiguously, to speak truth to power. Blake saw himself as assuming a similar role, as speaking truth to the political, ecclesiastical, industrial/mercantile, and artistic powers of his own day, powers which, as Blake recognized, were in league with each other, and which he saw as hopelessly hypocritical and corrupt. His poetry both bitterly indicts this regime and propounds a vision, in what he called his prophetic books, of what a redeemed human society might look like. The poem "London" is Blake's most brilliantly condensed indictment of the social order of his day.

One imagines that Blake would have had little patience with what he would likely have regarded as Stevens' indulgence in the uncertain, the undecidable, the ambiguous, and the evasive, particularly as regards matters political and aesthetic. Likewise Blake was seldom, unlike Keats, in a state of uncertainty or doubt, and had, again, quite definitively, made up his mind on almost everything. He was a passionate advocate of clear, bold outlines in art. He was repelled, for example, by what he saw as the muddiness, the murkiness, of much European oil painting, particularly that of Rubens and Rembrandt. He had a perhaps even greater contempt (a bracing intellectual contempt is a particular hallmark of Blake) for poets, like Pope, whom he considered to be "mere tame high finishers of paltry blots." His poetry betrays no uncertainty, no ambiguity about what is to be said. Helen Vendler's notion that the poet knows what he wishes to say and strives to say it as clearly and perspicuously as possible is far more applicable to Blake than to Keats or to Stevens.

For all their differences, however, Blake, Keats, and Stevens are alike in being difficult poets who resist easy interpretation. I have discussed at great length, of course, some of the kinds of interpretive difficulty with which Stevens confronts us. The difficulty of reading Blake—particularly of reading his long prophetic poems, which comprise, after the *Songs of Innocence and Experience,* of which "London" is a part, virtually his entire oeuvre—is notorious, and of a very different kind. The fact that his long, prophetic poems are allegorical does not, of course, alone account for their difficulty; some allegories, like *Pilgrim's Progress*, intended to be both read (by the literate) and read aloud (to the illiterate), are relatively straightforward and easy to decode. If allegories were ranked on a sliding scale in terms of difficulty, Spencer's *Faerie Queen*, addressed to a literate audience and drawing upon common theological and mythological points of reference, both Biblical and classical, would rank somewhere in the middle, while Blake's prophetic poems would surely belong among the thorniest.

Blake creates in his allegory a personal mythology, one whose *dramatis personae* and what they represent are initially unknown to us and provide us, as we plunge into these poems as though always in *medias res*, with few established points of reference. The prophetic books are to an unusual degree abstract and internalized, their main characters representing mental faculties enacting a kind of psychomachia. They are, of course, deeply concerned with political and social reality; they not only refer to but enact the kind of mental and spiritual struggle that Blake deemed would be required to sever at its root that power which not only enslaves men but causes men to enslave themselves. This is the struggle that Blake refers to as intellectual warfare. The prophetic poems seem to reenact Blake's own personal struggles as well as presenting a complex paradigm of the kind of obviously more than merely individual intellectual warfare that will be required for a general renovation and redemption of the social order to be possible.

Blake famously wrote, "I must create my own system or be enslaved by another man's." The remarkable extent to which Blake's poems, despite the difficulties just discussed, are in fact systematic and intellectually rigorous, has been largely recognized since the publication of Northrop Frye's *Fearful Symmetry*; it no longer seems plausible to view Blake as merely mad. And yet these poems acquire a kind of added pathos when one asks to whom they are addressed. One can only imagine the bafflement with which his long prophetic poems were met not only by the general ranks of the literate but by the intelligentsia.

Such is not the case with *The Marriage of Heaven and Hell* and with *Songs of Innocence and Experience*. Despite their very considerable complexity, they do not initially confront the reader as nearly impenetrable labyrinths. *The Marriage of Heaven and Hell* has an aphoristic wit to which only the determinedly dull can fail to respond. *Songs of Innocence and Experience* quite simply contains some of the most condensed and brilliant lyric poems in the English language. And, crucially, among the most seductive. Their force, if not their complexity, is felt upon a first reading.

3.

The political and social conditions that "London" indicts have been exhaustively addressed elsewhere, but I will fill in some of their broad outlines here before turning more narrowly to examine the operations of sense, and to a lesser degree of sound, in "London." Blake saw the London of his day as blighted by a privileged few, the elite of the hydra-headed monster of church, state, and an emerging mercantile class, who combined and conspired to suppress and to deny the rights of the many. Poverty was widespread. To make matters worse, failed crops and famine, with their threat of starvation, were a regular occurrence. For many the mere struggle to survive was paramount. The starving and disenfranchised flooded the city, many among them the young who had few options other than to enlist in the ranks of the hapless soldiers referenced in "London," or to become youthful harlots engaged in prostitution, spreading disease that blighted the offspring of shotgun marriages. The largely unoccupied soldiers were seen as potentially subject to sedition, and German mercenaries were hired to spy on them. The government, headed by Pitt, fearful that a revolution like that which had recently occurred in France would spread to England, became an elaborate and widespread mechanism of surveillance and political oppression, eager to stamp out dissent. At the same time the state was in a constant state of military mobilization, with the threat of a war with France always impending, which further lined the pockets of the rich, increasingly comprised of a rising industrial and mercantile class organized into corporations, which were granted charters that enabled them to monopolize land and power. It was widely assumed, by the self-aggrandizing and the self-interested, that a permanent impoverished underclass was an inevitable component of any society. The church doled out the hypocritical charity that, in Blake's view, exploited the poor in the guise of helping them. Rather than being educated, for example, the children of the poor were subject to brutal apprenticeships like those of the chimney sweeps mentioned in "London" and elsewhere in the *Songs of Experience*. In the name of pity and mercy, the hapless denizens of the underclass were thus subject to lives of indentured servitude, while of course outright slavery was likewise condoned as a necessary component of a growing empire.

Apart from or alongside Blake's literal accounting of the conditions prevailing in the actual city of London, lies, as always, his mythological, archetypal London. Like most of the great epic poets in the Christian tradition, Blake envisages four imaginative realms or states of Consciousness, which he calls Ulro, Generation, Beulah, and Jerusalem, corresponding to hell, to man's earthly condition, to an idiosyncratic version of an earthly paradise, and finally to the fourth and highest realm conceived of as the city of God. Many Christians have for millennia awaited the advent of the New

Jerusalem, for the fully regenerate city of God that will succeed the city of man at the time of the apocalypse. Augustine's *City of God* is a hugely influential expression of this vision. For Blake the highest, fully redeemed state of society always, likewise, takes the form of a city. He entitled his last great prophetic poem "Jerusalem." He always recognized, even while anatomizing London's fallen state, its vast, unrealized potential. He never lost his anticipatory longing for the advent of what he called "spiritual fourfold London," for a redeemed London that would result from an apocalyptic apotheosis of man's consciousness. This redeemed London was for Blake fourfold because it represents the fourth and highest state or level of consciousness, and because in such a state man's four major faculties would interact in a state of perfect harmony. For Blake, London was potentially a type of Jerusalem, and England, or Albion, was considered by Blake to have had a particularly important though generally unacknowledged role in providential history.

Albion in Blake's mythology is also the cosmic man, the "human form divine," the singular of which the city is the plural. Albion, the risen, redeemed, universal man, contains within him all that is both created and uncreated. With respect to him the terms subject and object, inner and outer, lose all meaning.

As an artist, Blake was, of course, not only preoccupied by political and spiritual concerns but by deeply held aesthetic principles. It is his preoccupation with this latter concern, again as both a poet and a visual artist, that is largely responsible for the brilliance of much of his poetry, particularly as exemplified by the short lyric poems found mostly in his *Songs of Innocence and Experience*, of which "London" is a particularly charismatic example.

The writing of any poem, of course, involves the choice of the words that in combination will comprise it, rescuing a particular, unique pattern of both sound and sense from the virtually infinite number of such possible combinations. We in turn, as readers, experience a select few of many such patterns, of many such poems, as particularly powerful, indeed as what used to be called inspired, as expressions of what Blake called the Poetic Genius. Again, preliminary minutiae aside, my primary purposed in this essay is to suggest that "London" itself demonstrates that something like what Blake called Poetic Genius is necessary to account for it. This is the task to which I will now turn.

4.

The sound effects of "London" are extraordinarily dense, brilliantly augmenting its sense, a point which here I wish simply to acknowledge. In what follows, however, I will mostly restrict myself to exploring Blake's lexical choices. I will examine the meanings or connotations of many of what I take to be key words of "London," all exhibiting a rich polysemy, and of how they operate within the semantic field of the poem as a whole. In contrast to such words I will suggest that the poem at the same time exhibits

—quite deliberately, of course—a kind of lexical poverty suggested by the striking repetition of many of its words, and by its repeated use of words that although not identical are so close in meaning as to be almost synonymous. I will have something to say, too, about what I take to be the significance of this contrast. Such an exercise, though it may sound dry and pedantic, I have found in the case of "London" to yield results that are revelatory and inexhaustibly rich.

On first reading "London" itself, one immediately notices that the poem is comprised of four stanzas of four lines, with four stresses per line, a form common to that of many Protestant hymns of Blake's day. Blake's multiple repetitions of the fourfold suggests, as well, that London is a kind of fallen anti-type of the spiritual fourfold London mentioned above.

The first thing that strikes one from this lexical standpoint is the repetitiousness of the poem's first stanzas:

> I wander thro' each charter'd street,
> Near where the charter'd Thames does flow.
> And mark in every face I meet
> Marks of weakness, marks of woe.

The words *chartered* and *mark* are both repeated, the former twice, the latter three times, within the close confines of the stanza that Blake has chosen, suggesting, at the outset, a kind of lexical impoverishment which, as we shall see, plays off against the lexical richness of key words that also operate more widely in the poem. The first stanza of "London" suggests a fixed and unvarying urban landscape, a fixity reflected, too, in the poem's obedient adherence to its strictly iambic marching orders. Even the presumably meandering Thames is chartered, bought like a piece of real estate, constrained. The poet/prophet's wandering sets him apart, as the sole possessor of relative freedom, from the hellishly frozen scene through which he moves, thereby discharging his task of marking, closely observing, and fiercely remarking upon all that he see and hears.

And yet even in the apparently repetitive, lexically impoverished first stanza of the poem, two words, the reiterated *chartered* and *mark*, both of which have multiple connotations, appear. As I continue to examine the sense of "London," it will be my contention that it contains a number of apparently simple words that are in fact highly polysemous, and that more importantly in virtually every case all of the various meanings of these words are at play, are fully relevant to the semantic field of "London" as a whole—a fact whose significance I will later have occasion to comment upon in some detail.

In one of only two corrections to the manuscript of the poem, the "dirty Thames" becomes the "chartered Thames." A purely descriptive word is exchanged for a word that is not only inherently more interesting but that resonates with much that is to come in the poem. The word *charter* refers to the appropriation and near monopolization of land granted by the state to mercantile corporations, increasing the wealth of the few at the expense of the many. I think, further, that it is impossible to hear the word *chartered* without also subliminally hearing the word *charted*, with its connotations of a world that has been thoroughly mapped and parsed, its dimensions fixed abstractly into place.

The second of the words in the opening stanzas that reap unexpected rewards is the word *mark*, used first as a verb and then as a noun. The poem's speaker *marks*, takes note of, the *marks* on the faces that he meets. The double use of this term draws the poem's speaker as subject into a kind of alignment with those about whom he is speaking. But the word *mark* has further connotations. That which is chartered or charted relies upon certain kinds of marks or marking, from signatures to the marks that delineate the boundaries of maps. Somewhat surprisingly, the first definition of mark as a noun in the OED is a "boundary, frontier, or limit," a distinguishing of one thing from another. Private property, of course, is one such inscription of limits. Another means of distinguishing one thing from another, is, of course, language, specifically writing. To mark, again to quote the OED, is to "record, indicate, or portray...to represent in writing." It is also "to inscribe." Thus an entire complex of meanings, from the mercantile to the cartographic, from signatures or seals (to mark is also to affix with a seal) on contracts to lines on a map to writing itself, is suggested. Marking as writing, and particularly as inscribing, and its power to do good or ill, were of paramount concern to Blake as poet/engraver. A mark on a face, of course, can be indicative of disease, and disease is very much a part of the world of London. Finally, there is some almost sinister sense that hovers around the word mark. The OED faithfully includes among its definitions of mark the mark of Cain and the mark of the Beast, indicative of fratricide in the first instance, and of the unregenerate who are stamped, in the Book of Revelation, with the seal of the Antichrist in the second. Blake was very much aware of the corrupt, the unregenerate forces at play in the London that he prophetically excoriates. At the same time, man, in his fallen state, can always enter the ranks of the regenerate, of those who are working toward the spiritual renovation of a city that he both reviles and loves, and of mankind in general.

I will quote the remaining three stanzas below, because the key words I will be examining accrue their full richness in the context of the poem as a whole. With the poem's second stanza we move into the beating, though afflicted, heart of London...

> In every cry of every Man,
> In every Infants cry of fear,
> In every voice: in every ban,
> The mind-forg'd manacles I hear

> How the Chimney-sweepers cry
> Every black'ning Church appalls,
> And the hapless Soldiers sigh
> Runs in blood down Palace walls
>
> But most thro' midnight streets I hear
> How the youthful Harlots curse
> Blasts the new-born Infants tear
> And blights with plagues the Marriage hearse

The second stanza not only picks up the regularity of the meter of the first stanza, but continues and thereby intensifies its extreme repetitiveness of diction. After the repetition of the word *chartered*, and the triple iteration of the word *mark* in the first stanza, the second stanza contains a triple iteration of the word *every*, which has already been used in the first stanza, and which is used for a fifth time in the third. The hammering away at the word *every*, in particular, suggests the kind of universal sameness and conformity that an authoritarian regime seeks to perpetuate. Finally, the word *cry*, repeated in the second stanza, likewise appears for a third time in the fourth, and is further perpetuated toward the end of the third stanza by the rhyming word *sigh*. The quite remarkable reiteration of these words has the additional effect of causing the meter of the poem, which would otherwise register as merely regular, to feel militantly, stridently regular, mind-numbingly selfsame. It also suggests the numbing, enforced conformity and selfsameness mandated by an authoritarian regime.

By contrast, the word *ban* in the third stanza, the third of the more polyvalent terms I will be exploring, contains within it a profusion of meanings, an embarrassment of riches, a polysemy richer even than the multiple connotations of the words *chartered* and *mark*. I will first recount, in somewhat condensed form, the various meanings of the word *ban*, like "mark" both a noun and a verb, listed in the OED: *(1) A public proclamation or edict. (2) A summons to war. (3) A sentence of banishment. (4) A proclamation of marriage. (5) To anathematize or curse. (6) A formal ecclesiastical denunciation; anathema, interdict, excommunication. (7) To prohibit.*

What is of note for our purposes is that all of the quite disparate meanings of the word *ban* are relevant, are again in play, circulating in the semantic field of the poem "London" as a whole. I will go through them, by your leave, point by point. (1) The government of London was in large part government by proclamation, or in common North American parlance, by executive order. The bans of both the monarch and the parliament further enriched the rich, further impoverished the poor. (2) The sense of a possibly imminent summons to war posed a constant, impending threat in Blake's London, which seemed to be in a state of perpetual mobilization, and is of course the cause of so many soldiers—including German mercenaries whose double role was to spy on English soldiers and civilians and to act as combatants in a potential war in

France—milling about on its streets. (3) Though formal banishment was no longer frequent in Blake's time, the surveillance state was elaborately ordered to uncover sedition, which could lead, of course, to prison, to a kind of internal exile. (4) A ban as a proclamation of marriage is related to the often-shotgun wedding of soldiers and harlots who figure prominently in the poem, and to the marriage hearse in the poem's final line. (5) Obviously, in context, the primary reference of the word *ban* is to curse, which expresses the inarticulate outrage of many at a reality they are powerless to change. (6) The church's power to denounce and excommunicate calls attention to its arbitrary power, including its power, in London, to exploit the poor, here in the pitiful form of the chimney sweeps, in the hypocritical guise of offering them charity. (7) Prohibitions of all kinds, finally, often in the form of unjust laws, were of course rife in Blake's London. In sum, every possible quite strikingly variegated meaning of the word *ban* is in full play in the semantic field of "London," its multiple filaments—or tentacles—reaching out to touch issues raised elsewhere in the poem, to augment and intensify its critique of both church and state. The polysemy of the word *ban*, like the words *mark* and *chartered*, is exploited to the utmost.

The next key term that I will discuss is the word *forged*, embedded in the remarkable phrase "mind-forg'd manacles." Here the primary dictionary meaning is to shape by "heating in a forge and hammering." The secondary meaning is that of "forgery or counterfeiting." But the various possible meanings and connotations of *forged* at play in "London" are generated not only by the dictionary but by mythological sources exploited by Blake. On the one hand, that which is forged in a crucible is analogous to a work of art forged in the crucible of intellectual warfare and of the imagination. For Blake as both artist and artisan, Hephaestus working at his forge was a kind of patron saint. On the other hand, furnaces are frequently associated in the Bible with the hellish, demonic realm that Blake called Ulro.

It is worth noting that "London" shares a manuscript page with Blake's great, enigmatic poem "The Tyger," in which the Tyger is initially depicted as burning in the forest of the night as though in some crucible, a crucible in which he is then depicted as being forged, hammered out, twisted, and torqued, and in general quite violently formed into being. The poem's first question—"what immortal hand or eye / Dare frame thy fearful symmetry?"—assumes, crucially and wrongly, that the Tyger is being created by some unspecified immortal being who is at least as dreadful, as awe- and fear-inspiring, as is the Tyger himself.

> And what shoulder, & what art,
> Could twist the sinews of thy heart?
> And when thy heart began to beat,
> What dread hand? & what dread feet?

> What the hammer? what the chain?
> In what furnace was thy brain?
> What the anvil? what dread grasp
> Dare its deadly terrors clasp?

Some terrible divinity, it seems, exerting the force of his powerful shoulder, and exercising some occult art, at the same time creates and subdues the Tyger by wielding and utilizing the hammer and chain—which seem more like instruments of torture than of creation—clutched by his dread grasp. At the same time, the act of creation seems like a kind of struggle between the artificer/creator and his incipient creation. The creator seems at times himself to be in danger of being overmatched by that which he is forging into being. Likewise, man's imaginative creations, like Frankenstein's monster or Milton's God, when no longer recognized as imaginative, as projections of his own mind, are granted a kind of specious, literal independence, and assume the power to terrify and oppress their creators.

But it is, of course, not some projected, alienated divinity, but man's imagination, the human form divine, that has created both the archetypal, wrathful Tyger, and the poem in which he appears. There is a hint of the Prometheus myth, of man as would-be creator and imaginative artificer, in the lines "On what wings dare he aspire? / What the hand, dare seize the fire?" It is man who has created and propagated the Prometheus myth in which man's attempt to snatch the torch of light and power from the Gods is seen by them as an intolerable usurpation. It is man, too, who has projected his imagination, his power, onto the fearsome deity, the sky God whom Blake calls Nobodaddy. As man's estranged imagination keeps withering, this counterfeit deity grows more awesome and powerful, finally coming to seem, in the Tyger's final stanza, perilously similar to The God of the Old Testament, a God who is alternately, capriciously, both wrathful and benevolent. "Did he smile his work to see? / Did he who made the Lamb make thee?"

The manacles forged by the mind in "London" have no independent reality and are in effect counterfeit instruments of the spirit's self-enslavement. Projecting his imagination upon some fearsome God, and fascinated and terrified by his supposed creations, man becomes enslaved by a phantom, or phantoms, of his own creation. The mind that forges manacles becomes a kind of hellish creator of the means by which he both binds and tortures himself, and he is given further impetus by a society comprised of those who are likewise self-bound and self-tortured, and who have squandered, from the outset, the very imagination through which they might free themselves. Such a society is based not on love but on an idolatrous worship of its own fear, and is perpetuated by violence or the threat of it. It can be redeemed only when man reclaims his imaginative power, when good works are forged in the crucible of love, and of the intellectual warfare that is a form of love.

I think it germane here to mention the second of Blake's two emendations of "London." In the manuscript the phrase "German forged manacles" was replace by "mind-forg'd manacles," which is surely a remarkably felicitous revision. The original phrase refers to the German mercenaries who were charged with spying on and in some cases arresting British soldiers. In the first version man is enslaved by an external, foreign agency. In the second version he is more clearly enslaved by himself—and presumably can only be liberated by himself, by his own redeemed imaginative powers.

Ideally, one would expect the prophetic artist as creator to assume this role, to become the acknowledged or unacknowledged legislators of a new order. But in fact, in Blake's view, most of the artists of his own time, Joshua Reynolds chief among them, had become co-opted by the very forces that Blake, as a prophet/poet, feels called upon to overthrow. Far from being revolutionary, Reynolds was quintessentially the sanctioned artist as academician, a slavishly imitative curator of the past, a smugly complacent champion of the status quo.

Before proceeding further with my lexical excavations I would like to point out that in the phrase the "mind-forg'd manacles I hear," what one would normally have expected to see, is instead heard. Inversely, a sigh, which would normally be heard, is seen, or envisaged, as running in blood down palace walls. We are not dealing here with Coleridge's perception of a sound in light, a light-like power in sound, signs of a visionary intensification of reality, but with a dark parody of such a state. Again, synesthesia, often taken to be a sign of a kind of sensory and intellectual harmony, here suggests something like the opposite. I am reminded not of Coleridge but of Rimbaud who, deeply interested in synesthesia, sought perversely to explore it through the "systematic derangement" and disorder of the senses. Though, of course, himself dedicated to no such program, Blake's heard manacles and seen sighs that run like blood down palace walls are instances not of the harmony of the senses, but of a disordered usurpation of one sense by the other. Hearing mind-forg'd manacles, and in particular seeing a sigh running down palace walls, has something of the quality of the hallucinations of a disordered mind, a mind that reflects the disordered and chaotic nature of the social order unsuccessfully veiled by an enforced conformity. These effects produce, too, in the reader, a feeling of disorientation and cognitive dissonance.

Similarly, the power of the chimney sweeper's cry to appall, etymologically to make pale, churches stained with grime and soot, and the power of the harlot's curse to engender an actual blight, disturbingly suggest that language has the capacity to exert an occult and an occasionally malevolent power. To believe that language, and in particular bans and curses, have this kind of dubious, illegitimate power is to succumb to a kind of atavistic magical thinking or the superstition against which Blake constantly railed.

Rather than imputing a disordered mind to the poem's poetic/prophetic narrator, the visions that he depicts can be seen as his perception or record of a pathological disorder, not only of the disordered senses, but of minds afflicted by the widespread hypocrisy of those in power who profess one thing but do another.

To continue, after this brief digression, with my examples of what I have been referring to as key words, I must refer again to the aforementioned word *appalls*, whose usual meaning is, of course, to shock and horrify. The church is here suddenly personified and said to be subject to a powerful emotional reaction. This irruption of personification feels like yet another instance of a kind of atavistic, disordered, at times superstitious language that, as we have seen, tends to become more prominent in "London" as the poem progresses. In the real world of London, of course, the grandees of the church, a bastion of cynicism and hypocrisy, were unlikely to be appalled by anything, least of all the by the cries, like those of the chimney sweeps, of those whom they have exploited.

As mentioned above, to appall also means to pale or dim; to become faint or feeble. To appall, to make pale, is the impossible task of the chimney sweeps in their losing battle to clear away accumulated ecclesiastical grime. The chimney sweepers, of course, breathed in vast amounts of toxic material that led them to wax pale and faint, to become subject to various diseases, and in some cases to die. But it was not only chimney sweepers who succumbed to the weakness and woe mentioned in the poem's first stanza; the dense smog of industrialized London, the gift of the captains of commerce, seriously compromised the health of all.

Buried within the word *appalled* is the word *pall*. A pall is a richly embroidered ecclesiastical garment; it is also a cloth laid over the altar during the Eucharist. Finally it is a cloth spread over a hearse, such as the marriage hearse referred to in the last line of "London," or the shroud spread over a corpse. The word *pallbearer* is related to these usages.

All of these ecclesiastical associations connote not life nor the promise of eternal life but literal and spiritual death..

The next key word in my—or Blake's—inventory is *sigh*, which, according to the OED, has not so much a number of definitions as a number of connotations. It defines the word *sigh* as an audible respiration suggesting or indicating dejection, weariness, longing, pain, or relief. To which might be added frustration and anger as well as the sighs generated by sexual congress—and finally the death sigh, the sound of the final expiration of the breath at the time of death. David Erdman in his book *Prophet Against Empire* indicates that the connection of sighing with death was far more prevalent in Blake's time than it is in our own. It is remarkable that a sigh, a mere ghost of a sound, suggests a kind of affective polysemy that is more than the equal to that of almost any articulated word.

The sigh is uttered in "London" by the hapless soldier who has sufficient frustration and anger to have earlier uttered bans, likely blasphemous curses. The soldier is associated with the harlot, and perhaps with the sighs of sexual congress. Finally, and preeminently, the soldier fears the possibility of death on the battlefield, that he will become the victim of some superfluous and unnecessary war, resulting in a final death sigh. Of course, we can well imagine him also issuing sighs of dejection, weariness, longing, pain, and even relief. And it is not only the hapless soldier whom one can imagine issuing such sighs. One can equally imagine the young harlot and the chimney sweepers uttering inarticulate though audible signs of distress. In fact, I suspect that the vast majority of the citizens of London, as opposed to the privileged few by whom they are they oppressed, might have multiple occasions to sigh as a result of experiencing the yoke of tyranny.

The final member of my little inventory of key words in "London" is *blasts*. The harlot's curse, corresponding to the soldier's ban, "blasts the newborn infants tear." The word *blast* also refers to the forges and furnaces discussed earlier. A blast is yet another term for a curse or a malediction; to blast is also to falsely and deliberately malign or destroy the reputation of others, an occupation perhaps much engaged in by courtiers, politicians, or merchants. In the particular context of the harlot's curse, the meaning of blast is not primarily to shrivel vegetation, to cause plagues, though it still carries these meanings, but is more simply and generally "to blight." What is being blasted and blighted here is not the vegetal but the human, the innocent tear, a newborn infant who is perhaps stricken by a venereal disease contracted between the harlot and some soldier she eventually weds. Their "marriage hearse," a terrible phrase, will thus be blasted by plagues.

Marriage is ideally a sacrament joining two people as one under God and holding forth a promise of a long shared life. Here we have, instead, the conjunction of marriage with a hearse, indicating a relationship that is doomed from the start. The relationship of the soldier and harlot, and the fate of their diseased infant, is emblematic of a future that is tragically foreclosed. And here, at the end of the poem, one senses that for Blake any viable future for most of the inhabitants of London was being denied by the tyrannical, unholy, death-dealing conspiracy of church, state, and the rising mercantile class. The poem ends, fittingly, with a plague, a plague reminiscent of the Biblical plagues that are the result of God's wrath.

In contrast with the polysemy of the complex words that I have been discussing is the kind of lexical poverty, the extreme repetitiveness of diction, to which I have already referred. Augmenting this literal repetition is the repetition of words that are similar in meaning or function. The words *ban*, *sigh*, and *curse* have much the same nature as the triply reiterated *cry*, suggesting not only the cacophonous ubiquity of sound in the poem, but the ubiquity of suffering, and once again, the brutal selfsameness of a society that enforces a strict and ruthless conformity. These words, too, are notable for either being inarticulate or barely articulate. Those who utter these curses/cries/sighs/bans clearly lack the capacity to articulate any kind of critique of the soul-destroying conditions that enslave them. They have been divested of the capacity for the intellectual warfare that might, eventually, have liberated them. Instead, their condition is for all intents and purposes hopeless.

Indeed, there seem to be two orders of words and of language in "London"; one characterized by lexical poverty, extreme repetitiveness and inarticulateness, or by mere inarticulate sounds; the other by the brilliant deployment of polysemous words and by striking rhetorical effects, such as the poem's strange use of synesthesia. The first order is that of the language of the sufferers in the poem, who are able to only barely articulate their sufferings and their anger at the conditions foisted upon them, with bans, curses, cries, and sighs, which either, as deployed, have one meaning or as mere sounds, properly speaking, have no meaning at all. The second-order language is that of the linguistically gifted poet/prophet, in which the multiple meanings of some apparently merely first-order words, such as bans and sighs, as well as others belonging to the second order, are exploited to their utmost, giving voice to the voiceless, anatomizing and indicting, with an extraordinary power and resonance, the conditions that are the cause of their pain and those who are responsible for it.

While the prophet wanders, the victim/sufferers are frozen in the hellish world of the selfsame, of single vision, the realm that Blake calls Ulro, the limit of contraction. Their torturers, likewise, are afflicted by the "single vision" of the tyrant and oppressor and their world too is ultimately hellish, imaginatively and spiritually dead. To use Blake's allegorical language, Urizen, the aged tyrant, the prince of a false and dissimulating reason, is bound upon the same wheel as Orc, the instinctual and vital energies he cunningly and savagely suppresses.

One normally imagines a prophet as clearly seeing the conditions and the moral waywardness that he indicts. Aside from the poem's first two stanzas, the poet/prophet who is the poem's protagonist, repeatedly hears, listens to, without judgement, the ubiquitous cacophony of barely articulate utterances, reminding us that hearing, too, of course, has a distinguished Biblical pedigree. The Israelites, after, all, occasionally hear but can never see God. Similarly, the individual worshipper hears, internally, the sometimes still, small voice of God. In either case, receptive listening is required of those who would act in accordance with God's grace and will. In "London," moreover, the protagonist's wanderings are often, it seems, conducted not by the light of day but under cover of darkness: "but most in midnight's streets I hear…" Blake's prophetic role is to bear witness to those who are suffering in the shadows. Listening, an empathic receptivity, is a kind of precondition of the prophet's speaking that articulates what those in pain cannot articulate, and to turning of his judgement and wrath not, of course, upon the sufferer but upon those who have created the conditions that cause their suffering. I have mentioned that Blake, like the Biblical prophet, exhibits a mixture of compassion and of wrathful indignation, the two principles, mercy and justice, that are preeminent in the Kabbalah, and whose proper adjustment to each other is of vital importance.

In the poem's first two stanzas, dominated by what I have called its first-order language, their very lexical repetitions—the lexical belonging, of course, to the axis of sense—at the same time register as sound effects. Sound and sense, augmenting each other, characterized by extreme repetition, cause the not uncommonly regular meter of the poem to sound oppressively strident. Likewise, in the poem's opening stanzas, alliteration, the triple *m* sound that is the result of the thrice-used *mark*, as well as the alliterative *weakness and woe*, reinforces the feeling of numbing, rote repetitiveness that characterizes the social order as a whole.

Later, the poem's sound augments the more complex sense of the poem's second-order language. For examples, the word *man*, included within the word *manacles*, suggests the significant cluster, related by assonance, of man/ban/manacles. Another such cluster, this time alliterative, is comprised of ban/blackening/blood/blasts/blight. The initial simplicity of the sound effects of the first two stanzas becomes more complex as the poem becomes increasingly phantasmagoric, almost hallucinatory—as it progresses toward its final emphasis on plague and blight that are the consequence in the Bible of both personal and state sponsored moral and intellectual malfeasance.

4.

Unlike Blake's long, sometimes almost impossibly dense prophetic books, "London" is a clear and extraordinarily condensed expression of Blake's vision of an unregenerate society, an expression in which each word—and all of its meanings and connotations, as I have tried to indicate—is fully exploited, mined for its maximal complexity and force, resulting in an extraordinary density of intellectual and affective implication and connotation in a poem whose denotative message is relatively straightforward.

Imagine, in a kind of homely and outdated metaphor, a poem as a kind of switchboard that contains a number of small light bulbs representing words, including both complex, polysemous words and simpler words whose usage is relatively straightforward and direct. Imagine that that each bulb lights up only when the fullest number of the possibles meanings or implications of a given word are achieved. Most poems would be like a switchboard that only lights up, with no particular pattern, here or there. "London" would be like a switchboard in which each bulb is fully and radiantly glowing.

Did Blake, when he wrote "London," deliberately, laboriously plot out a poem that would provide a structure and context in which the English language can be seen to operate, to resonate, at its highest pitch, each word of the poem not only vibrating with a maximal intensity but resonating with a myriad of other words? To the contrary, to all appearances the poem seems to have been set down quickly, with only one word crossed out and changed.

Because of its condensed form, "London" seems to me to be a particularly cogent empirical exhibit exemplifying what can never be proven, that currently much-maligned notions such as inspiration or the Poetic Genius or imagination, however conceived, are necessary to account for the greatest works of art. What Blake called the

Poetic Genius is homologous with what I have been calling creative intuition, the preconscious, synoptic, synthetic vision of what is later to be unfolded, enacted as a fully articulated work of art. Such intuitive insights are immediate, occur in what Blake calls the pulsation of an artery. They occur almost without exception to those who have long engaged in the struggle that Blake calls intellectual warfare, to those who thought long and hard about whatever problem, artistic or scientific, is to be worked out, just as Blake had pondered long and hard, pondered as a poet and artist, on the both the aesthetic and political issues raised in "London."

The Blake who claimed to write according to the prompting, or even, literally, the dictates of inspiration and Poetic Genius could well have been, and in fact was long considered, a crank, or worse, a madman, but nevertheless produced in "London" a poem that evidences that genius. I am, as promised at the outset of this essay, arguing from evidence that Blake produced in "London" a work that can be seen to authenticate his exorbitant claims for the powers of the imagination and of the Poetic Genius.

Of course, the senses of words work only in consort together, but in "London" they do so to an extraordinary, an exemplary degree. Here I will turn from my metaphor of the "London" as switchboard, and will invoke once again the less homely metaphor of Indra's necklace, each pearl of which reflects and is reflected by all the others. Perhaps language as a meaning-producing phenomenon, and great lyric poems like "London" as among its most potent, condensed epiphenomena, is/are in some way like Indra's infinitely imbricated, infinitely ramifying, endlessly shimmering necklace. Or one might think of such poems as like the gem-encrusted streets of Blake's fourfold Jerusalem, city of God, with its rubies reddened by rubies reddening, its diamonds reflecting diamonds reflecting diamonds. Or, indulging in the extravagant and the outlandish, one might even think of the lexical body of "London," comprised of its individual words and phonemes, as like the perfectly proportioned form of Blake's Albion, the redeemed, universal man in whom all is contained and transformed, the human form divine rising naked and unadorned, as in Blake's great print Glad Day, like the sun to his proper station.

5.

To Blake, as an intensely committed, even if unorthodox Christian, the London in which he lived and moved was not merely misgoverned but in a fallen and unregenerate state. Man, lest he continually enslave himself, was in need not only of a political, but also of mental and spiritual renovation and redemption.

Blake wrote in the midst of the upheaval of the industrial revolution, and unflinchingly looked at some of its consequences, at the "dark satanic mills" that were not only factories in which appalling conditions obtained, but a metaphor for the multiple ills of the society which Blake excoriated. The role of the poet/prophet is not to predict the future but to look with a clear, unflinching eye at the present and at the conditions obtaining in it. For Blake the present moment, the pulsation of an artery, is also, however, an eternal moment, one that grants access to a kind of timeless truth, to the kingdom or city of God. Blake never abandoned the prophetic hope for, indeed expectation of, the renovation and apotheosis of the fallen society he so unflinchingly witnessed.

I would like to end, as a kind of coda, with Blake's great short lyric "Jerusalem," the type with respect to which "London" is the antitype. Though it was not specifically written as a companion piece to "London," it expresses Blake's sublime anticipation of the building of a redeemed fourfold London that, as a city of God, will be one with the heavenly city of Jerusalem and the risen cosmic body of Albion.

Written in four stanzas of four lines each, with four stresses per line, the redundant fourfold structure of "Jerusalem" is precisely equivalent to that of "London," yet it does not produce anything like the same sense of lockstep regularity generated by the extreme repetitiveness of diction of "London." To the contrary, its use of a very different kind of repetition—that of beginning lines with the same word—produces, as is usual with this device (as deployed, say, by Christopher Smart, Whitman, and Ginsberg) an opposite kind of effect, one of gathering and intensifying momentum. The four-line stanza of both "London" and "Jerusalem" is typical of English hymns—and "Jerusalem," having been set gloriously to music, has in fact become one of the most beloved of these hymns.

Blake, in a move that is typical of him, displaces providential history onto England or Albion. Blake generally mistrusted the passivity of the pastoral. "Jerusalem," however, with its evocation of "mountains green," of "pleasant pastures," of England's "green and pleasant land," is a striking exception to this general rule. Blake suggests that the apocalyptic renovation that will manifest in a spiritual fourfold London, a city of God, has already been prepared for. The poem implies that holy feet have already walked on England's hills, that the lamb of God has already appeared in English pastures, and that the countenance divine has once been seen amid England's green and clouded hills. This reminiscence of a lost pastoral Eden paves the way, in the poem, for a vision of an imminent apocalyptic restoration of all that has been lost or squandered, and for the transformation of London into a new Jerusalem, a regenerate city of God.

I will quote the poem in full without further comment here, where it will serve the humble function of concluding this essay on a bracingly triumphant note.

JERUSALEM

And did those feet in ancient times
Walk upon Englands mountains green:
And was the holy Lamb of God,
On Englands pleasant pastures seen!

And did the Countenance Divine,
Shine forth upon our clouded hills?
And was Jerusalem builded here,
Among these dark Satanic Mills?

Bring me my Bow of burning gold:
Bring me my arrows of desire:
Bring me my spear: O clouds unfold!
Bring me my Chariot of fire!

I will not cease from Mental Fight
Nor shall my sword sleep in my hand:
Til we have built Jerusalem,
In Englands green & pleasant Land.

3.
Shelley: Beyond Idealism and the Daemonic Sublime

1.

To begin with a less than entirely distinguished sonnet (though its inaugural phrase "those who live / call Life" enshrines a fine disdainful irony) whose relevance, after a few intervening pages (I beg your patience) will become if anything too obvious:

> Lift not the painted veil which those who live
> Call Life: though unreal shapes be pictured there,
> And it but mimic all we would believe
> With colours idly spread, —behind, lurk Fear
> And Hope, twin Destinies; who ever weave
> Their shadows, o'er the chasm, sightless and drear.
> I knew one who had lifted it—he sought,
> For his lost heart was tender, things to love,
> But found them not, alas! nor was there aught
> The world contains, the which he could approve.
> Through the unheeding many he did move,
> A splendour among shadows, a bright blot
> Upon this gloomy scene, a Spirit that strove
> For truth, and like the Preacher found it not.

I have been searching for a way in to saying something meaningful and pertinent about Shelley, a poet who in some has ways cast a deeper spell over me than any of his Romantic confreres. Shelley is the most mercurial of poets. Indeed, we can imagine his spirit as mercury, but as mercury of a special kind that exists not merely in a solid or a liquid state, but also in many intermediate states as well, at least one of them combustible. In attempting to grasp one of these states, one loses hold of the others, and one is left with a partial and distorted perspective.

One conspicuous difficulty in writing about Shelley, in short, is that there were many Shelleys, and that the interactions between any two or more of them are difficult to evaluate. Which, if any, are central? Which are peripheral? How did their relative importance, and the relationship between them, evolve over time?

Among these multiple Shelleys are Shelley the platonic idealist; Shelley the skeptic, the student of Hume, whose intellectual philosophy deploys skepticism to clear the ground for the notion that all that we perceive is a function of our own consciousness; Shelley the satirist; Shelley the political radical steeped in the ideology of the Enlightenment; Shelley the meliorist who despaired of any meaningful renovation of society; Shelley the feminist and evangelist of free love who was the sole male in households of female acolytes, some of whom he cruelly banished under the pretext that they were too ideologically or spiritually impure, or immature, to embrace either his political radicalism or his lofty idealizations of love—households that were intended to be models of utopian values but were instead rife with dystopian tensions and anxieties. And, finally, there is the self-exiled Shelley, ever peripatetic, pulling up roots, while longing for some stable, sustaining home.

The constant, unsettled movement in Shelley's life reflects another endemic characteristic that first manifested itself in Shelley's childhood and continued unabated to his final days. I am referring to Shelley's intense restlessness, reflected not only in the impetuousness of his life but also in his impatient urge to thrust past the realm of phenomenal appearances and its quotidian manifestations, to mount a main assault on their mysterious, veiled source. Platonic or Neoplatonic idealism, with its promise of higher realms of experience, its apprehension of a kind of universal mind beyond the realm of mere sense perception, was thus initially attractive to him. But it did not, finally, appease his relentlessness, his quest to track down life to its hidden source, which perhaps lay beyond life's confines, including the final limiting term of death itself. From his early to his last days, Shelley was intensely impatient with and ambivalent about life itself as we commonly know or experience it. This impatience grew more, not less, intense as he grew older. More and more, life seemed to him a kind of brutal charade.

In my search to find my way into a discussion of Shelley, I might have set his many-mindedness aside and settled for writing about one Shelley, or about one poem (technically, of course, a play) by Shelley, *Prometheus Unbound*, which I regard as among the greatest achievements of English Romanticism, equal even to Keats' odes, or to that perpetual critical darling and front-runner, Wordsworth's "The Prelude."

One virtue of *Prometheus Unbound* is that, unlike the protean Shelley himself, it has a fine internal consistency, an intrinsic unity. The argument of the poem is extraordinarily simple. Prometheus, having sinned in his failed attempt to steal fire from the Gods, is chained to a rocky precipice by Zeus, who consigns him to perpetual torture. Meanwhile Asia, his one-time paramour, pines away in some antipodal Eastern realm, maximally distant from Prometheus. At some point, Prometheus is inspired to revoke the curse that he has directed toward the Gods, a ban which understandably rankles them, and forgives his tormentor—whereupon a world that had been completely fixed, frozen, bursts into vital motion. Prometheus is freed from his rock and Asia, under the power of some invisible influence that manifests itself as a kind of prevailing breeze, is wafted toward her erstwhile mate. At this point, after its first two acts, the poem's argument comes to an end. The last two books are taken up with the glorious pageant of Asia, regaled by her retinue of planetary spheres and sister spirits with sublime paroxysms of lyrical verse, as she draws ever closer to her apocalyptic union with Prometheus—a union which, I am keen to note, parenthetically, is a marriage between East and West.

This argument is uncannily similar to Blake's dialectic in the *Book of Los*, which is also elaborated elsewhere in his prophetic books. Urizen, Blake's embodiment of abstract reason, of the oppressive power of church and state in all their forms, has a vested interest in repressing Los, Blake's embodiment of the logos as imagination, who rebels against such repression. Locked in a frozen and endless conflict, both are given over to the Selfhood, to the ego in a limited and perverted form. The Selfhood is internally divided and is lorded over by a shadow of the self that Blake calls "the specter." A further aspect of this state of internal division is that the self is also estranged from its "emanations," figured as female, akin to Jung's anima or Stevens' "interior paramour," which in an integrated state of the self are related not only to man's capacity to relate productively to actual women, but also to his ability to unfold all that is creative within him, to produce works of art—in Blake's case, works of both plastic art and poetry, which serve as a liberating force and as an antidote to repression.

In *Prometheus Unbound*, Zeus is equivalent to Urizen, and Prometheus to Los. Locked in unremitting strife, both are given over to their internally conflicted Selfhood, to their repressive shadow selves, their specters, as a result of which Prometheus is self-divided, estranged from Asia, his emanation. As soon as Prometheus abjures his conflict with Zeus, his internal conflict or self-division is healed, and he is released from implacable hatred and defiance, from his oppressive specter, whereupon Asia, his emanation, rushes to reunite with him in what will be an apocalyptic consummation of their union.

The uncanny resemblance of *Prometheus Unbound* to Blake's dialectic is perhaps not accidental. Both Blake and Shelley, unlike the other major Romantics, with the possible exception of Byron, were and remained at heart defiant rebels, and both remained emotionally and spiritually committed to the dream of an apocalyptic renovation of society. However, the example of the chaotic depredations of the French Revolution led them to accept that much work, inner and outer, would need to be done to prepare for true and lasting change.

I have touched on *Prometheus Unbound* because it reflects Shelley at his most apocalyptically optimistic and single-minded—as a kind of counterexample, and hopefully an illuminating contrast, to Shelley's habitual many-mindedness, which I have alluded to above. *Prometheus Unbound* may uncannily echo Blake, but Shelley's work as a whole bears little resemblance to that of the prophetic Blake, whose point of view, whose unwavering critique of all within man and society that led to the terrible oppression he saw around him, was relentlessly single-minded and remained remarkably unchanged over many years.

Shelley's poetry, over the course of a much shorter career, is characterized by insistent, insatiable questioning, a questioning that never leads to satisfying, definitively conclusive answers but to still more ardent and sometimes more desperate questions. What I have been calling Shelley's many-mindedness is in part the result of the variegated and sometimes incompatible intellectual and philosophical perspectives that he so quickly and brilliantly assimilated, some of which he later abandoned. One might point, for example, to the ways in which the ethos of the Enlightenment and of what we think of as Romanticism are somewhat uneasily suspended in the brilliant rhetorical solution that is "A Defense of Poetry." Shelley was influenced not only by William Godwin and Thomas Paine, political conduits of Enlightenment values, but by David Hume, who ignited the strain of skepticism that serves as an unlikely ally of the platonic idealism in Shelley's work. This skeptical strain sometimes takes the form of a kind of aristocratic urbanity, as in Shelley's "Julian and Maddalo," in which Shelley's and Byron's alter egos are engaged, while riding on horseback on a beach in Venice, in a philosophical dialogue. Byron, an arch skeptic, or perhaps more properly a cynic, gives voice to a creed which Shelley resists, while at the same time finding it not entirely unpersuasive. The relatively light-hearted, mythopoetic "Witch of Atlas" has a unique kind of visionary urbanity, two terms not normally associated with each other that Shelley manages to make compatible.

Shelley, despite his political agitations, was hardly a man of the people, nor did he sound like one. He admired Keats and proffered him several small but heartfelt acts of kindness, but did so with a doubtless unconscious air of aristocratic noblesse oblige that Keats found not only off-putting but an insuperable barrier to the development of anything more than a casual relationship. Or perhaps Keats simply recognized that their difference in class, despite Shelley's efforts to annul such a difference, would nonetheless consign him to a kind of subordinate position.

The roots of Shelley's ambivalence run deeper than the often contradictory concatenation of ideas that seem to have been perpetually swirling in his mind. In attempting to settle on, and focus on, some manageably circumscribed and yet more fundamental aspect of that ambivalence, I have decided to examine Shelley's deeply conflicted attitude to power and to life, to the experience of being an embodied being, to the indignities and joys of being alive and subject to life's vicissitudes. I will focus mostly on the power of the imagination, with a particular stress, initially, on a triad of poems written in close succession, the first of which, "Hymn to Intellectual Beauty," recounts an experience of initiation that is at once of Shelley's spiritual awakening and his awakening to his vocation as a poet. The second, "Mont Blanc," a powerful exercise in the sublime, seeks to track to its source the awe-inspiring power that manifests as the created world. The third, "Alastor," Shelley's first fully mature narrative poem, and one of his finest, takes up and extends concerns addressed in the first two.

The "Hymn to Intellectual Beauty" begins by invoking a mysterious power. "The awful shadow of some unseen Power / Floats though unseen among us…" In the second stanza, this power is directly addressed: "Spirit of BEAUTY that dost consecrate / With thine own hues all thou dost shine upon / Of human thought or form…" Immediately following these lines, however, Shelley asks, "where art thou gone?" Much or most of the "Hymn to Intellectual Beauty" is a succession of metaphors, or of concrete instances serving as metaphors, that evoke this evanescent power, which visits this world with an "inconstant wing" and manifests as phenomena that seem—like the extraordinary image of imagination as a coal that fades even as it flares in "Defense of Poetry"—to vanish even as they appear. Addressing this power, Shelley plaintively complains,

> Man were immortal, and omnipotent,
> Didst thou, unknown and awful as thou art,
> Keep with thy glorious train firm state within his heart.

Which echoes the earlier complaint,

> Why dost thou pass away and leave our state,
> This dim vast vale of tears, vacant and desolate?

And again:

> Depart not—lest the grave should be,
> Like life and fear, a dark reality.

The poem concludes, however, with the wish "That thou—O awful LOVELINESS / Wouldst give whate'er these words cannot express" and with a confidence that this power—like Shelley's remembered bond, as a child, with a nurturing nature—will "…to my onward life supply / Its calm, to one who worships thee," a passage that reflects the influence of Wordsworth on the early Shelley. The poet shall eventually attain, under the aegis of the power of beauty and of loveliness, the calmness of what Wordsworth in "Intimations of Immortality" called "the philosophic mind," a cast of mind that is associated by Shelley with the higher, platonic realm of intellectual beauty, a beauty that gives to life whatever luster it possesses.

What I wish to emphasize here, however, is Shelley's deep ambivalence toward the power which he invokes. It appears as a shadow, a darkness that is twice referred to as invisible. When it touches us or our world it is thus already at two removes from its source. It is also twice referred to as "awful," as inspiring both awe and fear. It is also extreme in its capriciousness, in its almost simultaneous comings and goings. It evinces no concern, or at least no abiding concern, with man. Certainly it will not grant him immortality by taking up permanent seat in his heart.

And yet this same power is also associated with "Beauty," which far from being identified with the shadowy and the dark, consecrates all that it shines upon. When one lives under its aegis, one is granted a wise, philosophical, Wordsworth-like calmness, which in Shelley corresponds to "Intellectual Beauty."

Shelley's remarkable poem "Mont Blanc" is also highly ambivalent about such power. Here, "in likeness of the Arve" River, "Power" cascades down the face of the mountain, uprooting, overthrowing, destroying all in its path. At the same time, the Arve is likened to thoughts not only in the human mind but in a kind of universal mind, thoughts that are generative, creative, reflecting, perhaps, the even-greater power of their source. That source, however, must ever remain unseen by us.

> Power dwells apart in its tranquillity,
> Remote, serene, and inaccessible:

Shelley conjures up an image of the summit of Mont Blanc, a landscape which represents that which cannot be seen by us and therefore can only be imagined. The summit is described as being almost eerily tranquil, without motion except for that of gently falling snow. It is a scene strangely beautiful in its calm austerity and solitude. It is here, Shelley imagines, that the Arve, whose power generates the world of phenomenal appearances, originates. At its imagined, quiescent origin, the Arve is very unlike the restless, tumultuous power, gathering momentum as it flows, which visibly rages down the steeply pitched slope of the mountain.

This final section of the poem concludes with an abrupt question:

> And what were thou, and earth, and stars, and sea,
> If to the human mind's imaginings
> Silence and solitude were vacancy?

This enigmatic question seems to grow more enigmatic the more one ponders it. It has been a kind of koan for me, a code difficult if not impossible to crack. Perhaps Shelley intended it as such, as an expression of the very unknowability that shrouds the source that he seeks. Shelley's habitual state, reflected in his epistemological uncertainty, is in some ways akin to that of Keats's "Negative Capability" and of the remorseless but liberating not-knowing that is the outcome of Nagarjuna's logic. There is, however, a key difference: Shelley was by temperament profoundly discontented with and unable to rest in a state of unknowing. He had the intellectual integrity to recognize that both the working of his own imagination, and the dictates of what he called the "Intellectual Philosophy" (quite different, as shall see, from his essentially Neoplatonic notion of

"Intellectual Beauty"), kept landing him in an uncertainty which he experienced not as liberating but as an intolerable limitation. Quite often, as at end of "Mont Blanc," he leaves us as readers with a frustrated state of not-knowing as well.

And yet, one finds oneself making tentative feints at interpretation. On the one hand, the concluding question of "Mont Blanc" can be seen as suggesting that if the silent and inaccessible source of power were in fact a kind of vacancy, one could account neither for the human mind's imaginings nor for the things of this world. On the other hand, and to the contrary, perhaps Shelley is suggesting that the source of all might indeed be a kind of vacancy, like the Buddhist *shunyata*, or void, and that power in all of its manifestations, including ourselves, is a kind of illusory phantasmagoria projected upon the equally phantasmagoric painted scrim of this world. Shelley leaves this question, like so many of his insistent queries, open, thus leaving us, in our attempts to answer them, with nothing but our own insufficient resources.

Having provided the above as context, and on the principle of taking up first things last, I now return to the long-awaited scene of initiation that is of central importance in the "Hymn to Intellectual Beauty":

> While yet a boy I sought for ghosts, and sped
> Through many a listening chamber, cave, and ruin,
> And starlight wood, with fearful steps pursuing
> Hopes of high talk with the departed dead.
> I call'd on poisonous names with which our youth is fed;
> I was not heard; I saw them not;
> When musing deeply on the lot
> Of life, at that sweet time when winds are wooing
> All vital things that wake to bring
> News of birds and blossoming,
> Sudden, thy shadow fell on me;
> I shrieked, and clasped my hands in ecstasy!
>
> I vow'd that I would dedicate my powers
> To thee and thine: have I not kept the vow?
> With beating heart and streaming eyes, even now
>
> I call the phantoms of a thousand hours
> Each from his voiceless grave...

This remarkable account of Shelley's spiritual initiation veers close to suggesting that the young Shelley was a Faustian practitioner of the dark arts. It has a kind of gothic, necromantic air. It reminds me of yogic practitioners of the so-called "left-hand path," frequent haunters of the cremation grounds. Shelley was temperamentally an antinomian through and through. Beginning with his stint at Oxford, from which he was expelled for writing a pamphlet advocating atheism, both his ideas and his behavior were regularly regarded as scandalous or outright blasphemous, a state of affairs that led to his permanent, if unofficial, banishment from England. Characteristically, musing deeply on life, Shelley is drawn to the precincts of death, calling "the phantoms of a thousand hours / Each from his voiceless grave."

If we ask ourselves with which of the two apparently contradictory views of the power of the imagination suggested by "Hymn to Intellectual Beauty" this scene of initiation comports—the dark, shadowy, capricious power, invisible, at two removes from its source, blithely unconcerned with man, sovereign in its sublimity; or the beautiful, luminously harmonious power conducive to calm, repose, and the philosophic mind—the answer is clear. It resonates primarily with Shelley's dark vision of awful sublimity.

Does this mean that Shelley's ambivalence regarding the two faces of poetic power set forth in "Hymn to Intellectual Beauty" has simply been resolved? Not at all. Shelley will continue to be attracted to the radiant spirit through which beauty is apprehended, which is exemplified by "the best and happiest moments of the happiest and best minds," and which is allied with the contemplative, the philosophical and the higher, platonic realm of intellectual beauty. This Neoplatonic strain in Shelley, though never entirely abandoned, will ultimately be superseded by what Shelley calls the intellectual philosophy, about which we will have more to say later.

In any event, Shelley's conception of the imagination here seems to be Janus-faced. In one of its aspects the imagination is a daemonic, capricious, inconstant power that visits the poet whenever and wherever it will. It is beyond the conscious control of the poet. It provides him only the briefest intimations, subsiding even as they arise, of its mysterious source. Its visitations can seem, at times, more unsettling than inspiring. Shelley was troubled throughout his life by nightmares, sleep walking, and deeply disturbing, almost hallucinatory visions. The daemonic power to which Shelley had pledged himself at times seemed to master him more than he mastered it, and it proved anything but an easy master. And yet it has a kind of undeniable, beneficent aspect as well. Like the river Arve in Mont Blanc and the implacable West Wind in Shelley's great ode, it overwhelms, uproots, dislodges all that is in its path. In doing so, it clears the ground for future creations. It is bound up with the great, ever-turning cycle of life and death.

Even in *Prometheus Unbound*, with its healing of internal divisions, with its exultant Neoplatonic apocalypse, with its chorus of Asia's attendants chanting hymns extolling an intellectual beauty that is on the verge of triumphant realization, this dark, daemonic force makes a mysterious appearance. It does so in the figure of Demogorgon, a kind of demiurge who dwells in shadowy, unfathomable depths. He is a master of the fated and fatal whose main function seems to be to turn the wheel of time. There is a disturbing suggestion here that the regenerative apocalypse of *Prometheus Bound* has not, in fact, been engendered by free will, by Prometheus' seemingly spontaneous revocation of his curse, but has been predetermined by the cyclical movement of history itself. If this is the case the apocalypse portrayed in *Prometheus* will not, like the Christian apocalypse, be final. It, too, will pass as the grinding wheel of time continues to turn.

But Demogorgon is not merely the turner of the wheel of history. His shadowy nature is itself not fully graspable, is profoundly mysterious. With respect to him, Shelley writes the "deep truth is imageless." The depths of the daemonic are as unfathomable and nameless as the nameless and unimaginable heights of the inscrutable One that in Neoplatonism is the source of all.

If Shelley's imagination holds commerce with this kind of shadowy, daemonic realm, nevertheless his Neoplatonic muse is its equal. His insatiable drive toward the realization of ideals perhaps too lofty to be accommodated within the confines of life itself, his drive toward ecstatic union with the One, the source of all, or at least with its manifestation in the radiant, ideal forms of intellectual beauty, remains insatiable.

In "Alastor," these two strains of the power of the imagination, working together in the poet who is the poem's protagonist, lead not to some higher synthesis, but on the contrary to what seems an inevitably tragic outcome.

The preface of "Alastor" has been confusing to many critics. Some see it as emphasizing, with only a minor reservation, the nobility of a figure who in the poem itself is treated in almost entirely, and rightly, glowingly positive terms. Others see the preface as laying appropriate disapprobation and blame upon a solitary, essentially narcissistic figure whose quest is at its outset rightfully doomed to fail. Those in the first camp consider the poet's quest, though doomed, as an essentially valiant exercise by a figure who is perhaps too good for this world, but whose purity and magnanimity are to be admired, not condemned. Those in the second camp see the poet as a self-obsessed dreamer, infatuated by his own delusions, who meets the fate that he deserves.

The preface itself begins by depicting the poet, at considerable length, as a kind of paragon of all that is virtuous and noble. However, in one brief passage, spanning the end of the first paragraph and the beginning of the second, Shelley suggests that the poet has lost his way first by imagining a figure, a kind of spectral double, possessed of all his virtues, with whom he might converse, thus freeing himself from the burden of too great a solitude. This strange encounter has disastrous consequences. Shelley concludes this passage by asserting that his depiction of the poet and his fate is "not barren of instruction to actual men." He writes of the poet's untimely demise:

> The Poet's self-centered seclusion was avenged by the furies of an irresistible passion pursuing him to speedy ruin. But that Power which strikes the luminaries of the world with sudden darkness and extinction, by awakening them to too exquisite a perception of its influences, dooms to a slow and poisonous decay those meaner spirits that dare to abjure its dominion.

Before addressing this rich passage, it is worth noting the Alastor of the poem's title refers not to the poet himself but to the spirit of solitude. Thomas Love Peacock, who suggested the title to Shelley, noted that in Greek, Alastor is defined as an evil genius, and that in his view of the poem, the spirit of solitude is none other than this evil genius. Shelley's view on the matter was far more complex.

In "Alastor" itself the poet, goaded by the spirit of solitude, a daemonic power rather than an evil genius, sets forth on a quest during which he is awakened, as a result of his too exquisite perception, to the influence of a power that destroys him—or that enlists the vengeful furies, agents of an irresistible passion, to destroy him.

I would suggest that the agents just represented as external to the poet—the spirit of solitude, the influence of a daemonic power, the implacable furies—are in fact at least equally internal. Shelley's imagination is instinct with a creative/destructive force that not only obliterates all in its path but motivates the poet's drive to discover the ultimate source and nature of things and in so doing, inadvertently, to court death. Shelley seldom describes this aspect of his imagination as having a seat within himself. It is almost always depicted as an external, fateful force, with respect to which the poet is a kind of passive instrument. Its darkly inspiring visitations are entirely beyond his conscious control.

The second source of the poet's downfall—the drive to embrace the projection of an ungraspable ideal consonant with his own soul or with his own ego—comports with what I have been describing as the Neoplatonic strand of Shelley's imagination, which also seeks to drive beyond the confines of the experience of the phenomenal word, to enter the precincts of a higher, intellectual, formal beauty, and ultimately to pierce beyond them to the One true reality with respect to which all realms, both the intellectual and the physical, are emanations, mere copies of an originating power.

As to where the sympathies of the preface, and therefore of Shelley, lie, it seems obvious that Shelley is deeply sympathetic to the figure of the poet, who more than any other character in Shelley's narrative verse seems a portrait of Shelley himself. Even the faults ascribed to him in the preface can equally be regarded as virtues. However, I do not think that the poem was barren of instruction, particularly to Shelley himself. He, more anyone, would have been aware of the potentially destructive and even self-destructive forces of his own Janus-faced imagination. Indeed, Alastor is a kind of working out of the potentially tragic implications of such an imagination.

Finally, before proceeding to a brief consideration of the poem itself, it is important to note that the mysterious, destructive power referenced in the preface is not only that of the daemonic imagination, but also political power as capriciously exercised by those who are corrupted by possessing it. Like Shelley's father, such figures demand that life be led as it is expected to be led, as it is conventionally, unquestioningly, unselfconsciously and in fact unconsciously led, a life that is to Shelley no life at all but a kind of progressive deadening of the spirit. It is toward those who lead such lives and insist that others lead or be led by them towards whom Shelly directs his fulsome opprobrium in the preface.

As for Shelley himself, he could never have lived his life as he would have been conventionally expected to lead it. He could never have been content with the life of a landed, reactionary aristocrat. As soon as Shelley sensed this, I suspect quite early in his life, he must have had an intimation that his fate was to be that of one who is homeless, an exile. His rash actions as a youth were thus a hastening of the inevitable.

Toward the end of his life one senses that he was quite literally wishing for a hastening of the inevitable, eagerly if fearfully anticipating death. He seems to have sensed even early on that his life would not be a long one. Shelley closes his preface with the epitaph:

> The good die first
> And those whose hearts are dry as summer dust
> Burn to the socket!

2.

Turning toward Alastor itself, the poet's quest is from the outset framed in simple and direct terms:

> The fountains of divine philosophy
> Fled nor thirsting lips, and all of great,
> Or good, or lovely, which the sacred past
> In truth or fable concentrates, he felt
> And knew. When early youth had passed, he left
> His cold fireside and alienated home
> To seek strange truths in undiscovered lands.

We are told that the poet's quest is an attempt to discover strange truths. It is a quest for a possibly illicit gnosis. That quest itself is recounted in great detail. We are not, however, told anything further about the cold fireside and alienated home from which the poet is fleeing. We are told of what he is moving toward but not of the alienated, clearly intolerable life that he escaping. And yet escape from an intolerable given seems every bit as much the motivation of the poet as is the pursuit of an imagined ideal or of a deeper knowledge.

The poet's quest seems, initially, to be going well enough. After having passed through, like any proper hero, a succession of primal, wild, threatening, more than merely natural landscapes, he is indeed able to peruse the archives of a sacred, no longer distant past. His quest for a still deeper, possibly daemonic knowledge, for the primal source of all things, nonetheless, of course, continues unabated. This quest is also implicitly a Promethean attempt to amass greater power, to track down and to capture the unseen power that generates all things at its source. As Shelley makes clear in "Mont Blanc," this source is inaccessible to mere mortals, and so the poet's quest is indeed doomed, destined to fail, even at its outset.

The poem swiftly progresses to the two incidents that are the only interruptions of the poet's solitude in a narrative poem of considerable length. They occur in quick succession. Taken together they seal, or perhaps merely signal, the poet's doom.

The poet, apparently briefly resting from his quest, is fed and tended to by an Arab maid who steals time from her duties to take care of him, and who is secretly in love with him. The poet is oblivious to her ministrations, and seems barely to register her presence at all.

Soon after continuing his quest another, stranger, encounter ensues. The poet dreams of a veiled maid. She speaks in entrancing tones that are like the voice of his own soul heard in the calm of thought. Herself a poet, the poem that she speaks is at first restrained, Apollonian, quietly melodious, imparting a vision of ideal beauty. Her song gives melodious voice to the ideals of knowledge, truth, virtue, and divine liberty the poet most cherishes in himself, all virtues of the philosophic mind. Then, her frame permeated by the fire kindled by these ideals, she raises "wild numbers." Her song suddenly becomes ecstatic, dithyrambic, Dionysian, ascending into the regions of the daemonic sublime. Inspired by the power of her song she rises up and stands before the poet, an ethereal vision who is nonetheless depicted in exquisitely erotic terms.

The veiled maid embodies both aspects of Shelley's imagination, first its idealizing, philosophic bent, cherishing the beautiful and true, then its attraction to dark, daemonic sublime; its yearning for the compelling visitations of a power that is always depicted, like the maid, as outside of the poet. Responding to the once-veiled maid in all her sublimely Dionysian glory, the poet is enthralled.

> His strong heart sunk and sickened with excess
> Of love. He reared his shuddering limbs and quelled
> His gasping breath, and spread his arms to meet
> Her panting bosom:...she drew back a while,
> Then, yielding to the irresistible joy,
> With frantic gesture and short breathless cry
> Folded his frame in her dissolving arms.
> Now blackness veiled his dizzy eyes, and night
> Involved and swallowed up the vision; sleep,
> Like a dark flood suspended in its course
> Rolled back its impulse on his vacant brain.

What has happened here? The veiled maid is the ideal projection of the poet's own idealized self. Significantly, the preface refers to her as a prototype, not an anti-type.

Though clothed in seductively female form, she is a dream image of the poet himself, of his imagination, and of his poetry. Having refused to embrace a genuine other, he seeks a kind of narcissistic, monozygotic union with an externally projected version of himself, a union that is impossible to realize. His obsessive idealism has rendered him oblivious to the Arab maid, and thus to the possibility of communion with an actual other, the antidote to isolation for which he so desperately longs. In his unconsciousness he has rejected the genuinely other, the embodied other, and in so doing has rejected not only his own embodied self but by extension life itself. He has delivered himself up, unwittingly, to a kind of annihilation. His frame is held in the arms of a vision that dissolves it, and sleep, the cousin of death, dissolves all else in darkness, until nothing is left of the poet but a vacant brain.

Awakening, the poet becomes obsessed with recapturing a vision that will continue to elude him, and that he knows will continue to elude him. From this point on the poet becomes almost entirely passive. The only remaining action in the poem is the compelling movement, the current that bears along a hopelessly disillusioned poet with a kind of unnatural speed toward an inevitable destination. The poet traverses a consistently sublime and awful terrain. Shelley depicts not nature as we know it, but shifting visionary landscapes that are a more than naturally vivid hallucination of nature, a kind of surreal hyper-reality. Ultimately, the ever-shifting vistas of the sublime themselves become oppressive. Deathward toward an inevitable death progressing, the poet's body, a body that, in rejecting the Arab maid, he has implicitly rejected, rapidly wastes away.

Toward the end of the poem the refrain "He fled. He fled. He fled" keeps recurring. The movement forward of the quest has become a movement away from the motive, which I have indicated was little elaborated at the outset of poem. His quest is a movement that leads away from a life that has become intolerable toward a death that has become the poet's only possible salvation.

The poet who has sought for the ultimate gnosis, for the source of all things, for power as well as for virtue and wisdom, meets only, like all of us, death, a death which in the case of the poet, who has at least dared to aspire beyond the confines of life as we live it, at least has the virtue of being swift.

Finally, and somewhat parenthetically, it seems to me that Keats' "Endymion," published in 1818, was considerably influenced by "Alastor," which had appeared in print two years earlier, and provides an instructive contrast to it. Keats would have surely read, and read with some intensity, the work of a respected contemporary. In "Endymion," the title character pines away for Cynthia, the inaccessible, unobtainable Goddess of the moon. Eventually, however, he comes across and falls in love with an Indian maid, a mere mortal. Cynthia, in what will prove to be a kind of test, whisks Endymion to heaven, and attempts to seduce him. She offers herself to Endymion, who remains impervious to her seductions. Remaining faithful to the Indian maid, he quits the realm of heaven and rejoins her, whereupon it is revealed that all along Cynthia and the Indian maid have been one. In his steadfastness, his faithfulness to the Indian maid Endymion has passed the test, and wins the appropriate reward.

The situation in "Alastor" is the obverse of this. The poet ignores the Arab maid and chooses to embrace, instead, an ethereal phantasm. Keats, in effect, reverses the tragic terms of "Alastor" and creates a comic denouement instead.

3.

Shelley's ambivalence toward power and toward life itself continue to be worked out in a number of his later poems, particularly in "Adonais," "Epipsychidion," and "The Triumph of Life."

"Adonais" is Shelley's great pastoral elegy mourning the death of Keats, one of those too good for this world, and thus likely to die young; in this case a death that Shelley represents, if only for the purposes of his poem, as having been precipitated and hastened by reviews of Tory aristocrats who, abusing their power, have mocked and derided an impressionable young poet. Their destructive work is seen in the poem as conjoint with the malign power of life itself. According to the rueful and disenchanted speaker of the poem, "Life, like a dome of many coloured glass /Stains the white radiance of Eternity," an eternity that in this poem is something like the Neoplatonic One with respect to which all else, including and perhaps especially life as we are constrained to live it, is a kind of degraded copy.

"Epipsychidion" is a reprise of the poet's dream vision in "Alastor." Its similarly enigmatic title, likewise drawn from the Greek, was taken by Shelley to mean something like "soul of my soul," though it would have been more pertinent to the poem had it meant soul out of, derived from, projected from my soul. "Epipsychidion" is an idealized account of Shelley's platonic affair with a young aristocrat, Emilia Viviana, who was consigned to what Shelley viewed as imprisonment in a nunnery by her powerful father, the governor of Pisa. Emily is one of many female figures whom Shelley has briefly regarded as miraculous embodiments of his own most cherished ideals. Once again there is an intense desire for complete union with the other, or with the no longer other upon whom Shelley has projected a version of himself, a union that is portrayed as impossible to realize in this world, and which necessitates a retreat, an escape, into the idealized, imaginative realm of an island paradise unbuffered by the vicissitudes of life. And yet, ironically, this paradise cannot help but be seen as every bit as isolated, imprisoning, and other-worldly as any nunnery.

The poem presses beyond the Neoplatonic duality-in-unity so exquisitely realized in Donne's "The Ecstasy," in which the lovers, though one, remain other to each other, and praise their bodies, which have conveyed each to each. "Epipsychidion" instead idealizes a state in which the lovers are subsumed by and annihilated in each other, in which their physical bodies are seen as barriers to union. Hence the poem, although feverish, is like many of Shelley's love poems oddly sublimated and chaste. Once again, as in "Alastor," the poet is sick with love. Once again love so conceived is doomed to failure. Shelley came to regard "Epipsychidion," rightly, as an embarrassment. The movement, or movements of the poem seem willed, forced, disjointed. Written in oddly inapposite couplets, it has none of the formal elegance or visionary power of "Alastor," written in a blank verse whose suppleness and virtuosity have been too little acknowledged. In the end, "Epipsychidion" seems like a faded copy, a weak parody, of "Alastor," the originality of whose conception far outshines that of its derivative successor.

The platonic affair with Viviani herself was one of many episodes in Shelley's life, not all of them platonic, in which he conceives of an actual, human, female other as a kind of acme and embodiment of his own political or spiritual ideals and who, when his imaginative projection fades, as all such projections eventually do, is regarded by a disenchanted Shelley as having betrayed those ideals, as having been a fraud and impostor all along. This pattern first manifested in Shelley's unspeakably cruel and appallingly self-righteous abandonment, both physical and financial, of his first wife and their infant son, an abandonment that stripped her of any definable social status and left her emotionally and physically homeless, resulting in her eventual suicide. Shelley's idealizing tendency, too often resulting in narcissistic idealization and projection of himself, wreaked tremendous damage upon several such women.

"Epipsychidion" manages to include a cruel depiction of his wife, of the one woman who was his intellectual equal, upon whom he depended, and to whom he remained, after his own fashion, committed. Mary Shelley is allegorized in "Epipsychidion" as part of a *ménage a trois* that includes Emily. She is associated with the moon, a figure for a kind of cold, chaste, and passionless love. Shelley abandons her and elopes, as it were, with Emily. Of course, Mary Shelley would have read the poem and would, one presumes, have been deeply hurt by Shelley's portrait of her.

Toward the end of his life Shelley seemed to have awakened to his culpability for the damage he had caused to so many women. They had not betrayed him; he had betrayed them. The older Shelley finally felt the burden of this belated self-knowledge. His valorization of free love was defrocked as a kind of self-serving travesty. He, too, finally was implicated in the pageant of life, was himself among those who had wantonly and destructively abused his power. As noted earlier, Keats was startled when, in the course of one of their conversations, Shelley confessed his terrible remorse over his treatment of his first wife.

By his mid-twenties Shelley's hair was turning gray. His vital powers, like those of the poet in "Alastor," seemed to him to be prematurely waning.

Shelley's last, unfinished poem, "The Triumph of Life," entirely unlike "Epipsychidion," shows Shelley in full command of his virtuosic powers as a poet. Like Keats in his late, unfinished "The Fall of Hyperion," Shelley takes Dante as his final model. "The Triumph of Life" is written in a strict, remarkably skillful *terza rima*, a form famously invented by Dante in his *Divine Comedy*. It consists of three-line stanzas with a complex rhyme scheme that ties, with a gorgeous, mellifluous fluidity, each stanza to the next. It is an almost impossibly difficult form to pull off in English, which has far fewer rhymed words than does Italian.

The poem depicts Life as enthroned, in the manner of some particularly brutal Roman tyrant, in a chariot, his triumphal procession not only uprooting, mowing down all in its path, but sewing panic and chaos in the ranks of those in its rear, a panic that then spreads concentrically to those on those on all sides. A number of figures whom Shelley had imagined to have been heroes, leading lights of the Enlightenment, champions of liberty, Rousseau chief among them, are revealed to have been blighted by the cruel reign and spectacle of life, which all are constrained to witness. It seems clear that Shelley, in his more self-aware later years, must have seen himself, too, as having been blighted and corrupted by this brutal spectacle. He knew or feared that, in Blake's words, we become what we behold. "The Triumph of Life" breaks off after a typically Shelleyan question: "then what is life? I cried..."

The poem was interrupted by Shelley's death. Shelley had had a particularly disturbing vision or hallucination, an encounter with his doppelgänger or double, who asked him yet another typical Shelleyan question: how long do you intend to rest content? Shelley, terrified, interpreted this encounter as a possible harbinger of his imminent death.

Several weeks later, on what appeared to be a calm afternoon with only a slight breeze blowing, Shelley set sail in his beloved small skiff, not much more substantial than the shallop that bears his wasted form in "Alastor," and steered a course that was imprudently far from the shore. A summer squall blew in, engulfing and capsizing Shelley's boat. Thus he, too, like the hero of "Alastor," and like Keats, died young, the fate of those too sensitive to be oblivious to the influences of power and of life in all of their cruel guises.

In "Adonais," Shelley had consigned Keats to the realm where the immortals are. He was writing, of course, of literary immortality. Though no doubt harboring hopes to the contrary, Shelley, the confirmed atheist, was likely to have seen death as annihilation, as mere vacancy, a key term that occurs not only in the "Hymn to Intellectual Beauty," "Mont Blanc," and "Alastor," but elsewhere in his work as well.

If Shelley was not a heroic figure in the mode of Keats, he was, however, a genuinely tragic one. His flaws, like those of the poet in "Alastor," like those of the protagonists in many Greek tragedies, were also virtues. These, in concert with his many unequivocal virtues, which I have insufficiently emphasized here, led to the production of deeply probing, insistently questioning, many-minded and open-minded works of art, many of them instinct with a peerless beauty and radiance. Of his unequivocal virtues, courage was perhaps paramount. To revert to terms discussed in the third chapter in this book, few poets have probed the limits of the sayable more insistently than did Shelley, and fewer have then sought to push them still further, to breech the limits that circumscribe the precincts of the unsayable, the regions where the deep truth remains imageless. I mentioned in a previous chapter that poets who attempt to breach these boundaries almost always come to grief. And yet the records they leave behind are invaluable.

4.

I have, in this essay, been scant in my treatment of the comic, satirical Shelley, an unlikely disciple of Pope, and more importantly of the political, revolutionary Shelley, the proponent of the values of the Enlightenment, author of "The Revolt of Islam" and "On Liberty." I find that Shelley's poems that address the political directly are less effective than those that address it obliquely, but this is perhaps a too-convenient excuse. My own interests and prejudices, quite simply, direct me elsewhere.

However, and finally, there is yet another Shelley to be encountered. This Shelley is not, in my view, merely one of many, but is the perhaps the quintessential Shelley, at least at times encompassing and comprehending all others.

Shelley wrote, in his beautiful short essay "On Life," to which I will now turn, that in living we lose the apprehension of life. This Shelley sought to live life, regarded here as precious and valued, fully consciously, with an open heart and mind, to live it with the greatest possible degree of intensity and responsiveness, and was determined above all never to become dead to life, to lose or squander life in the living if it, to become one of the walking dead whom he castigates at the end of the preface to "Alastor." This Shelley wished never to be merely immured to life, never to take it for granted.

At the beginning of "On Life," Shelley writes:

Life and the world, or whatever we call that which we are and feel, is an astonishing thing. The mist of familiarity obscures from us the wonder of our being....Life, the great miracle, we admire not, because it is so miraculous. It is well that we are thus shielded by the familiarity of what is at once so certain and so unfathomable, from an astonishment which would otherwise absorb and overawe the function of that which is its object.

After reiterating Wordsworth's notion, propounded, of course, not only in the immortality ode but in much of "The Prelude," that children in particular are close to this sense, this apprehension of the miraculous and the wondrous, Shelley laments that "As men grow up this power commonly decays, and they become mechanical and habitual agents." Such agents are precisely those whom Shelley, as we have seen, roundly condemns in the preface of "Alastor." To recover, in living, the apprehension of life is to overcome this kind of death in life, is to enable a process of de-familiarization, to rediscover that which the repeated combinations of our habitual thoughts have extinguished in us. Such a renewed apprehension strips, as it were, the curtain from the scene of things. There are, of course, many iterations of the trope of life as an illusory painted curtain in Shelley. In this case, it becomes clear that this obscuring curtain is not some regrettable quality inherent in the very nature of things but is the product of our own deadening habits of mind.

Having renounced and denounced the vulgar materialism of his youth, Shelley avers that he must now confess, or profess, that, despite the fact that it is a view against which all of our persuasions struggle, "... I am one of those who am unable to refuse my assent to the conclusions of those philosophers who assert that nothing exists but as it is perceived." Later, freeing himself from a thicket of double negatives, Shelley more straightforwardly declares that the view of life presented by the "most refined deductions of the intellectual philosophy" is that of unity. Nothing exists but as it is perceived. The difference is merely nominal between those two classes of thoughts, which are vulgarly distinguished by the names of ideas and of external objects.

Shelley's intellectual philosophy is sometimes confused with a Neoplatonism that he never completely abjures. It is important that the two not be conflated. That nothing exists apart from the perception of it, *esse est precipi*, was the motto of Berkeley, the great English proponent of subjective idealism. It is related to, but not identical with, the Shaivite axiom that nothing exists that is not Consciousness, which differs from subjective idealism in that Consciousness, at least in the Spanda Shastra, is not ascribed to any subjective agent, whether human or divine. What is most of interest to me in this context, however, is Shelley's notion that the difference between ideas and a supposedly fixed, external material reality is merely nominal. Neither ideas nor idealism, on the one hand, nor a reductive materialism, on other hand, have any independent basis in reality. Their status is conjured up by one aspect of the inbuilt tendencies of language. Again, it seems to me that Shelley, like other figures whom I have addressed in this book, is intuitively working his way toward some notion of reality that lies between and beyond both subject and object, or any such merely nominal antinomies.

More radical still is Shelley's notion the pronouns *I, you, they,* which we accept as reliably representing ourselves, are themselves merely nominal grammatical devices, habits of thought, with no substantial, independent reality behind them. Shelley's skepticism with respect to merely nominal distinctions, as well as merely nominal antinomies like that between subjective ideas and objective realities, reflects an intense skepticism with regard to language itself. Poets, again, are particularly prone to run up against the limitations of language, all the more so in the case of a poet like Shelley, who chafed against limitations of any kind, and who was determined to track both language and the appearances of the visible world back to their hidden source—an enterprise that Shelley came to recognize as doomed to failure. And so, in "On Life," Shelley exclaims: "How vain is it to think that words can penetrate to the mystery of our being!" The images associated with words are equally useless. "The deep truth," Shelley writes in *Prometheus Unbound*, "is imageless."

The intellectual philosophy to which Shelley frequently refers in "On Life" is Shelley's peculiar mix of skepticism and the notion that all that we perceive is a phantasmagorical function of our own consciousness. Shelley occasionally reverts to what he formerly referred to as intellectual beauty, his version of Neoplatonism, as becomes clear when Shelley professes the doctrine of a universal mind in whom all individual minds participate. The roots of this notion in Shelley take us back to the "Hymn to Intellectual Beauty" itself, a poem which I have discussed here in some detail.

I would like to suggest, however, that it is clearly not merely the most refined and logical deductions of philosophy of whatever kind, mere words alone, that have led to Shelley's fundamental conception of the unity of all things. His prose essays are essentially inspired rhapsodies. They betray no penchant for or interest in sustained logical argument.

An extraordinary, central passage in "On Life" gives a more likely account of the genesis not merely of Shelley's conception but of his experience of an overarching unity:

> Those who are subject to the state called reverie, feel as if their nature were dissolved into the surrounding universe, or as if the surrounding universe were absorbed into their being. They are conscious of no distinction. And these are states which precede, or accompany, or follow an unusually intense and vivid apprehension of life.

To refer to such experience as a mere reverie is surely among the choicest specimens of English understatement. Clearly Shelley himself is one of those who have experienced the state to which he refers. His account of that state is about as typical and straightforward an account of one kind of mystical experience as can be imagined. Surely there is ample evidence that Shelley experienced such states. He was, as well, exquisitely sensitive to their too rapid departure, to the inevitable dispiriting reversions to a quotidian and diminished apprehension of life.

Shelley remained subject to disturbing, daemonic visitations, to which he was if anything increasingly vulnerable toward the end of his life. But such visitations, as we shall see, are very different from Shelley's experiences of the creative imagination, of that in him which inspired the production of poems. Though the experience of inspiration, too, was fleeting, it is always represented by Shelley as joyful, as a respite from the dullness of the quotidian or the visitations of the daemonic.

As is the case with many of his unfinished prose works, and with "The Triumph of Life," "On Life" breaks off at crucial point. After discussing the universal mind, Shelley makes a more general statement. "Mind, as far as we have any experience of its properties, and beyond that experience how vain is argument! cannot create, it can only perceive."

Coleridge would have heartily approved of this notion. He regarded not only the mind, whether rational or perceptive, as devoid of creative power but viewed even the primary and secondary imaginations as, respectively, echoes, then distant reflections, of a primal, originating power which he called God. The final sentence of "On Life" is particularly pregnant: "It is infinitely improbably that the cause of the mind, that is, of existence, is anything like the mind." The next logical step in this development of Shelley's argument would likely have been to account for that which does have the capacity, as a cause, to create; it would have been to point to some creative power beyond the static universal mind and the unchanging One posited by the intellectual philosophy—to some force akin to the sublime power or powers broached in both "Mont Blanc" and "The Hymn to Intellectual Beauty," which is a constant concern of Shelley's poetry. One would expect a more maturely conceived, more refined, account of such a power. Fortunately, three years after writing "On Life," Shelley provides such an account in "A Defense of Poetry."

I will here simply quote my own précis of Shelley's mature view of the imagination as expressed in that great, rhapsodic essay.

In "A Defense of Poetry," Shelley describes the mind in the act of creation as a "fading coal [awakened] to transitory brightness" by a force, "some invisible influence," a "power [that] arises from within" but which eludes not only the will but "the conscious portion of our nature," an inspiration whose "original purity" somehow carries within it the presentiment of profound, "original conceptions."

Here imagination is no longer regarded solely as a daemonic force impinging from without but also as a power arising from within. That which is within and without are ultimately regarded as one, or as twin facets of one power that Shelley almost always addresses in the second person, as thou, and with whom his relationship is dialogic. He represents himself not as the possessor of this power, nor as identified with it as a sublimely inflated, all-consuming, daemonic idealization the ego. Rather, this power, when intimately connected to the imagination as creative, is no longer experienced or represented as daemonic, but rather as that which provides intimations of profound conceptions which but for the imagination would be lost in obscurity.

It is this Shelley, inspired by the quickening of an intuitive, synoptic, creative imagination, who ardently wished to apprehend life in the living of it, who wrote, in his "Defense of Poetry," of poetry as a record, an archive recording "the best and happiest moments of the happiest and best minds."

It is this Shelley who is perhaps the most intensely gifted lyrical poet in English, who had at times the ravishingly lucidity and radiance of a Mozart, who writes, in his "Hymn of Apollo,"

> I am the eye with which the Universe
> Beholds itself, and knows it is divine;
> All harmony of instrument or verse,

> All prophecy, all medicine, is mine,
> All light of art or nature; —to my song
> Victory and praise in its own right belong.

And who also wrote, in *Prometheus Unbound*, declaiming a particularly eloquent vision a redeemed, universal man:

> Man, O not men! a chain of linked thought
> Of love and might to be divided not,
> Compelling the elements with adamantine stress...
>
> Man, one harmonious soul of many a soul,
> Whose nature is its own divine control,
> Where all things flow to all, as rivers to the sea...

It is this Shelley who invoked, in his "Ode to the West Wind," a revivifying wind that is a classical, Biblical, indeed Hindu metaphor for the universal life force and/or the breath of the Spirit itself. At once, like Lord Shiva himself, the creator, destroyer, and preserver, the West Wind sweeps away the dead and the deadening, preparing the way for renewed life. The poem itself, at once an apostrophe, a prayer, and a prophecy, imagines that renewed life as a redeemed society.

Finally, it is this Shelley—the Shelley who, in his best and happiest moments intuited presentiments of profound, original, conceptions— whose imagination succeeded in glimpsing the power of Consciousness closer to its source than did the two subsidiary, conflicting aspects of the Shelleyan imagination that I have earlier traced. These glimpses did not simply dissolve Shelley's experience of the conflicts, dichotomies, or antinomies, however nominal, to which I have referred. But they did grant him in privileged moments, access to a power that encompassed and transcended them, suggesting to him, if all too briefly, a vision of the fundamental unity of all things.

Surely to be the receiver of such intimations, vouchsafed only to a few, was not simply to feel a burden and a responsibility, but to experience joy and wonder—a joy and wonder that are also an essential part of Shelley's poetic repertoire.

Of course poems, the translations of these intuitive, synoptic intuitions, these presentiments of profound conceptions, into discursive language, are, in true Neoplatonic fashion, faded copies of their originals, and yet they too are sublime. Such intuitions, such sublime, happiest moments, are granted, again, only to those fortunate few among poets who have the rare capacity to translate them into exquisitely patterned speech.

And so in the end, we are left not with many Shelleys nor with one Shelley but with two Shelleys: the despairing, defeated, tragic author of "Triumph of Life," and the author of *Prometheus Unbound* and "Ode to the West Wind," the author who proclaimed that "to my Song / Victory and praise in its own right belong."

Toward the end of his life Shelley experienced, on the one hand, disturbing intimations of the daemonic, counseling despair, and on the other intense periods of creative intuition, still granting ecstatic glimpses of life as keenly apprehended in the living of it. During this time, he was working on a translation of Goethe's *Faust*. There had always been something not only Promethean but also Faustian about Shelley's experience of the daemonic sublime, some sense of having made a pact with forces as much dark as light. meanwhile, he was working on translations of his beloved Plato, for him unambiguously an angel of light. He experienced the daemonic, then the ecstatically, luminously creative, as a kind of oscillating current. These two currents were not, in Shelley, ultimately reconciled or reconcilable. Their increasingly rapid oscillation, along with the continual uprooting and relocation of his household (itself fraught with tension), occasioned by financial exigencies, was exhausting, overtaxing his never robust constitution, draining his vital powers.

At some point Shelley reached what must have seemed a kind of insuperable impasse. He could no longer imagine a way through it or beyond it.

Envoi: Afterword as Prelude

It has been my contention in this work that explores and then re-explores in different contexts a set of loosely and hopefully dynamically interrelated themes and motifs, themes that touch upon the triad of poetry, mysticism, the imagination, and finally Consciousness itself—of which the prior three terms or fields of activity are manifestations—that the works of poets of genius are instinct with, and tap into, through a creative, synoptic, preconscious intuition, the tremendous potential force of Consciousness itself as an ongoing act of pure self-reflective awareness; and that through their acts of imagination, the poems they produce are instinct with and energized by this ineffable power. This power, moreover, pervades the prelinguistic matrix of energies that manifests as language itself—a matrix that precedes and exceeds any given language in potential form as *la langue*, or in actual form as *la parole*, and that, when rendered articulate through the creative power of Consciousness, is constitutive of and enacts the phenomena to which it seemingly—to us in the West, at least—merely refers.

I have traced a kind of analogy between poets and mystics, both of whom, in achieving their respective ends, tap into this power of the ongoing act of Consciousness as pure, self-knowing awareness. The characteristic act of the mystic is the attempt to fully assimilate him or herself, in subtly different ways, to Consciousness itself. The mystic's activities need not entail the imagination but neither do they exclude it, especially in the case of those mystics whose vocation it is, like that of poets, to communicate either orally, as a kind of direct transmission, or in written form, what is essentially ineffable by means of language. The act of the poet, on the other hand, whose primary task it is to translate the ineffable into articulate form, necessarily entails the act of the imagination.

With respect to the imagination, I can only reiterate what I stated in the introduction to this volume: it reflects, as a noun, the mind's, and particularly the Western mind's tendency to hypostasize or reify not only the abstract but also the dynamic into reassuringly stable, seemingly substantial categorical niches. Whereas, in contradistinction, I have stressed that the imagination is not a faculty, but a force. Who knows—it may even be dependent upon an energy that is in some way independent of the human mind, a forcefield upon which the mind draws, experiencing a subsidiary stirring, a resonance, generated by some greater vibration that pulsates indifferently through all thoughts and all things.

Hopefully, in this largely speculative volume, I have fleshed out and made a case for the view of the imagination first suggested above. A notion that is tentatively, and perhaps coyly, framed in the interrogative, "Who knows?" in the preceding paragraph, is one for which I have made, instead, something of an affirmative case, a brief that I do not attempt to prove, as it is by its nature not amenable to proof, but simply to put forth as it has been put forth by the many figures discussed in this text who are far wiser than I, who seem to have adopted a similar notion—or more properly, to have been granted a similar experience—of Consciousness.

With respect to poetry, which has been my main concern in this text, I want to stress yet again, in this wholly inadequate postscript, that the writing of it, like taking a walk, is a kind of act, an act of the imagination. It is an act that has as its purpose the creation of works of art of whatever kind, whether musical, or visual, or verbal or, as in the case of dance, kinesthetic. Imagination is not to be confused with fantasy, which is an undirected activity of the mind, which has a value of an entirely different kind. Just as various mystics take different paths in the pursuance of their vocation, and as people walk in characteristic ways and with different motives, ranging from a stroll in the park to a competitive 100-yard dash, so the act of the imagination assumes, with respective to different poets, characteristic forms, and is pursued either as a kind of end in itself, as in Stevens' poems of the pleasure of merely circulating, or with a specific end in view.

I have stressed that the act of the imagination is aligned with, resonates with the pure ongoing act of Consciousness itself, and is, again, expressed in different ways by the several mystics and poets discussed in this text, ranging, for example, in no particular order, but beginning with those who are primarily mystics, from Abhinavagupta's and Longchenpa's expression of the act of Consciousness as pure, self-knowing awareness; to Nagarjuna's expression of Consciousness as logic, as an ongoing act of the mind that suggests a radical state of indeterminacy free of all conceptual reification; to Lao Tzu's expression of Consciousness as the way of action in inaction, of inaction in inaction; to Jnaneshwar's poetical/philosophical evocation of Consciousness, the ultimate trickster, as that which acts both to conceal and to reveal itself.

With respect to those who are more specifically poets, the act of Consciousness assumes the form of the act of the imagination, and it, too, ranges widely, from Li Po's ecstatic, shamanic, sometimes drunken poetry of the imaginative act or going out of the self in radical identification, annulling the limitations of time and space, either with the things of this world or with others; to Basho's and Williams' poetry of the imaginative act of pure perception; to Stevens' poetry of Consciousness as the exorbitant, inexhaustible imaginative act of the mind; to Blake's works limning the prophetic imagination as the purgative act of intellectual warfare that separates truth from error; to Shelley's writings conveying his almost tragic sense of the imagination as the act, fading even as it flares, of translating the awakened mind's sublime intimations of glorious original conceptions into faded and inadequate, though nevertheless vital, copies; to Coleridge's poetry of the imagination as the echo or tributary of the eternal act of creation of the infinite "I Am"; to Wordsworth's poetry of the imagination's sublime enactment of the interpenetration of mind and nature, and finally to Rumi's and Keats'—and in the end, to Jnaneshwar's—poetry as a radical, imaginative self-abandonment to Consciousness as the act of love .

I have stressed that words, too, are acts, are quanta of energy, and that their force is greatest when they most align themselves with and resonate with the prelinguistic energy of the ongoing act of pure, self-knowing awareness or Consciousness that is their source. The more they are instinct with this force, the greater their power will be.

I have touched upon the nature of a certain kind of poem, the kind that most fully realize the designs of the poet, as being like the human form divine itself, like the bodies of enlightened Tantric masters, microcosmic embodiments of the macrocosm with which they are one, as containing all, as subsuming, as Stevens says in "Asides on the Oboe," all external referents.

I have touched upon the poet and the same-hearted reader as alike inspired by the imagination as creative intuition, as alike co-creators of the poem. I have touched on the synchronic and diachronic, the sacramental and the secular aspects of language and of experience, of the qualitative and the quantitative, of the intelligence of the head and of the heart, of poetry as the medial, as the liminal, as the path between all mind-born pairs of opposites, as that which evades not only categorical niches but the kind of disembodied abstractions which I am, in the words you are now reading, indulging in with a none too fine excess. And I have touched upon about much else besides, much that this too abstract and reductive précis leaves out.

But enough! Or too much! Or too little! It remains for me to declare in what way this perhaps ill-advised afterword is also a prelude.

Directly after composing this text I found myself writing a long series of essays on English Romantic and American Neo-romantic poets, the successors to the essays in Stevens, Keats, Blake, and Shelley in this text, essays that are related to this volume as the practical is to the speculative. Though in some sense rooted in this volume, they took on, as I wrote them, a life of their own. They are more granular examinations of the many related yet different ways that individual poets, through the exercise of their imaginations, have assumed the sometimes arduous burden of translating the ineffable into the lineaments of the articulate. It is these essays that together comprise what is in effect a kind of second volume of this book, *Elective Affinities: American Poetry from Whitman to Ammons*.

Selected Bibliography

While many poets and texts were mentioned in the text, this bibliography is restricted to those texts from which substantial quotations were taken.

Basho, Matsuo. *Narrow Road to the Northern Interior.* Boston, Mass: Shambhala Publications, Inc., 202

Bate, Walter Jackson. *Negative Capability: The Intuitive Approach in Keats.* New York: Contra Mundrum Press, 2012.

Bevis, William. *Mind of Winter: Wallace Stevens, Meditation, and Literature.* Pittsburg, Pa: University of Pittsburg Press, 1988.

Blake, William. *The Complete Poetry and Prose of William Blake: With a New Foreword and Commentary by Harold Bloom. (Revised Edition).* Berkeley, California: University of California Press, 1982.

Bloom, Harold. *The Poems of Our Climate.* Ithaca, New York: Cornell University Press, 1977.

Buddhaghosa, Bhadantacariya. *The Path of Purification: Visuddhimagga.* Onalaska, WA: BPS Pariyatti Editions, 1975.

Coleridge-Taylor, Samuel. *The Major Works Including Biographia Literaria.* Oxford, England: Oxford University Press, 1985.

Dickenson, Emily. *The Essential Emily Dickenson.* New York: HarperCollins, 1996.

Dyczkowski, Mark. *The Doctrine of Vibration.* Albany, New York: SUNY Press, 1987.

Dyczkowski, Mark. *The Stanzas of Vibration.* Albany, New York: SUNY Press, 1992.

Ginsberg, Allen. *Collected Poems 1947-1997.* New York: HarperCollins, 2007.

Gupta, Neerja. *Abhinavagupta's Comments on Aesthetics in Abhinavabhrat and Locana.* Newcastle upon Tyne, United Kingdom: Cambridge Scholars Publishing, 2017.

Isayeva, Natalia. *From Early Vedanta to Kashmir Shaivism.* Albany, New York: SUNY Press, 1995.

Jnaneshwar. *Amritanubhav.* Adapted by the author from a version by Swami Abhayananda: https://www.nonduality.com/jnan.htm

Keats, John. *John Keats: The Complete Poems (Penguin Classics).* London, England: Penguin Books Ltd., 1973.

Keats, John. *Selected Letters.* London, England. Penguin Books Ltd., 2014.

Li Po. *Poems of the Masters: China's Classic Anthology of T'ang and Sung Dynasty Verse.* Port Townsend, Washington: Copper Canyon Press, 2003.

Longchenpa, Rabjam, Barron, Richard (trans.). *The Precious Treasury of The Basic Space of Phenomena.* Junction City, California: Padma Publishing, 2001.

Selected Bibliography

Maritain, Jacques. *Creative Intuition in Art and Poetry*. Providence, Rhode Island: Cluny Media, 2018.

Mishra, Giriratna. *Sri Tantraloka of Abhinavagupta*. Dehli, India: Chaukhamba Surbharati Prakashan, 2018.

Mitchell, Stephen, translator. *Ahead of All Parting: Selected Poetry and Prose of Rainer Maria Rilke.* Modern Library: New York, 1995.

Mitchell, Stephen, translator. *Tao Te Ching.* New York: HarperCollins Publishers, 1992.

Nagarjuna, author, Garfield, Jay (trans.). *The Fundamental Wisdom of the Middle Way: Nagarjuna's Mulamadhyamakakarika*. Oxford, England: Oxford University Press, 1995.

Olson, Charles. *Collected Prose*. Berkeley, California: University of California Press, 1997.

Ortega, Paul Muller. *The Triadic Heart of Siva*. Albany, New York: SUNY Press, 1989.

Pound, Ezra. *Cathay: A Critical Edition*. New York: Fordham University Press, 2018.

Pound, Ezra. *New Selected Poems and Translations.* New York: New Directions Books, 2010.

Sensharma, Deba Brata. *Paramarthasara of Abhinavagupta*. New Delhi, India: Muktabodha Indological Research Institute: 2007.

Shakespeare, William. *The Complete Works of William Shakespeare*. San Diego, California: Canterbury Classics, 2014.

Shelley, Percy Bysshe. *A Defense of Poetry*. Charleston, South Carolina: BiblioLife LLC., 2009.

Singh, Jaideva. *Shiva Sutras: The Yoga of Supreme Identity*. New Delhi, India: Motilal Banarsidass, 2012.

Singh, Jaideva. *Spanda-Karikas: The Divine Creative Pulsation*. New Delhi, India: Motilal Banarsidass, 2012.

Stevens, Wallace. *Stevens: Collected Poetry and Prose (Library of America)*. New York: Library of American, 1997.

Stevens, Wallace. *Letters of Wallace Stevens. (Paperback edition)* Berkeley, California: University of California Press; December, 1996.

Vendler, Helen. *Wallace Stevens: Words Chosen Out of Desire*. Cambridge, Mass: Harvard University Press, 1986.

Wordsworth, William. *The Collected Poems of William Wordsworth*. London, England: Wordsworth Editions Limited, 1994.

Wright, James. *Above the River: The Complete Poems.* New York: Farrar, Straus and Giroux, 1990.

About the Author

George Franklin graduated in 1975 from Harvard University, where he studied poetry with Elizabeth Bishop and Robert Fitzgerald. He subsequently received an MFA in Creative Writing from Brown University, and an MA in English literature from Columbia University. He lived for over ten years in the ashrams of his spiritual preceptor in India and in upstate New York, where he developed a keen interest in Kashmir Shaivism. He has published two books of poetry, *The Fall of Miss Alaska (*Six Gallery Press, 2007) and the chapbook *Contour with Shadow* (Frolic Press, 2016). A forthcoming book will be published by Ristretto Press. His uncollected poems, including "Talking Head," a forty-page poem in blank verse, have been published widely, most prominently in *Epiphany Magazine* and in *The Recorder*, the Journal of the American Irish Historical Society. He had the honor of serving as editorial assistant to the great scholar and pandit of Kashmir Shaivism Debabrata Sensharma on his translation of and commentary on Abhinavagupta's *Paramarthasara*.

www.ingramcontent.com/pod-product-compliance
Lightning Source LLC
Chambersburg PA
CBHW080119020526
44112CB00037B/2782